THE · D·E·S·I·G·N·E·R'S

C·O·M·M·O·N·S·E·N·S·E

B·U·S·I·N·E·S·S · B·O·O·K

THE DESIGNER'S COMMONSENSE BUSINESS BOOK

Barbara Ganim

3443

NORTH LIGHT BOOKS
Cincinnati, Ohio

99 98 97 96 95   5 4 3 2 1

Library of Congress Cataloging-in-Publication Data

Ganim, Barbara
    The designer's commonsense business book / by Barbara Ganim — Rev. ed.
        p.   cm.
    Includes index.
    ISBN 0-89134-618-X
    1. Commercial art — Practice — United States — Handbooks, manuals, etc.   I. Title.
NC1001.G36   1995
741.6'068 — dc20   94-47295
                                          CIP

Edited by Mary Cropper and Diana Martin
Designed and illustrated by Kristi Kane Cullen

DEDICATION

To Liliana who helped me discover the writer inside myself

ACKNOWLEDGMENTS

As I thought about the people who deserve some credit for not only contributing to the contents of this book but also to the philosophy behind it, I remembered Miss Roberts. She was my third grade teacher, who always said, "*Can't* never did anything!" I've carried that phrase with me throughout my life—it's the concept that I live by and the underlying current of this book.

I especially want to thank: James Mullen, who taught me to see the world in a new and beautiful way. He was my inspiration and the model for the teacher I became. Lili Costa, for her supportive friendship, unending patience and expert editing. Her brilliance is an eternal flame of ideas and resources. Susan Fox-Michaud, my long-time friend and business associate. Her belief in me and constant encouragement helped to make this book a reality. She was always there to help me remember all those things I wanted to forget about clients, employees and being in business. Judy Scarfpin, a treasured friend who ignited the spark that started my writing this book. Virginia Chapin, who taught me to reconnect with the inner self I thought I had lost. John Palumbo, who showed great patience in answering my constant questions about taxes and accounting. My parents, whose love and support through the years gave me the confidence to tackle every challenge that came along. My Aunt Frances who always told me, "You only get out of things what you put into them." Tobi, my ever-faithful German Shepherd, who walks me an hour every day—a sure cure for writer's block.

I must also include some additional acknowledgments for those people who were so important in the writing of this revised edition: My appreciation goes to Mary Cropper, my editor and advisor at North Light Books. She honored my voice as a writer, and I honor and appreciate her insight and ability as an editor and collaborator. She is the person most responsible for the completion of this revised edition, because without her, I'd still be stuck back in the organizational and research phase of this project. I also want to thank Diana Martin, my second editor at North Light, whose gentle prodding and encouraging words kept me on target and on time with each and every deadline. She made phase two of this project enjoyable. Without the help of a very special personal acquaintance, Susan Catenzaro, I could never have put all those financial spread sheets into a comprehensible form that my readers could understand. My gratitude also goes to my present business and personal accountant, Steven Hatch, who provided me with information on all the new tax laws. I wish to thank Michael Hamel, Jr., from ABAR Imaging Center, Providence, RI. His willingness to help me understand the complexities of graphic imaging and the function of service bureaus in the design business was like a breath of fresh air to a writer almost suffocating from information overload. And finally, I want to thank all the other people I've had the pleasure of working with at F&W Publications/North Light Books. Their support, assistance and always rapid responses to my questions, concerns and needs have been greatly appreciated.

INTRODUCTION

When I set off on my own as a freelance graphic designer, people always told me they envied me. Why? What did they think was so great about being a freelancer? After all, I had become one out of necessity, not by choice. I was teaching graphic design and illustration at a local college on a part-time basis while waiting for a full-time position to open up. But teaching jobs were scarce then, and I had bills to pay. I loved teaching, and I just couldn't bring myself to think about taking a different kind of job. Besides, something inside me screamed at the thought of finding a regular, forty-hour-a-week job sitting behind a drawing board in a high-pressure ad agency or stuffy corporation. So the best choice, the *only* choice, for me at the time was to continue teaching and get some freelance design work to bring in the extra money I needed to survive.

Why then did others envy me, when I was just doing what I *had* to do? Because they thought it must be so exciting to have my own business and do fun projects. Because they envied my freedom: I wasn't stuck behind a desk or someone else's drawing board doing what someone else told me to do. And they were absolutely right. Hearing why they envied me made my spirits soar.

But every flight must have a landing, and reality soon set in again. I loved the freedom and the work I did, but there was another side to the shiny coin called "being on my own." That side wasn't quite as bright. There were financial pressures and business hassles. Will the phone ever ring with another job? What if I don't make enough money this month to cover the rent? Will this client really hire me if I do ten sample designs or is he just stringing me along? How do I find some new clients? Did I fill out this sales tax report correctly? When can I afford to get health insurance? How can I keep track of my time and expenses? Why is billing, which I hate anyway, always such a hassle? My envious friends never thought about that side of having your own design business. The trouble is, most designers don't think about that either — until it's too late.

I was a solo freelance designer for only a year. Not because I couldn't take it or didn't make it. In fact, my business grew so fast that I joined forces with a fellow designer to handle the workload. We combined our names and services, and our fledgling graphic design studio, Ganim & Fry Associates, was born. We moved our equipment into a separate room in my house that would serve as our business office. But it didn't stop there. Pretty soon, we had to move into a rented office. The next thing we knew, we were changing our business name again. We landed our first advertising account, became a full-service advertising agency, and replaced the word "Associates" with "Advertising" in the name of our studio. In addition to designing ads and brochures, we were buying advertising space for clients, writing and producing radio and television commercials, and making presentations to boards of directors. It didn't happen overnight, but it did happen. Now I was no longer an insecure freelance designer and illustrator working for myself, but an agency director hiring other designers to work for me.

Why did I survive when so many who start their own graphic design businesses don't? Luck? Sometimes. Persistence? Always. But those weren't the only reasons. I succeeded because I treated my business like a business and spent as much time working at the business side as the creative side. I consistently delivered good work on time at a reasonable cost. I actively sought new clients while keeping my present ones happy. I kept careful track of my expenses and time and billed promptly. It just seemed the commonsense thing to do.

Sure, I made a lot of mistakes, but I learned from them and tried not to make the same ones twice. Sometimes, I'm amazed I got through at all. I guess I must have had a little leprechaun on my shoulder, and I wish one for each of you. But you'll need far more than a lucky charm. Today there are more designers than ever before and fewer clients to go around. Talent alone isn't enough — it never was. You've got to also be dependable, knowledgeable and professional.

You can make it as an independent designer. You can run your business and make a profit. That's why I want to share with you what I learned from my own mistakes. I wish someone could have shared this information with me back then, but I had to learn the hard way. Trial and error may be a great way to learn, but it sure takes the joy out of living sometimes. So why waste precious days, months and years struggling for every little rung of the ladder when you can profit from my mistakes instead? I hope you'll find answers to all your questions here — including those questions you never thought you had.

1

You're in Business!

Page 1

Presents the concept that all freelancers and independent designers are in business. Describes the joys and perils of having your own business. Explains business plans and organization strategies. Shows how to present yourself as a professional — and tells why you should.

2

Taking Care of Business

Page 35

Explains why you need systems and procedures. Presents a system for working on and tracking a project from start to billing — with ready-to-use forms. Includes special tips to make every step easier.

3

Money Talks

Page 85

Shows how to calculate what you need to charge, and how to price projects to stay financially healthy. Provides a system for managing expenses, billing for your work and tips for collecting your money. Explains what taxes affect you.

4

Work Smarter, Not Harder

Page 115

Demonstrates taking a job from start to finish, illustrated by a sample project. Includes special tips for making a job go faster and easier — and solutions for typical problems.

5

Collaborators and Competitors

Page 133

Describes roles, titles and work of various design professionals. Covers collaborating with other creative professionals such as illustrators, photographers, copywriters, printers, service bureaus, and others with whom you'll work. Offers solutions to typical people problems.

CHAPTER

one

You're
in
Business!

hat does having your own studio mean? It means you can choose to do absolutely anything you want to do. You make all the creative and business decisions and answer only to yourself and your clients. You choose when, how and where you'll work (depending, of course, on what you can afford).

Having your own studio also means you need to have a business structure, keep records of what you do, charge for your services, and pay taxes. You're responsible for bringing in enough money to cover your bills and having some left over to pay yourself—and maybe others—a salary. All this is true whether you're just doing a little design work on the side, running a one-person studio at home or in an office, or managing several employees.

For the first few years, you will have to work hard just to build a solid client base. Once your base is established, you can begin to be more selective about the clients and the projects you'll accept. In time, if you develop a reputation for outstanding work, especially with an area of specialization or expertise, you'll be in an excellent position to pick and choose your clients and projects.

Being in business for yourself will give you a wonderful sense of freedom. Your clients will be your bosses, but they won't be looking over your shoulder eight hours a day. You will still have deadlines and schedules—and be responsible for meeting them with quality work on time—but you will set those schedules rather than have someone else setting them for you. You will also have the freedom to create exactly the kind of working environment that best suits your individual needs and taste.

Most designers would love to have office space that resembles a spread from *Architectural Digest* or *HOW* magazine—looking plush and professional while reflecting creativity and personal style. What they can afford, however, is often more a matter of function than style. In fact, many designers just starting out work out of their homes.

One of the greatest advantages to starting a graphic design business is that you *don't* have to rent an office. Almost every designer I've ever known started in his or her home. The ideal working space is a private room large enough to comfortably hold a drawing board and/or computer work station, a desk, files, a copier and maybe a client. Any variation on this description will do, but try to avoid basements, especially if they are damp, cold or dark. Good lighting, especially natural daylight, is essential not only because most of us work with color, but because daylight replenishes our spirits. I worked for six months in my basement and found myself very depressed. If you work outside your home, the space you rent will depend on what you can afford.

There are some disadvantages to working at home. For example, you can never leave your work at the office. Also, some people—including certain clients, friends and family members— may not take your work seriously or may interrupt you frequently. In spite of these and other drawbacks, the decision to move out should be based on only one factor—your financial situation. If you can afford to do so, then you can search for space that fits your budget, requires a minimal amount of fixing up, and is convenient and comfortable for both you and your clients. No matter where you choose to locate your studio, a great working environment is one that is comfortable, practical and affordable.

Getting Started

All too often, people never take that final step to start their own design businesses. While they may think about it for years, they eventually give up the dream because they've convinced themselves they don't have what it takes to succeed. What does it take to succeed? What do you really need to start your own business and make it work?

It takes far less to get started than most people think. In fact, a design studio is one of the easiest businesses to start, because all you need is yourself—your talent and skills—and a place to work. Okay, I admit it; this is simplifying things a bit. But keep in mind that a design studio is one of the few businesses that doesn't require inventory, rented office space or other costly up-front investments.

What Training or Experience Do You Need?

When I started my part-time freelance business, the only real experience I had was a summer job during my junior year in college doing pasteup and, later, illustrating several children's books. I had my B.F.A. with a major in drawing and printmaking, but that hardly constituted formal training in graphic design. What I did have was the ability to draw well, in a style that reproduced well in print, and a thorough grounding in design principles. As for business experience, I had absolutely none. Although I wouldn't recommend starting out with as little to offer potential clients as I had, it is possible to start a business from practically nothing if you also have another job to support yourself while you learn what you need to know to run your business full-time.

But there is an ideal set of circumstances from which one can successfully launch a full-time independent design business. Few

Forty Hours Aren't Always Enough

Now that you are your own boss, no one can tell you when, where or how to work – except you. At times you will enjoy that kind of control over your work life. At others you'll find yourself putting in sixty- and seventy-hour weeks just trying to keep up.

This will seem vastly unfair when quiet evenings at home are just a memory and weekends seem to get squeezed into a few measly hours. You may even start to wonder why you ever wanted to be out on your own, anyway. That's natural. When you're up to your ears in alligators, it's hard to remember that your original goal was to drain the swamp. But the cold hard truth of the matter is – that's life. Mess around in swamps and you find alligators.

Everything has a price and not always one paid with cash. You can't buy success in business, you can only work your way to it. So think of every eight-hour day as maintenance just to keep your business running in place. Every hour beyond that will move it forward. The more time you put in, the faster and farther you will go. If you stick with it, produce quality work and manage to stay ahead of your bills, eventually you will experience the rewards of owning your own business.

of you will have every characteristic and experience described in this ideal situation. The following checklist should help you evaluate what experience and qualifications you *do* have and encourage you to take that leap toward launching your own graphic design business.

☐ Graduation from an art or design school with a major in graphic design.

☐ Coursework or self-study of both the theory and application of design methods and principles.

☐ A well-rounded education that exposed you not only to art, but also to literature, history and science.

☐ Some practical courses in advertising and marketing, communication skills and business management (or self-study in these areas).

☐ An interest in motivational psychology (why people do what they do) and social trends.

☐ At least two years' work experience in a small- to medium-sized graphic design studio or advertising agency.

☐ Experience in production, conceptualizing ideas, working with clients and supervising staff members or freelancers.

☐ Hands-on experience dealing with vendors and subcontractors, working with budgets and cost-accounting projects.

☐ Experience working with pricing and billing jobs; an understanding of how a business makes money in graphic design.

If you checked all these, you are golden. But if your background is more limited, don't worry. Just do your best to learn what you don't know. You can find most of the information you'll need in books. You can also take courses on starting and marketing your own business. Most colleges and community col-

Determine Your Peak Periods

If you're not familiar with your own time clock, keep a daily log of activities for one week. Try doing this at one-hour intervals throughout the day and evening, until bedtime. Write down the time of your entry, what you are doing, and how you are feeling mentally, emotionally and physically at that time. By week's end, you should know when you can expect your peaks and lows. Trust your body to know when it is full of vim and vigor and when it would rather kick back and take a short nap or a break of some kind. By shifting gears throughout the day according to your own body's cycles, you will be less frustrated and, in general, a happier, healthier human being – and a whole lot more productive.

Opportunity Only Knocks When You're Ready

My opportunity knocked when a series of events created a chain reaction that changed my life. When I was teaching and running my small design business on the side, I gave my graphic design class an assignment to design a logo. One student asked to redesign the college's logo. "Okay," I said. "Why not?"

Later that day, I spotted the Dean of Continuing Education sitting in the cafeteria. Remembering that she had once mentioned that she really disliked the school's logo, I decided to tell her about the student's project. Maybe the dean would want to see it. What a great opportunity for my student! My long shot paid off. The dean did want to see the logo and would recommend its use, if she thought it would work. As the dean and I continued to talk, the conversation turned to the agency who was handling the advertising for her division. She wasn't happy with them. Suddenly she looked at me and said, "Why don't you do it?"

"Me? I'm a graphic designer; I don't know anything about advertising."

"So what? You're a good designer, and what you don't know about advertising, you can learn. From what I've seen of your work and heard about you, I'm sure you'll be better than this agency."

I was thrilled, flattered and convinced that I wanted to say yes. Was I crazy? Did I really think I could pull this off, when I knew zip about advertising? I didn't know how, but I knew I had to try. I've always believed that people can do just about anything – if they really want to do it and are willing to work hard enough. I felt that applied to me, too. I told the dean I'd take the account.

I soared off to tell my partner, Pat Fry, the good news. I shouted exuberantly, "Can you believe it, we've got our first advertising account?"

"Our first advertising account, indeed!" she said. "We weren't even looking for one."

Pat wanted to be excited, but she had some serious doubts about this. She pointed out that designing ads or catalogs was one thing, but writing press releases, developing an advertising strategy, and placing ads were other matters entirely. "Besides," she declared, delivering the clincher, "newspapers won't let graphic designers place ads. Only legitimate advertising agencies can do that!"

"No problem," I responded, swallowing hard but trying to hide it. "We'll form our own agency tomorrow. Ganim & Fry Advertising, how's that?"

Becoming a legitimate advertising agency was the easiest part. Pat's fears about our lack of experience and knowledge of advertising were well founded. It wasn't easy, but we dug in, did our homework, and became very good at advertising. Although Pat later left the agency, I spent the next eight years building a Rhode Island agency that earned a solid reputation for quality work. By the way, the agency still has the dean's account – and has the account of the rest of the college, too.

Of course, you could say that a lot of this was good luck. My student just happened to want to do the college logo, the dean just happened to be in the cafeteria that day, she just happened to be unhappy with the advertising agency, and we just happened to talk about it. But there's much more than luck involved. The dean did *not* just happen to offer me the account. She knew I had a reputation for being a good, hardworking designer and teacher and gave my best to everything I did. Those qualities, in her mind, outweighed my lack of actual experience in advertising. I had *earned* that opportunity and was ready when it finally came. Discipline, concentration and vision paid off for me, and they will for you.

leges offer noncredit evening classes on related topics that take only a few nights to complete. And finally, don't be afraid to talk to other people in business – any business. Most small businesses share the same day-to-day concerns. Businesspeople love to help others who are just getting started. Someday your turn will come to do the same for another newcomer.

Although you can go directly from design school or college to being a freelancer, I would strongly suggest you work for someone else first. That way, you can build your portfolio and get experience making business decisions. You'll also have the chance to fill in any gaps in your production background. It's a big leap from the classroom to preparing mechanicals and doing real world projects. Working for someone else gives you additional expertise to draw on – and help at hand when you need it. Try to work for a designer whose work you really respect and who will let you have greater hands-on involvement at earlier stages in a project as you are able to handle it.

If you do have a part-time job to help support you, start gradually with a few projects or only one client. As you gain confidence and experience, you'll be ready to take on more. And if you have some special talent, such as exceptional illustration skills, airbrushing, typesetting or computer design experience, you will be able to carve out a market for your services more quickly than the generalist. (See chapter seven, "Pounding the Pavement," for more on positioning yourself in the marketplace.)

The best rule to follow is this: Move slowly, and don't take on more than you know you can handle.

Working Capital

How much money should you have put aside to start your business? This depends on three things: how much you need to live on; one-time start-up expenses—furniture, equipment, telephone, legal and license fees, etc.; and continuing expenses—rent, gas and electricity, stationery, materials, etc.

If you plan to leave your present job and begin a full-time business, in addition to your basic start-up costs and operating expenses, you should have enough money in the bank to support yourself (and family) for at least six months. Add a cushion of approximately 10 percent of that amount to cover health insurance and any emergencies that may come up. (If you have another job, subtract that income from the total you'll need.)

Determine what furniture and equipment you must get in order to do business. Make a list of essentials such as drawing boards, filing cabinets, a telephone and legal costs. Then pin down costs on as many items as possible and comparison shop for the best buys. Add that to what you need to live on. If you have a job and are freelancing on the side, invest in furniture and equipment gradually out of your freelance income. This will not only reduce your start-up costs but give you some good tax deductions along the way.

You should have enough start-up financing to carry your business for at least six months. This isn't just rent, telephone and utilities; you'll need to cover working materials, mail, insurance, stationery, dues and subscriptions among other expenses. If you plan to rent office space, include a deposit on the space and moving costs to the amount you'll need.

It's always wise to start out slow, investing

The SBA and You

The Small Business Administration exists to help all small businesses, including design businesses. One of the SBA's most valuable free services is providing you with a consultant who has expertise in graphic design or a closely related business. This consultant will come to your home or office, once or twice a week for as long as necessary, to advise you on any aspect of getting started. You can even request someone with specialized skills, such as computer graphics, accounting or project management to teach you whatever you'd like to learn. The SBA can't guarantee that they will always have someone with the exact skills or experience you need, but they will do their best to make an appropriate fit. The consultants the SBA uses are called "Resource Partners" and come from either the Service Core of Retired Executives (SCORE) or the Small Business Development Centers located nationwide.

In addition to consultation services, the SBA can provide you with specific guidelines to help you get a bank loan. Those guidelines show how to determine what you need money for, how much it will cost, and how to put your financial proposal package together. If your particular situation is complex, they can recommend a professional loan packager who will do it for you. You will have to pay for that service, but it may be well worth it in the long run.

The SBA guarantees participating lenders that all business loans approved by the SBA will be repaid. The guarantee covers 90 percent of any loan up to $155,000 dollars and 75 to 85 percent for loans between $155,000 and $750,000. The SBA will not guarantee any loans above $750,000. So if you have a good credit rating, but a bank turns you down, check with the SBA. If you qualify, the SBA's backing may be what you need to get your financial institution to reconsider your proposal. There are three basic stipulations the SBA requires:

1. You must put some of your own money into the business.

2. You must have enough expertise to successfully run the business.

3. And most important, you must be able to show that the loan can be paid through the cash flow of the business.

To find the SBA office near you, call their national toll-free number: (800) U-ASKSBA.

The SBA also has a number of special programs for women and minority businesses. For more information about these and other services, you can write to the Office of Public Communication, U.S. Small Business Administration, Mail Code: 2550, 1441 L St. NW, Washington DC 20416.

only what you can afford out of your own pocket. But there may come a time when you will need to tap other resources to make your studio survive and thrive. If you lack the funds to cover your needs, you need to explore borrowing money from a bank or other sources.

Since the economic recession of the late 1980s, it has been almost impossible for small businesses like yours to get loans, especially start-up loans, from banks and other lending institutions. However, if you need to secure a bank loan, be well prepared. Put together the most thorough and professional-looking loan proposal you can muster. (For a source of help in preparing a proposal for a start-up loan, see the sidebar on the SBA, page 5.) To do this, you will need the following:

♦ A statement describing your business and the clients you have and/or the potential clients you are targeting.
♦ A statement of both your short-term and long-range business objectives and goals.
♦ A formal five-year business plan (see page 7 for information on how to put that together).
♦ Copies of your tax returns for the last three years.
♦ An itemized list of all your business-related expenses.
♦ A written request for the amount of money you need that explains why you need it, and an itemized list that shows how the money will be spent.

If you have been in business for a while, ask your accountant to prepare the financial statements, including a projection of your future earnings based on your present status. She should also give you the copies of your tax returns and help you list your business expenses.

If your request is rejected by the bank, don't be afraid to ask why. You may only need to provide more information. Or you may need to find someone to guarantee repayment with or for you. (See "The SBA and You," page 5, for more on their guarantee program.) Since bank lending policies differ, check with every bank in town before you give up. There are also alternative sources for business financing you may want to explore. (See "Alternative Sources of Financing" on page 8.)

If you do borrow money, be sure you get enough money—undercapitalization can be fatal—without incurring bigger payments than you can afford. There is a tremendous temptation to say, "If I have to pay this much back, I might as well get enough to really start out right." Bad idea! You're asking for trouble—and hefty loan payments that could break your new business's back.

Shop for loans *very* carefully. Take your loan application to at least three banks and compare deals. Although the bank where you have your personal finances may offer you a better deal on that basis, avoid mixing your business and personal finances if at all possible. For instance, don't offer your home equity to secure a loan unless there's no other way. If you must use your personal equity, try to get a reduction of a percentage point or two on interest or a delay on the first payment due.

Be prepared when you go to apply for a loan. Have your business plan ready (see pages 7-11 for how to put one together) and show that you've done your homework. Use concrete numbers for costs, even if you have to estimate. Work up forecasts of your earnings: how much you'll make and where it will come from. Be as specific and detailed as possible.

Ask for a single payment, simple interest note rather than an installment loan. As you make monthly loan payments, the original loan amount (the principal) decreases and the interest is charged only on the remaining principal. With an installment loan, you're still paying in the percentage agreed upon for the full loan amount up until you make your last payment, even though at that point you may owe the lender only a tiny fraction of the principal.

If you have projects already under contract, you can use those signed contracts as leverage in negotiating for a loan. When you get a loan, don't forget to include loan payments in your overhead expenses—and always make those payments on time.

Never agree to include credit life or disability insurance in a loan package. Don't let the bank convince you that such a provision can be a condition of the loan; that's not legal. Buy any insurance you need from an independent insurance broker, not a banker—you'll get better coverage at a fairer price that way.

Clients

Do you need to have one or more clients lined up, ready to put you to work, before you make the big move? That would be great, but it's not absolutely necessary. If you have enough start-up capital or a part-time job so you can pound the pavement for a month or two, then you should find a few jobs to get you going.

If you are working for a design studio or an ad agency, don't try to persuade your employer's clients to come with you when you leave. That can ruin your reputation before you even get going. In addition, you could be liable for legal action if your company has solid grounds to prove that you diverted business or stole clients. (If former clients approach you *after* you've gone, that's different.) Start clean and on your own. Business is hard enough without enemies or legal headaches.

Writing a Business Plan

You must have a written business plan when applying to a bank or lending institution for a loan or line of credit. In fact, that's about the only time that most people ever think about putting together a business plan. But you'll need a plan. You have to think about what you want to accomplish in business, how you intend to do it, and where you foresee your business going in the future. Reflective thinking and planning are necessary. Remember the old adage, "Most people don't plan to fail, they just fail to plan."

A business plan is the map that will guide you toward each of your goals. It makes you focus on why you want to start your business, what your business philosophy is, who your clients will be, and what strategies you'll use to get those clients. Knowing all this can save you from costly mistakes and the frustration that comes from just getting by each day. A business plan can motivate you to follow through on each action you set down—ac-

tions that will bring you closer to your goals.

Even though the ideal business plan should be a broad document that outlines your anticipated goals and growth for the next five or more years, those goals may change long before that. It's good to review your plan once a year to see if you have strayed off course or if your goals have changed. If either does happen, you can easily alter your course and revise your plan to accommodate any changes in direction.

When you write a business plan for a bank or other lender, have concrete numbers for everything and be prepared to explain and defend your figures. You may also have to explain in detail what a graphic designer does—many bankers won't have had any previous contact with designers. You must establish yourself as a professional who will have steady income; the perception that professionals in the arts are rather fly-by-night persists with many people.

The following is an outline for a formal business plan. You can use the headings shown here as part of an actual plan (section VIII is optional). The more detailed and specific you are when you prepare it, the easier it will be to actually use it to guide your business. (For help in developing your business plan, see pages 7-11; for creating a marketing plan, see pages 158-159; for figuring out costs and fees, refer to chapter nine, "Planning Your Future.")

The Business Plan

I. Name of Business: Select a name for your business. This should tell something about who you are and what you do. (See page 162 for more on choosing your business name.)

II. Mission Statement: State briefly what your business will focus on, and who and what your market is. Don't just put down "graphic design"; list the types of design work you will do and the clients who will want those services. You won't need detail at this point—that's the next step—but include enough information so that someone who knows nothing about design can figure out what you do.

How to Get a Federal I.D. Number

If you incorporate your design studio, you must apply to the IRS for a Federal Identification Number (FID) which is also called an Employer Identification Number (EIN). This number is used to identify and track for the IRS your corporation's financial activities such as income, expenses, payroll, bank accounts, and federal income tax reports and tax payments. You cannot open a corporate bank account without your FID.

You must use your Federal Identification Number when you file and pay your employees' (once you incorporate, you're an employee, too) and your corporation's share of state and federal withholding, social security taxes, unemployment taxes, and in some states TDI or Temporary Disability Insurance.

To get a FID/EIN, call your local/regional IRS office and ask for the TELE-TIN number service (telephone taxpayer identification number). Or you can request an SS-4 form, fill it out, and send it to your regional IRS service center (the same place you send your federal taxes).

Alternative Sources of Financing

If you run into that proverbial brick wall when trying to secure a bank loan, don't give up your dream of a studio of your own. There are other ways to find the money you need to start or expand your business. Your first, most reliable and perhaps smartest source of financing is you.

If you are currently employed and want to go out on your own, put a percentage of every paycheck into a "saving to start my studio" account. Although interest rates have been low for some time, a savings account is still an excellent tool to pay for your start-up or growth costs. (Depending on how much money you have available and your tolerance for risk, putting at least some of your savings into another kind of investment can increase your return, but consult an investment or financial planner about these options.) Plan to save both enough for your business needs and to cover any personal emergencies that might come up within one calendar year, and at least three to six months of backup funds to cover personal living expenses during lean times.

If you have built equity in your home (owned it long enough to recover part of the cost of buying it), consider a home equity loan. These loans are based on the appraised value of your home and are the only kind of loan on which the IRS still allows you to deduct the interest. Shop around, since some lending institutions offer programs in which you can avoid points, closing costs and application fees in order to be more competitive in this area. The interest rates may be higher when the up-front costs are eliminated: Remember nothing is free, especially when it comes to a loan.

A home equity line of credit is similar to a home equity loan. You still borrow against the value of your home, but you only need to borrow what you need, as you need it, rather than a lump sum.

One source of loans many people overlook is their life insurance policies. The amount of a loan against your policy that you are eligible for will depend on how much equity you have built up in your payments. This works just like any loan in which there is a fixed rate of interest and the balance can be paid back over a specified period of time. The only thing to keep in mind is that should you die before the loan is repaid, the balance due will be deducted from your benefits.

If you cannot tap your current funds or wait till you can save more money for financing, there are still alternatives.

Find a business partner or two to help foot the bill for a business start-up or for growth. (For more information on the pros and cons of partnerships, see page 10.)

Ask friends and family members for help. If you do this, keep the arrangement strictly professional. Offer to pay interest and set up a schedule for repayment. Before you make an offer, have a lawyer help you decide on a fair rate of interest and a manageable payment schedule and draft a legal contract. Doing this will present your intentions in the most honorable light, and it will also cover your bases with the IRS. Otherwise, the IRS might classify the loan as a gift subject to a gift tax.

Seek out investors among your acquaintances and area businesspeople. There are always people who are looking for good ways to invest their money, and your studio could be exactly what they are looking for. Investors put a certain amount of money into a business with the intention of not only making back their investment, but also earning some form of repayment such as interest, dividends, or a percentage of your profits.

III. Statement of Purpose: Describe your personal business philosophy—your principles and values—for example, delivering quality work on time at a reasonable price. Discuss in detail the services you plan to offer (those you listed under your mission statement) and any areas you plan to specialize in. Also, list the reason(s) you are going into business, what needs you expect to fill, and why the clients you have targeted will benefit from your services. (See chapters five and six for a discussion of the different kinds of design work you will do and which clients might want those services.)

IV. List of Goals: Include what you expect to accomplish in terms of the kinds of clients you'll get, the types of projects you'll handle, how much you want your business to earn,

what you expect to take as a salary for yourself, etc. Set a time line for achieving all of these goals. Be realistic! No matter how good you are, unless your work is already well-known it will take time to build a solid client base.

If you're not currently doing corporate identity, annual reports or major advertising campaigns in an advertising agency or a design studio, don't plan to get these kinds of projects right away. Realize that you'll probably begin with fairly basic, low-budget projects if you're just starting out, or with the same level of project you're currently doing for someone else.

Work out careful income projections based on what you plan to charge (see pages 86-87 for determining your fees) and the number of projects you can reasonably expect to

To find investors, put the word out through the business community grapevine. You can also take out a small classified ad in a local business newspaper. Study potential investors as carefully as they will study you and your business. Check out their reputations, credit ratings, and any other business investments. Don't accept deals that sound too good to be true or give away more control over your studio than you are comfortable with. Also protect yourself by never engaging in any legal agreement without the advice of your lawyer.

If the business grapevine proves to be unfruitful, you can contact the Association of Venture Clubs, 265 E. First South Street, Suite 300, Salt Lake City UT 84111. This group helps match up investors and businesses in need of financing.

Try commercial finance companies instead of a bank. These companies offer loans to businesspeople, but usually at a higher interest rate than a bank. You will also be required to put up some type of tangible collateral, such as your car or house. Consider the costs and risks carefully before you get financing from one of these companies.

Look for Economic Development Agencies. These are state and local agencies that are set up to work with area businesses. Call the Government Printing Office, (203) 783-3238, to obtain for a fee a biannual list of state aid programs called "States and Small Businesses." Since every state is different, check your local government directory for relevant listings. You can also call the town hall or your mayor's office for information or assistance in locating appropriate government agencies or programs that can offer advice and sources of federal or state financial aid. There are also some programs especially for women.

American Women's Economic Development Corporation (AWED) offers training and support programs for women in business or those who are planning to start a business. Their address is 641 Lexington Ave., 9th Floor, New York NY 10022. You can also reach them by calling (800) 222-AWED or New York: (212) 688-1900; Washington DC: (202) 857-0091; Los Angeles: (310) 983-3747.

National Association of Women Business Owners (NAWBO) exists to assist women business owners. Many cities have local chapters, so check your directory for listings. You can call for more information or the location of the chapter closest to you at (800) 892-9000 or (312) 922-0465. The address is 600 S. Federal St., Suite 400, Chicago IL 60605.

Minority and Women Owned Business program (M/WBE) began in New York state in 1988 and has spread to a number of other, but not all, states. M/WBE offers loans and puts out a directory of women and minority owned businesses that is circulated to state agencies and contractors. The organization also provides bonding programs (a business often needs to be bonded in order to work under contract for a state agency). You can get more information by calling (518) 474-3256; or write P.O. Box 2072, Albany NY 12220.

National Chamber of Commerce for Women provides some of the same services as local chambers, with the exception that the focus is specifically on women in business. Thus all programs, such as networking, technical assistance, mentor matches, business plan and resume assistance, support and advocacy, are geared toward issues that concern women. You can reach this organization at (212) 685-3453; 10 Waterside Plaza, Suite 6H, New York NY 10010.

get. Work up estimates of how much time different types of projects will take.

You should already have worked out a personal and a business budget to establish how much money you'll need to make to cover your first year's operating and living expenses. Use that to determine what you'll pay yourself as a salary.

V. Strategies: This is a step-by-step plan of how you will reach each goal. For example, how you intend to target your market, what research you will do, how you will make contacts, and what contacts you already have as leads into your selected markets. Describe your competition and how you'll position yourself — what you can offer that is different or perceived as different — to compete with them.

Give specifics; don't say your competition is every other designer in the world. You're competing with other one- and two-person firms or others in your specialty. You don't need to work out a detailed marketing plan, but you should know whether you'll get clients through direct mail, local contacts or by visiting trade shows.

VI. Structure: Decide what kind of business organization you'll operate under — sole proprietorship, partnership, association or corporation. If you have partners or associates, state who they will be, what they will do, and why you're working with them. If you intend to work alone, spell out what responsibilities and tasks you will handle, what you will subcontract out to others and who those others will be.

List only subcontractors you will use regularly. If you're not a copywriter, state that you'll hire one on a freelance basis as needed. If you don't expect to do projects that use photographs, don't list photographers. Will you have enough work initially to use freelancers? Will they do mechanicals, layouts or more general tasks?

VII. Location: State where you'll locate your business and why it's a good location. Describe how your office will be set up and equipped. List which aspects of your work can actually be performed in-house and which will have to be sent out — typesetting, stats, etc.

The three main issues in where you'll locate your business and why are expenses, convenience and image. If you're starting out on a shoestring, you'll have your office at home. If you can afford an outside office, explain your choice of location in terms of what benefits you'll achieve in exchange for the costs.

VIII. Action Plans: Write out a step-by-step plan for meeting your goals within a set period of time. Pull together all the information

Choosing the Right Business Structure for You

You can set up your design studio as a sole proprietorship, an association, a partnership or a corporation. Each business structure has its own pros and cons, so choose the one you'll start with carefully. Since a design studio can grow and change, reevaluate your business structure every few years. A rapidly growing partnership that is adding employees frequently is a good candidate for a change to incorporation, for example.

Sole Proprietor: Nearly every designer starts in business this way, because it's the simplest form. You get all its profits but have sole responsibility for its operation and its debts. You are *personally* liable for everything related to your business. The law doesn't distinguish between your business and personal debts, so you could be in big trouble if you don't make enough money to cover your expenses. You could lose everything — even your home and stereo.

You need to register your business with your state's division of taxation and get a sales tax permit (or resale number). If your studio will operate under a name other than your personal name, you need a Doing Business As (DBA) certificate. If D. Designer opened a studio and called it "Top Cat Designs," D. D. would need a DBA certificate; in other words, D. Designer is doing business as Top Cat Designs. On the other hand, D. D. wouldn't need a DBA certificate to operate as "D. Designer Designs." In some areas, you may need additional permits or licenses. Find out what applies in your area and check out local zoning regulations.

Association: If you team up with one or more people but each remains officially a sole proprietor, you've created an association. For example, a designer named Smith and a copywriter named Jones might publicly call themselves Smith and Jones Associates, but to the government they are still Doing Business As (DBA): Smith, Graphic Design/Sole Proprietorship and Jones, Copywriting/Sole Proprietorship.

Partnership: When two or more people form a legal partnership, they share the financial earnings and liabilities of a joint business. Each person's share is based on a percentage of interest in the business. The percentage of interest is based on the partner's contribution to the business: money, reputation or expertise. Once the contribution and interest are determined, the lawyers draw up a partnership agreement. Don't believe problems can't happen to you. Be very businesslike in drawing up the agreement. Protect your interests by getting your own lawyer.

Unlimited liability applies to partnerships, too. But there's another catch. Because the law treats the business and personal life of a partner as the same, the actions of any one partner, or even a partner's spouse, can affect the other partner's assets. In other words, your partner's creditors could go after your personal possessions if he or she gets into debt. Partnership insurance, another means of self protection, covers you if your partner dies or skips town.

Incorporation: A corporation is a legal business entity that is totally separate from you as an individual. Most important, you aren't personally liable for the corporation's debts and would lose only the money you've put into the corporation. In fact, you become an employee of your own business. As such, you are paid a salary and pay personal income taxes on that salary. The corporation pays separate taxes based on its earnings and deductions.

The freedom from personal financial liability for business debts is a major benefit of incorporating. If a client leaves you with a large printing bill, only your business assets could be taken away; you would still keep your house and car (unlike the sole proprietorship or partnership). Incorporating may also save you some money. Corporations can often get tax

you compiled under sections IV, V and VI and translate it into specific actions and a schedule with definite dates for completing each step.

●*Phase I/Action Plan (Years 1-2):* Outline exactly what you plan to do and how you plan to do it during the first two years.

●*Phase II/Action Plan (Years 3-5):* Assuming you accomplish your goals in the first two years, what will you tackle in the next three to five years? How will you do it?

●*Phase III/Action Plan (Years 5-10):* This is a projection of where you want your business to go during years five to ten. Why do you think this can happen? How will you make it happen?

You'll get the return on the time you spend writing your business plan — even if things turn out differently — in the time and money you'll save by knowing where you're going. It's like getting a map and marking out the route you'll take to your destination before you leave home. So, take the time now to map out where you want your business to go and how you plan to get there. You will be glad you did.

breaks the self-employed person can't; have your accountant check current IRS regulations to discover if this will happen for you. You might even qualify for a corporate discount from some suppliers.

But incorporating is expensive. The initial cost alone is enough to make you think twice — $200 to $300 to do it yourself and at least $1,000 if you use a lawyer. Your annual bookkeeping and accounting costs will be higher than for other structures because record keeping is more complex, and you must have corporate state and federal tax statements prepared each year. Another major cost is corporate taxes. If you have a traditional corporation (a subchapter C corporation), you have to pay corporate taxes on all profits earned by the studio. Then you have to pay personal taxes on the profits you distribute to yourself and other stockholders, if any, at year's end.

One or more people can form a corporation. You can incorporate without a lawyer, if you're careful and thorough. But don't try to incorporate without the help of an accountant who thoroughly understands your financial history and goals.

Contact the Corporate Division of your Secretary of State's office for the information you need regarding your state's regulations on and procedures for incorporation (every state is different). Then pick a name for your corporation. Since no two businesses in a state can have the same name, you must have your corporation's name cleared through the Corporate Division's office. You must get a new Federal Identification Number (FIN), also called an Employer Identification Number, or EIN (see page 7), even if you already have one. Finally, you will file a Certificate of Incorporation; when the certificate and your choice of name have been approved, the state will issue your corporate charter.

Every corporation must issue stock. If you own the whole corporation, you can hold all the stock. If you have partners, the stock is divided up among you based on your shares of the business. Most states require that a corporation have a board of directors and officers. If you are the sole owner, you can be the board of directors and the officers or invite people to serve in those positions. Being a director or officer usually involves nothing more than a few signatures and attending an annual meeting to review the corporation's business. However, if you and they choose, your directors can become an active board that provides advice and guidance for your studio, meeting several times a year.

The Subchapter S Corporation: This is a variation on the traditional corporation (subchapter C) that has all the advantages of incorporation plus some additional tax benefits. With a subchapter S corporation, all profits are taxed once at the personal rate unlike the traditional corporation, where you pay both corporate and personal taxes on profits you make. You avoid the tax liabilities of the traditional corporation, but you still have the same protection from personal financial liability.

There are some eligibility restrictions for forming a subchapter S corporation, but these generally do not affect freelancers and small design studio owners. You set up a subchapter S corporation through the same process as a traditional corporation, but you must notify the IRS no later than the fifteenth day of the third month of your corporation's life that you are electing to be subchapter S. If you fail to do so, you will automatically be classified as a traditional corporation.

The combination of limited personal financial liability and avoiding double taxation makes the subchapter S corporation a good business structure for designers. But before you make any final decisions, verify the potential financial advantages and disadvantages with your accountant.

Working at Home vs. the Outside Studio

There are advantages and disadvantages to either arrangement. What you do depends on your needs and finances. The economic issues are the most obvious — it's cheaper to have your office at home. But then you have issues of appearing professional, finding appropriate work space, and dealing with cabin fever. (Cabin fever can strike in the rented office, but that seems less common.) It's probably significant that most designers start out working from home but move into rented space as soon as they can afford it. But that doesn't mean a rented studio is right for you.

Although rented studios do cost more to occupy and operate, and you need to consider location and leases carefully, there are advantages: You're far more likely to build a long-term relationship with a Fortune 500 company if you look like one yourself. You may enjoy having a clear separation between your work and home life. You've got to weigh all the costs and benefits and then do what's best for you.

If You Work at Home

The least expensive option is working at home. That's how I started out myself. The economic advantages are obvious: the rent and utilities are cheap (you have an "in" with the landlord), you won't need a lot of furniture, you won't have daily commuting costs, and you get a healthy tax deduction from having a home office. Working at home can also help reduce your child care costs, if you can handle the distractions.

There are psychological benefits in addition to the obvious economic ones. If you wake up in the middle of the night with a great idea, you can go right into your studio and work it out. You can wear jeans and sneakers all day, if you don't have an appointment. And you can run a load of wash or let in a repairman *while* you're working (not after or instead of).

There are, of course, disadvantages to the home studio setup. Location is a problem if you live any distance from your clients and vendors. You have to schedule meetings and appointments carefully so you can make the best use of your time without racing frantically from one place to another.

Many designers find working at home too distracting. There's always something else that you could do: watch TV, eat, go for a walk, even do chores. Then there are your family and friends who blithely assume that you'll always be free to visit, run errands, or look after the children. Good luck getting any work done between all those interruptions!

Expanding your business and adding new employees is difficult if your studio is in the main part of your home. You can only have as many people or as much equipment as you have space. Once you've run out of usable space, you face having to build an addition to your home or moving to larger quarters. Some of these problems can be solved, and we'll look at some ways to deal with them later in this chapter.

Projecting a Professional Image

When you're working from home, you have to be careful not to appear to clients, vendors or even family and friends as an "amateur." This is true even if you're working only part-time as a freelance designer. To get the respect you deserve as a professional, you must first think of yourself that way and then project that image to others. When you think about your image as a designer, remember the phrase, "What I *see* is what you *are*." People will develop an opinion of you and your business based on how your office looks and how you look and act when you're in it. Want respect? Then show you deserve it.

Your home studio can do a lot to promote or hurt your image as a design professional. Ideally, it's separated from the rest of the house; maybe you've converted your garage for your use. This makes it easy to separate your work and personal lives as well as create the sense that your studio is a place of business. If that's not possible, the next best option is a private space of your own: the attic or a converted spare room. This gives you some privacy and control over your space. Least suc-

How to Find and Hire a Lawyer

You can set up your new studio as a sole proprietorship (see page 10) without hiring a lawyer, if you do your homework carefully. If you have or want to have a more complicated structure, such as a partnership, an association or a corporation (see page 10), you should have a lawyer. And it's wise to have a relationship with a lawyer before you need one for a specific problem.

How can you find a lawyer you can trust? Begin your search by using the business grapevine – ask other designers or your suppliers for recommendations. If your sources are comfortable with their choices, ask why. You can also call your local bar association for referrals or the Small Business Association. Once you have several referrals, call and ask for an information interview. Be sure to ask if there is a charge for that. If there is, I usually eliminate that one right then and there. A lawyer who is going to charge me for the time it takes to decide whether or not I want to work with him is more interested in getting my money than in meeting my needs.

During that first meeting, ask if the lawyer's fees are hourly, per project or on a retainer – a base payment against which fees and expenses are deducted. If you are asked to pay a retainer, be sure to ask if the unused portion is refundable if you terminate services. Then find out if she has a written agreement detailing fees and services. Also ask if she has any experience dealing with a design or graphics business. Be sure you understand what you are being told. Does she use simple, non-jargon filled language?

Ask who will handle your account. If it is an associate, ask to meet that person and examine his qualifications. Also ask how much time that lawyer spends in the office during the week. There is nothing more frustrating than waiting days for your lawyer to return an urgent phone call because he is always tied up in court.

If you are going in with a specific problem, ask for the lawyer's recommendations and the reasons for them. He should take your questions seriously and answer them directly, without excuses or complicated explanations. You should feel that the lawyer took the time to understand your problem. If you feel rushed or pushed into a decision, he's probably not the right lawyer.

If you decide to give a lawyer a specific issue to work on, ask for a clear and, if necessary, written timeline outlining what will happen and when. Ask what she expects the outcome to be, and why. Again, look for clear and direct answers.

Protect yourself when dealing with lawyers by keeping a written record of all phone conversations (date, length of time spent, topic and outcome), personal meetings and correspondence. Also keep track of how long it took her to return each phone call. That way, if you question your lawyer's services or fees, you have documentation. If you do question a bill, always do it in writing, using your log as evidence of your understanding of what transpired.

Some people feel embarrassed to question a lawyer about the services they've received. Don't be. It is your right to receive all the services promised to you and to understand what is happening with any legal matters being addressed. If at any time you are unhappy with the service you receive, it's your right to fire that lawyer. You may do so in person, but I recommend doing it in writing. I once fired a lawyer who continued to work on my case and bill me for it. Because I had a copy of the termination letter I had already sent, I quickly got the matter straightened out through my new lawyer. It's a rare problem, but if you feel that your lawyer has acted unethically in any way, call your state bar association about a disciplinary board review.

---

cessful, unless you live alone, is partitioning off part of a room with a screen or some kind of curtain. Although it's not very private or professional looking, it does at least give you a space of your own.

Avoiding Cabin Fever

Cabin fever is one of the biggest problems designers with a home studio setup face. You don't have to go out to the office every morning. In fact, you don't have to go out at all except to meet with clients or to get supplies, type or stats. This may sound great at first, but it can get old very quickly. Watch for the telltale signs of cabin fever:

♦ Extreme loneliness
♦ Excessive irritability
♦ Short attention span
♦ Stalking the postal carrier just to have a conversation
♦ Leaving the TV on all day to hear the sound of voices
♦ Running unnecessary errands to get out of the house
♦ Doing the one chore you most hate to stay out of the studio

Don't worry. There are cures for this dread disease that don't involve moving out of your house into a new studio.

A Copier in the Living Room?

If the only work space you can afford is extremely small, consider creative alternatives for storing large equipment. I knew a designer who had a copier in a very tiny studio off his living room. He needed the copier, but it really got in his way. There was seldom a day when he didn't swear at it or kick it out of pure frustration. I suggested that he put it in the living room. "Put a copier in my living room!" he gasped. "What will people think?"

"They'll either think that you have a copier in your living room because you need it or because you assume everyone has one there."

He thought for a moment, then said, "Well, I don't really care what other people say is or isn't standard furniture for a living room – and it would be much more convenient."

"So, there you go," I said cheerfully. "Problem solved."

"We·e·l·l·l·l, maybe," he said rather guiltily. "I think my wife will get really upset if I plonk a copier in the living room."

"Have you ever asked her if she'd mind having a copier in the living room?"

"Uh, no. It's not the sort of thing that comes up every day."

"Then why not ask and see what she *does* say, instead of assuming that she'll be upset. If she does get upset," I continued, "find out what her objections are. If she thinks it'll stick out like a sore thumb or is afraid you'll leave copies all over the floor, *then* you can look for ways to resolve those problems."

He thought about that for a few minutes as he looked around the living room. Suddenly his eyes lit up. "See that little alcove in the corner of the room? If we set it there and put a large plant or a Chinese screen next to it, it wouldn't even be noticeable." He discussed it with his wife, and that's what they did. So, don't be afraid to apply a little creativity to your space problems.

1. Establish a daily routine and stick to it. Set yourself regular office hours, allowing for unavoidable overtime. Sticking to a regular rhythm of work and leisure time as much as possible helps take away the feeling that you never get away from your work. Setting a regular work schedule has the added benefit of reducing unwanted interruptions. If you're firm about not dropping everything to run errands, pick up the children, or just chat, family and friends will come to accept (and respect) you as a businessperson.

2. Plan to get out of the office at least once a week for business-related reasons. Unless it's much cheaper to buy a month's supply of everything you use, plan your purchases so you can get out of your home office regularly. If most of your clients are local and their businesses aren't too far away, drop off materials for approval yourself. *Join a local design or advertising organization or club.* Participating in such a group will be helpful because this will not only get you out of the house, it will give you a support group and a sounding board of fellow professionals. Joining the AIGA, AAAA or local Art Director's Club will put you in touch with fellow designers. Also consider joining local business groups such as the Chamber of Commerce. You'll meet new people (and potential clients).

3. Develop a daily productivity schedule for yourself. It will give you a sense of structure and accomplishment. Assign time slots throughout the day to specific tasks. For example, use the first hour of each business day to make and return phone calls to clients and vendors. Then three hours of design or production work. A lunch hour could be combined with picking up materials or delivering work to clients — or even a walk! Back to the office for another two or three hours of work on various projects. You take another short break toward the end of the day, then do paperwork.

4. End each day by writing out a list of things you need to do the next day. This makes it easier to walk away from your studio and forget about work. Don't panic if you didn't finish everything on each day's list! As a general rule, if it's not done by five P.M. (or the end of your regular working day), it can wait till the next morning. Just roll it over to the top of the next day's list. The only exception is a deadline for something due first thing the next morning. You wouldn't make a habit of asking your employee to stay late every night, would you? Save burning the midnight oil for the client's deadlines rather than those you impose on yourself.

5. When you make a list, assign a priority number to each day's planned activities. Establishing priorities in addition to noting deadlines helps you keep a sense of perspective about what you're doing. Once you've marked work on tight or immediate deadline

projects with a #1, think about what else you need to do that's most important. That's not necessarily the job due at the end of the week. You could assign a #1 on a certain day to working on a new self-promotion piece or following up with a client you're trying to get. After you choose those priorities, choose the items that are important but not as urgent. Mark these with a #2. The "Get to if I cans" are a #3 priority. At the very least, push to get through all the #1s each day. That way you'll be sure to get the most urgent and important jobs done and feel like you're getting somewhere.

6. Take frequent breaks. When you work alone, you can get caught in the trap of grinding away hour after hour until you can't concentrate and your work's not as good. Keep yourself fresh and relaxed to stay at your peak creativity. You're also less likely to fall prey to cabin fever if you don't keep yourself chained to the drawing board. Plan regular breaks throughout your workday. Get out of your studio, even if it's only to go into the kitchen for juice or coffee. Better yet, go for a walk, jog, meet a friend for lunch, exercise or shopping. If you have children, plan a long break for late afternoon so you can spend time with them without feeling guilty about work that's not getting done. Usually one long break combined with lunch and two shorter breaks will keep you not only at peak productivity but ward off cabin fever.

7. Know when you've had enough. Some days, no matter how many breaks you take, you just won't be able to do your best work. At these times, your body or mind is trying to tell you that you've had enough. When this happens, stop work for the rest of the day if that's at all possible. You run the risk of making serious mistakes if you try to keep going, so dump the guilt and kick back.

Continuing to work when you've had more than enough can bring on a good case of cabin fever. Although you do have to be disciplined and work regularly, there are exceptions to even that rule of business life. Take a mental health day (or days) when you really need to. And try not to work when you're so ill you wouldn't go in if you worked for some-

body else. Unless you've got a screaming deadline or major emergency, that will only make matters worse — and make you long for a job in a studio where you *could* call in when sick!

Also, caring for someone else who's ill can require staying away from work. You'll probably only end up frustrated and upset with both yourself and your patient if you try to run back and forth between studio and sickroom. (On the other hand, don't let someone who's home with an illness take advantage of your being there because you work there, too!)

If You Rent a Studio

There are also advantages and disadvantages to having a rented studio. It projects a very professional image to business contacts, family and friends. Giving your business a space of its own shows you care about and are committed to it. You'll have more opportunities for and space to make a statement about who you are and what you do. You can structure your studio to reflect your work and the types of clients you will have.

You may also enjoy having a definite division between your personal life and work life. Most designers report a sense of relief from knowing they can leave the office *and* their work behind. When your studio is always right there with you, it's too easy to keep popping back in to do just one more thing. And there's no more worrying about children, pets or both chasing a ball through your work space and accidentally destroying the massive project that was waiting for delivery the next morning.

Although you have more expenses with an outside office, the opportunities for tax write-offs are much greater. You can deduct the full rent as well as all operating expenses. You can often recover most of the costs of remodeling, furnishing and expanding your office space. Expansion is easier with a rented office. You may have to be cramped while a lease runs out, but then you're off to bigger and better quarters. If you buy an office, such as a condo or building (redoing houses and barns is popular), you will have a mortgage, in-

A Business Phone Line

You can use your home phone line for business calls. This may not be the best solution, however, if there are other people at home during the day, such as children, who might tie up the phone for long periods of time or answer business calls. Even if you train your children to say "Answering for . . . ," the effect will still be less than professional. An answering machine is one solution, but only if you can convince your children that the phone really is off limits to them between 9:00 A.M. and 5:00 P.M. That rule can in practice, however, be especially difficult to enforce.

The alternative is a separate business phone line. A business line costs more per month than a private line, but you can deduct the entire cost—installation, equipment and monthly charges—from your taxes. From an image and privacy standpoint, this is the best way to go. It's also more convenient to have a separate business line if you're going to use a fax machine. You'll need to be able to receive faxes, such as rush corrections, without the line being tied up. A long fax tying up the phone may also prevent you from receiving an emergency call from family members.

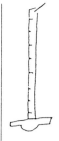

terest payments, depreciation, taxes and other expenses that will benefit you at tax time.

The biggest single disadvantage to an outside studio is the increased expense. You'll reap benefits at tax time but feel the sharp impact on your monthly cash flow first. And in lean times, there will be even less left over than you had when working at home. You may have to do some general belt-tightening to keep your head above water. Turning down jobs to give yourself plenty of time off may have to go as well.

Location and Leases

Choose your studio's location carefully. You don't have to move into the high-rent district to get nice space, but don't take a space solely because it's cheap either. Moving into the Bowery sends the wrong message — and could get you mugged! Research a number of neighborhoods; a studio in an area where renovation is just beginning can be an excellent long-term investment.

Consider convenience, too. Will your new studio be close to clients and suppliers? You don't want to waste too much time commuting back and forth to clients' offices for meetings or running all over town to suppliers. Some suppliers will deliver only within a certain area, and that service can be a great time-saver for you. This doesn't mean that you should instantly reject a less convenient space, but you should consider the trade-offs before you sign.

How much work will it take to make your new studio ready for you to use? Although you can save a lot of money by rehabbing your space yourself, you must consider the time trade-off, too. If you're spending more time and effort renovating than you are on design or self-promotion, you're not doing yourself any favors. And don't fall into the trap of taking a less desirable space because, "I can always fix those problems." Inadequate lighting or storage space are difficult and expensive to correct.

If you can afford it, hiring an architect to oversee your new or revamped offices can save money, time and your sanity when you need extensive renovations. An architect will work with you to create a space that reflects both your needs and creative personality, then find contractors to actually do the work for you. You won't even have to supervise the workers; a decent architect handles that as well.

Finally, you've found just the right space for your studio. And here's the landlord with the lease all ready for you to sign. Great, let's do it, you think and reach for his pen. Whoa! Stop right there. No matter how perfect the space, you don't want it on the wrong terms. Before you sign, have your lawyer review that lease thoroughly with you. Remember, though, that you know best what your business needs, so make sure the lawyer gets it for you. Be careful about restrictions in the lease; for example, a lease that permits you to use the space only for "graphic art design" would prevent your sharing space with a photographer. And be sure you understand what you're getting for your money. There's a big difference between getting 1,000 square feet that are usable feet and 1,000 square feet that include your share of public corridors, elevators and bathrooms. Your responsibilities for the space are also important. Will you or the landlord be responsible for electricity, cleaning service or repairs and improvements? If you're bearing most of the expenses, you should ask for lower rent in compensation.

Try to get a short-term lease that gives you the option to renew for a year or two at the present price. If you outgrow your space during the term of the lease, you're free to move. If you don't, you can renew.

Studio Space Alternatives

There are alternatives to working at home or renting an office on your own if neither option appeals to you or fits your budget. Instead, share space with other designers or creatives as owners of independent businesses. This kind of arrangement can save you big bucks on rent, utilities and even equipment. For many designers, this is a practical step to take in order to start out in business at all. Sharing the cost of not only space but also computer equipment, a photocopier and a fax may mean you won't have to postpone your dream of your own studio until you've got the money to invest.

If you are already renting but have more space than you need or are paying more than anticipated, you may want to think about subletting some of your space. Before you do, review your lease or talk with your landlord. Some rental agreements prohibit sublets. However, your landlord might approve it, even if the lease forbids it, if you are planning to bring in a business similar to your own, or if it means losing you as a tenant because you can no longer afford the rent.

Artist/designer co-op rentals have also become popular in the last few years. These are usually located in large buildings, like old factories, warehouses or mills where space is unimproved. The rent is cheap, but it's up to you to make the best of it—whatever the condition. Each renter is responsible for putting up partitions or otherwise separating his or her space; crates or curtains may be used by some. Other people don't mind the open space and may prefer to remain one big, happy family.

Many designers are moving into business incubators. This type of setup is usually owned by someone who purchases a building for the sole purpose of providing inexpensive rental space for small and starting-up businesses. The attraction, however, isn't just the reasonable rent. These incubators also provide—as part of the rent or for an extra fee—secretarial/reception services, which can include answering your phone, taking messages and typing. Most incubators offer the use of copiers and fax machines, a conference room and a kitchen to their tenants. Some will even provide furniture, such as desks and files, and sometimes phones, too, for those who need them. Executive suite leases often provide the same services, but are more upscale and expensive than a business incubator.

In addition to the obvious advantages of these various forms of shared space, there are other considerations to bear in mind before you make a final decision. If you are in a build-ing that rents to other types of businesses besides designers, this can be a great way to pick up new clients. Convenience is one of the major motivators when businesspeople look for support services. Also, you have the opportunity to meet people and network.

The presence of other designers or related creatives in their building or space helps ease the sense of isolation many solo designers experience when in business for themselves. Many creatives who share building or studio space end up freelancing for each other or collaborating on projects.

While there are financial advantages to shared space, there are disadvantages, too. Sharply contrasting work styles can wreak havoc on shared space arrangements. Designer X might love to play hard rock or heavy metal CDs all day long, while your beloved Mozart gets drowned out by his blasting boom box. If you're a neat freak, can you share space with slobs?

You should also be concerned about the reputations of your studio mates. Honesty and integrity are critical qualities when you're sharing the costs of space and expensive equipment. They're also important when it comes to client confidentiality. There's also the question of being able to trust someone not to swipe your clients.

Before you jump into any shared space situation, explore all the alternatives in your area. When you find some possibilities worth considering, spend time there to see what people's habits are. Evaluate the facilities for convenience, comfort and safety. If you have to sign a rental agreement, read it carefully and run anything you don't understand by a lawyer. Know what your rent includes and get a detailed listing of all additional fees. If your group is jointly leasing equipment, be sure everyone understands the terms and accepts the financial obligations. Develop a written agreement to cover what happens if someone leaves before the lease ends. If you are subletting, prepare some form of written agreement spelling out expenses, use of equipment and all other details.

Once you do decide to share space, get your working arrangements ironed out first. If

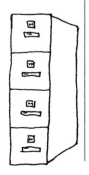

you and your office mates will use common space, phones and equipment, establish rules for who does what when. When moving into space already shared by others, ask what the house rules are. If there aren't any, ask — no, politely insist — that they be written up and posted for all to observe. This will save time and tempers later.

Go slowly when it comes to friendly chit-chat with your neighbors. Don't let someone looking for an excuse to avoid work interfere with yours. And don't tell anything that you're not prepared to have become common knowledge. Respect other people's privacy, too. Good manners go a long way toward making it easier to live together; they're good business, too. And don't forget the golden rule of sharing space with other creatives: "Thou shalt not steal thy studio mates' clients."

Setting Up Your Studio

You can set up your own studio to suit your personal tastes, needs and interests — and to fit your budget, large or small. You can display objects, posters or artwork that you like to have around and even have the style of furnishings that you find most comfortable. Because you're the boss, you decide whether the look is futuristic high-tech or classic and comfortable.

Whatever look you choose, there are some basic elements every designer's work space should have. You must have good lighting (preferably with natural light) and enough electrical outlets to handle your equipment. Your work area should be as clean and neat as possible. Some disorder is unavoidable (and there are those who work best in what others would describe as a mess), but sloppy and dirty surroundings send the message that you don't care about your work. Having a space to meet with clients that is located away from your work area will also help. And it's more impressive.

You should have enough floor space so you won't bump into furniture or equipment every time you turn around. Having room to move can sometimes make the difference between meeting a deadline or not. It can also

make the difference between your being in a good or a bad mood. There's nothing more maddening, time-consuming and painful than running into or knocking over something all the time.

Consider the environment in your prospective studio space, too. Watch out for too much humidity. Dampness can warp mechanical boards and paper, cause things to stick together, encourage mold growth and affect computer equipment. Also, check your space for leaky ceilings or windows. Air that is too dry can be a problem, too, because static can mess up your computer's drive, monitor and printer. Check where your electrical wires fall behind your desk or copier. Don't let any wire touch baseboard heating units or radiators because they can get hot enough to melt the plastic insulation on the wires, shorting out the wires or even causing fires. Putting your computer equipment or copier too close to a heat source can also result in hefty damage.

If you live alone and work at home, you can have a work area anywhere you want, as long as it doesn't interfere with the rest of your life. Avoid areas where you might often have food, however. What if your breakfast coffee splatters all over a client presentation? You might also think twice before using your bedroom as a work space. One woman who worked in her bedroom found herself unable to stop working on jobs until the wee hours of the morning — simply because they were there in front of her.

Careful selection of a location for the home studio is critical if you have a family or roommates. What if your children are playing in the room where your studio is located, and a stray ball knocks a plant over on a set of finished mechanicals? Sometimes sharing household space with other activities is absolutely unavoidable, but working in a spare room is best. I knew a man who lived with his wife and child in a fairly small two-bedroom apartment. After some intense pleading, he got his wife to give up a large walk-in closet. It was no bigger than 6 × 6 feet, but he turned it into a work space that allowed him to close the door at the end of the day. That gave him his privacy and kept him from being tempted to do just one more thing before he quit. (His wife liked that, too; she felt it made up for losing the closet.)

Give as much thought to designing an efficient, effective work space as you do to designing an effective layout. Begin by deciding what equipment and furniture you absolutely must have or just plain want. Then consider how to fit those pieces into the space available.

The most efficient way to use any space that you designate as your studio, especially a small space, is to arrange your work area in a U-shape. You can put your drawing board on one end of the U, a desk and/or filing cabinets on the other end, and your computer work station in the middle. Get a chair with rollers, and you can quickly and easily move from desk to drawing board to work table. This saves time and energy. Put your phone within arm's reach, closest to the work space where you will spend the greatest amount of your time. If you will be using a computer, arrange your space so that the computer screen is at a right angle to any window to reduce daylight glare and reflections.

Even if you're going to use a computer most of the time, you will still need a large, flat work surface such as a desk or a table to sort project records and materials, write checks, and use the waxer. You'll also need file cabinets or other storage units to keep samples of finished pieces and business records. If space is limited, you can use a tabletop or flush surface door (you can get tabletops without bases at most hardware/furniture/household-type outlet stores or flush doors at lumberyards). Lay either of these across the tops of two filing cabinets to get an inexpensive combined work/storage space.

Once you've assembled the equipment and furnishings you need and can afford and figured out the safest and most practical place to put them, you can fine-tune your work space setup. Consider what furniture and equipment you use most often and in what combination. For example, do you go back and forth between computer and drawing board? Then they will need to be positioned together. Do you have your phone

where you can grab it without killing yourself? Plan your floor space so the things you use most often are located relatively close to each other. Be sure you can get to the phone or fax or whatever in a hurry if you have to.

Then think about the order in which you use your equipment, work tools and surfaces. Try keeping a mental log during a typical project to determine what that order is. Once you're aware of your work pattern or order, you can plan your work and floor space so that the most frequently used materials, equipment and work surfaces are within arm's reach or a one-motion body swing in a freestanding position or from a rolling swivel chair.

You can cut some costs by buying inexpensive, even second-hand furnishings — for those with some painting and restoration talents, salvage houses and junkyards are a treasure trove. But never skimp on comfort. Spending 90 percent of your day sitting at a desk or drawing table can result in some painful and even long-lasting damage.

If you can afford it, outfit your workspace with ergonomic furniture — chairs designed to reduce back strain, keyboard shelves with wrist rests to prevent carpal tunnel syndrome (CTS), and antiglare attachments for monitor screens. Think of these costs as an investment in your future. Time lost because of a bad back or a wrist in a sling, not to mention medical and physical therapy bills, can cost far more than the right equipment in the long run. Be considerate of any staffers you have, too; what you find comfortable, someone else may find sheer torture. So make sure each employee's work area fits that person's physical needs.

If and when your studio grows beyond being a solo act, plan any expansion or rearrangement carefully. Try to avoid giving your studio a patchwork appearance as you add people and equipment. Everything will look better and everyone will work better when the new is integrated smoothly into the old. If you wait until the day before a new employee starts to work in a new area, you may find that you don't have adequate electrical outlets or floor space where it's needed.

What You Don't See Can Hurt You

I just learned what could have been an expensive lesson. The laser printer in my studio at home started printing ghost images of type and graphics from pages I had printed days before. I cleaned the inside of the printer and nothing changed.

The computer technicians were stumped, so I decided to call the man who replaces my toner cartridges in case I simply needed a new one. When I told him about the overprinting, he asked me if the house was particularly dry. I didn't know. Then he asked whether I woke up with a scratchy throat every morning. "Yes!" I said, thinking he had to be psychic. How else could he know that?

Well, he wasn't psychic, but he turned out to be a good detective. He told me, "Your scratchy throat means your house is too dry – and that dryness is causing the problem with your printer. Static causes the printed image to burn into the drum. You're lucky this is all that happened." He knew an accountant who had had a static problem. The accountant had lost all of a client's records one day just by building up a big electrical charge on the rug with her shoes and then touching a turned-on monitor. Zap, a whole client file was gone.

The toner cartridge man advised me to get a humidifier that can keep the room at 60 percent humidity. He also told me not to turn the heat way down at night, which of course I always did. Cold makes the dryness in the room even worse.

Equipment such as computers and photocopiers also have special requirements; you can't just park them in a vacant corner or closet.

Remember that any change in work areas results in a certain amount of downtime for everyone involved. Build in a margin for time that work will be disrupted, but minimize the negative consequences by getting the space set up right the first time and planning for the long-term rather than just the immediate situation.

Consider your own comfort and that of your employees when planning new or expanded work space. Make sure everyone has enough space to work and easy access to frequently used materials and equipment. If the studio is primarily a large, open space, consider setting up areas where people can have extra privacy and quiet for tasks that require extra concentration, such as checking color proofs. Maybe a conference or meeting room can be used for private space when it is not being used for client meetings.

At this stage of your business growth, appearances count. Although a certain amount of clutter is unavoidable, make sure that the reception area and conference rooms are never affected. It's also time to upgrade the furnishings and decor if you're pursuing mid-sized to large companies trying to win those top-level corporate accounts. Your public areas can have any personality and show creative flair, but make sure your clients will still feel comfortable there.

The more projects you do, and the more materials you have, the more storage problems will result. If you haven't already done so, it's time to establish a large, separate area for storage. You may want to have several separate areas: one for storing business and financial records, one for archiving materials from past projects, and at least one for frequently used supplies. Use separate supply cabinets for storing quantities of small items such as tape, markers and pens. You can buy in bulk for greater savings and quickly find everything later. Take time to thoroughly analyze both short- and long-term storage needs to develop the best solutions possible for your design studio.

Storage: Problems and Solutions

There comes a time when you start losing things, only to find whatever you'd lost practically under your nose. (You couldn't see it for the stuff lying on top of or around it.) Your piles are giving birth to piles. You can't find anywhere to store materials, projects or records. You have a **storage problem**. Cleaning up may relieve some of the symptoms temporarily, but there's only one cure. You need to drastically add to or revamp your existing storage space and systems. The following storage treatments are ones that have worked well for me both when I worked at home and when I had a rented studio. As your business grows, you may want to consider consulting with companies that deal strictly with solving storage problems.

Problem 1: Small, tabletop items are getting all over. It seems you have jars of ink, paint or glue sitting on every surface, including the floor. Another common symptom is never being able to find pens, markers or rulers.

Solution: Desktop organizers and desk accessories are available in every imaginable size, color and price. You can often get bar-gain basement prices at discount supply stores or from wholesalers who specialize in working with small businesses. Check to see if there are any in your area. Hardware stores and the kitchen departments of discount stores are also good sources of inexpensive storage units. Small shelves, maybe four or five inches deep, hold ink pots and pens nicely. Because they're so small, you can add these shelves above or below existing shelving or tuck them into space that you might not otherwise use. Thrift shops operated by charitable organizations are excellent sources for found materials that you can turn into shelving or storage units with a little work.

Problem 2: Business papers are getting misplaced. Correspondence, invoices, time sheets and other vital documents manage to disappear just when they're needed most. If a client calls with a question about a bill, you can't pull all the necessary documents without leaving them on hold for an hour!

Solution: File folders are an absolute must. Since they come in a variety of sizes, colors and styles, you'll surely find a type that works best for you. Be sure to clearly label each folder as part of a consistent system. Otherwise, you'll never remember where you put what. For files you need at your fingertips daily, desktop file holders are great. You can find a wide variety of expanding file folders, racks to hold hanging files, and even systems you can hang on the wall. Use stackable trays for sorting papers or stacking folders to be re-filed.

Solution: File cabinets are fairly inexpensive and especially convenient for storage. Small, rolling units can be tucked under or behind other equipment if space is at a premium. Or turn a desk drawer into a filing cabinet. A system for hanging file folders works quite well. Or you may want to make your own dividers and insert them in your drawers.

Problem 3: Work in progress scattered all over and presentation materials and samples missing. Many designers start out storing such critical, and sometimes irreplaceable, material as logos, photos, artwork and mechanicals in drawers, desktop heaps or even on the floor. But they quickly learn a harsh lesson when hours are wasted trying to find a missing project piece.

Solution: Manila envelopes come in all sizes and are wonderful for holding project materials. There are racks (some on wheels) made especially to hang and store medium to large envelopes. Many of these racks come with plastic, see-through envelopes as well. You can also stack manila envelopes on shelves or stacks or in flat files. We went a cheaper route for storing project materials in my agency. We bought large (40 × 60 inch) sheets of oak tag and folded them in half, taped them along the sides with 2-inch-wide masking tape and, presto, we had sturdy folders for all our bits and pieces. We stapled a 3 × 5 inch unlined index card to the side edge of each folder for a label. We wrote the client and project name on the card with a big marker. The folders were stored in vertical stacks with the index

Clients, Disks and You

Clients often think they are entitled to the disks their electronic mechanicals were created on, so they can make changes or updates to the piece without having to pay for your services again. However, unless you specifically agreed to give them all rights and the disks – in exchange for adequate payment – you own the copyright to and the disks for any materials you produce for a client. Any changes or additional uses beyond the original agreement cannot be done without your permission and additional compensation.

This doesn't mean dozens of greedy clients will try to rip you off, although that can happen. More often problems arise from the client misunderstanding what you do and its value. It's quite simple to the client: Why should she have to pay you all that money again just to replace one picture and its caption in that brochure? It's simply a matter of deleting the old caption and typing in the new one.

If you wait until the issue arises to explain matters to a client, it may take a lot of effort to clear up the situation. Clearly tell the client *before* you begin work that you will retain the copyright to and the disks for all work you produce, unless you agree otherwise in writing. (Put the copyright symbol with your name and the date into every electronic file you create.) Then negotiate a purchase price determined by the work's value and the client's future use of the work as part of a written work agreement.

Always use a written agreement, even it's only a purchase order, that spells out in detail exactly what rights the client is buying and what uses must be negotiated. Often a client won't know when or if your work might be used again. You can then suggest that the agreement specify that charges for any additional usage be agreed on later. Head off fears that you'll gouge the client for each usage by giving some idea of what such a charge might be.

You will sometimes run into clients who challenge you over usage rights and restrictions. If that happens, you may want to show them a copy of the *Graphic Artists Guild Handbook, Pricing & Ethical Guidelines*. The Guild sets up guidelines in its Code of Fair Practice that all artists are encouraged to follow. This code raises the standards within the communications industry to a fair and ethical level.

card sticking out for quick reference.

Solution: Flat files are a great way to get your project pieces, samples and presentation materials under control. (You can buy several units and place them on top of one another.) Flat files also provide excellent protection for work in progress and finished pieces awaiting client approval or reprint orders, not to mention your collection of drawings, designs, mechanicals, printed samples and presentation pieces. Flat files protect them from your children, yourself or even earthquakes or fires.

Solution: Vertical files, sometimes called art racks or stacks. These are large boxes with Masonite or plywood separators, usually placed three or four inches apart, positioned vertically in the box. A vertical file works extremely well for client and materials folders. Be careful how you store mechanicals or other mounted artwork in vertical files or they will quickly begin to curl or warp. Turned on its side, one of these files makes a nice enclosed shelving unit—perfect for lightweight materials like paper or mat boards. Although you can purchase these units at art or office supply stores or through catalogs, they can be made very easily. All you need is a plywood frame or box with evenly spaced grooves cut into the inside top and bottom surfaces. Plywood or Masonite can then be cut to fit securely into the grooves. Simply cut the grooves into each side of the wooden box and place your shelves if you want to use it for horizontal storage.

Solution: Traditional on-the-wall or modular shelving units can help get your storage problems under control. You can find many units in home and office furniture stores, art supply stores or through catalogs. Discount and hardware stores offer inexpensive imitations of the fashionable designs on the market. If you can't afford even those, you can find bricks or cinder blocks, pine shelving boards, plywood or knobless hollow doors for very little money. The most expensive Scandinavian-designed units won't work any better than boards and blocks.

Problem 4: Equipment that's permanently in your way. This problem is more common when you're just starting out and can't afford much floor space. But if your business and staff are growing rapidly, you may find yourself facing the occasional space crunch.

Solution: Try built-in or movable units that can be stuffed under or behind other furniture. For example, a small rolling file cabinet

could be stuffed under your worktable or under a computer table. Perch the fax machine or a personal copier on top of a vertical file unit.

Solution: Take over a closet, or part of one, and park the offending item in there. Roll it out when you want. Install shelves in closets to handle those things you don't want often but don't want to get rid of either.

Keeping in Touch With Clients

In an ideal world you could do all your design work and answer every call from each current and potential client. But that's seldom possible for a designer, especially if you're designer, production artist, owner and receptionist. An answering machine can be your most important investment and the key to maintaining client contact when you can't answer the phone or be in your office. It gives them the feeling that although you are not available, their needs will be attended to as soon as you receive their message.

The message on your machine should be friendly but also professional sounding. Be sure you give the name of your business clearly, so your clients will know they've reached the right number. The message itself can be quite simple—you are currently unavailable but will return their call as soon as possible if they leave a message at the tone. (Have a friend or associate listen to your message and evaluate how clear it is as well as how friendly and professional.)

Always return your calls immediately or folks will stop leaving messages—that could mean not getting that next big job. (Saying, "I'm sorry I missed your call," when returning a message both acknowledges their call and tells them it was important to you.) If you will be out of the office for several days on business, doing a press check or photo shoot for example, you may want to change your message to tell callers that you are out of the office but call in regularly for messages in order to return their calls as soon as possible.

You should try to always answer the telephone when you're in the studio—unless you're doing something that you can't stop without ruining your work—or have someone

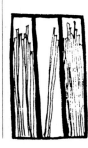

answer for you. Some clients can't or won't leave messages on a machine. A friend told me that widespread, strong client resistance to talking to a machine rather than immediate contact with a person can definitely cost you work in her area.

An answering service is another, more expensive solution to office absences. With an answering service, your clients get to talk to a person instead.

The Computer in the Studio

Computers have had more impact on the graphic design industry than anything else in the twentieth century. Illustration and layout programs can be used to create complex artwork, develop logos, set type, design, work out layouts and comps, create graphics and illustrations and prepare mechanicals. Some studios even prepare their own color separations and deliver film to the printer. Others create slides, transparencies, videos and multimedia presentations. Computers can also handle many routine business chores: generating invoices, tracking projects, preparing time sheets, etc.

Although most designers still prefer doing the conceptual stages of a project by hand, they take advantage of the computer's ability to let them experiment with many approaches quickly and easily. For example, once the concept for a logo has been developed, they use the computer to try out many variations quickly and easily.

Doing production on the computer makes it easier to handle — and sometimes even head off — client changes. Type corrections can be easily made, reproofed, and faxed off to the client for approval. Because you can use your computer to create comps that closely approximate how the finished piece will look, clients understand what they're getting at an earlier stage, reducing the number of "I didn't know it would look like that!" changes during the proofing stages. You don't absolutely need a computer to start your own design studio, but you'll find it difficult — if not impossible — to stay in business

long without one. Many designers who are setting out on their own now have spent at least six months to a year working for someone else (and some are staying much longer). This lets them get the computer expertise they need to go it alone. Freelancing on the side while holding down a full-time job is also common, with the freelance income being invested in computer equipment. Designers who do this leave their jobs for their own studios without taking on a heavy burden of debt. Based on the changes I've seen computers bring into the field of graphic design, I think getting experience with computers and having cash in hand to buy computer equipment is the way to go for those serious about wanting to have their own studios. Graphic design is becoming increasingly competitive, and you need every bit of help you can give yourself.

Computers have also changed the areas of production that designers are responsible for. In the past, we developed the concept, did a layout, and then sent the layout off to the typesetter, the photos out to the color separator. Finally the printer created the film from the mechanicals and ran our jobs on press. If a vendor or supplier made a mistake, he had to correct it. Not anymore! With computers, we can — and often have to — do it all. That means the buck stops with us. We have more control over the final quality and appearance of our pieces, but we have to take full responsibility for all phases of design and production.

When it comes to quality control, the best defense is a good offense. We must learn to anticipate potential problems and prevent them from happening rather than focus on how to fix something that's gone wrong. I know several design studios that now employ professional typesetters to ensure the quality of their type, including the proofreading. We have to proof and reproof everything carefully, and then make the client take the responsibility of proofing before approval as well. (That also means reading for sense and legibility; fancy text wraps full of bad hyphenation won't impress clients.)

We also have to work closely with our printers because computer-generated mistakes on films can be tough to spot. There are also gaps between what the computer can create on the monitor and what traditional printing presses can do; the problems of color variation from screen to printed page are merely the best-known of these. Your printer can help you avoid and, if necessary, correct problems when you let her know what you're trying to achieve. She can also supply good ideas for faster and better ways to get the results you want. A good service bureau is another invaluable ally, who can not only untangle your computer files but also help you communicate with printers and other vendors who are less computer literate.

Clients and Computers

Clients have always been notorious for wanting everything—yesterday. Unfortunately, the speed and power of computers have led clients to believe that you can do anything faster with a computer. Now, with a computer on every designer's table, they want it last week!

When your clients don't understand why what you do takes so long, try to gently educate them by explaining or demonstrating how computer design and production works. Help them understand the steps you have to go through—even with a computer—to produce a quality design. When offered a choice between quality and speed, clients opt for quality every time.

Clients also love to say, "What if we just add this one little thing?" at the last minute. Often the computer makes it possible to accommodate those last, little changes when you couldn't have done so with traditional production. Or you can use the computer to show quickly how that "one little change" can totally disturb the viewer's eyeflow with the end result that the design lacks impact. Given the choice between a design with impact and one that incorporates their proposed change, most clients will agree that a design is nothing without impact. Print out a laser proof showing the impact of copy changes and attach it to a change order for approval to persuade a client who just can't understand the costs of that "one little change."

But what if the client wants it now and doesn't care how it looks? Then you have to decide whether the job is worth taking. It's hard to turn down paying work, especially when you see bills mounting up. But taking a project where you can't do good work or maintain the proper level of quality can hurt you more in the long run. The client who didn't care about taking the time to do it right will blame your design when the piece doesn't get the desired results. Getting a reputation for poor-quality work—although you don't deserve it—can cost you plenty.

As a consequence of the computer revolution, some clients believe that, with a computer and the right software, a secretary or even their cousin Eddie could produce all those graphic things they pay you for. Misguided clients may even have the nerve to tell you what they are planning to do and ask your advice on how to do it. Before you get angry and tell them to . . . well, you know, try the old "gentle education" approach.

Demonstrate that computers are not a substitute for design know-how. Show them an ad or a brochure you designed. Point out how the graphic elements are not random choices but are based on the principle of how a viewer's eye moves from left to right across a piece of printed material. Also, explain that the selections of color, type, illustration styles and photo placements are made to enhance that eye movement. In other words, demonstrate that you are more than a computer jockey; you are also an expert on how an individual reacts to a visual image and how to use that reaction to persuade the viewer do what the client wants. When the art of design is put in these terms, clients often decide that the money spent on your services is well worth it.

Clients who are driven primarily by cost considerations may listen to all your arguments and still choose to produce their own graphics in-house. (Others may decide to hire a full-time, in-house designer instead of you and then swamp that designer with work to justify the salary.) You can wish such clients well and let them go, or you can offer to help them get started. For example, you can show them how to set up their new computer system and then teach them the basics of their software graphics programs. All this assistance, don't forget is consultation — that is, billable time.

Offer to produce basic design templates for the client's new in-house projects and put them on disks so cousin Eddie only has to plug in the information that will change. Charge the client accordingly for all rights to use the templates. You can also offer to provide additional consultation services and be available for special design projects when needed. This way, you won't be burning any irreparable bridges, and when the client eventually realizes that you do a far better job than cousin Eddie, you are still in the picture.

The best way to avoid losing work to secretaries with computers is to limit the number of low-end, straightforward, primarily production projects you accept. These are the kinds of jobs that are disappearing to in-house staff most quickly. The more specialized your work becomes and the more you become known for accepting only high-end quality projects, the less often you will have to contend with a client who thinks "I can do it myself."

What Do I Need to Compute?

By itself, the only thing the computer will do for sure is put a big dent in your bank account. A basic system can run several thousand dollars while software packages average several hundred dollars apiece. Start adding in the bells and whistles — scanner, color printer and color monitor — and your costs accelerate even faster.

Before you decide to go into hock for the rest of your life to get the latest and best of everything, ask yourself some questions. To determine what you'll need to invest up front, ask yourself this:

◆ What will I use it for right away?
◆ What quality of output do I need?
◆ What kind of material will I need to input?
◆ What hardware and software do I need to do it?
◆ What can I afford?
◆ What kind of support do I want from the seller?

Be as specific as possible with your answers to these questions. Weigh the costs against what you want and decide what possible trade-offs you can make. "I will do primarily layouts, comps and mechanicals, so I must have a computer with a hard drive with at least 8 meg RAM and as much memory as I can afford, a monitor, a page layout program, and some fonts. I will probably have more one- and two-color jobs than four-color and expect to do many pieces where I'll need to see a whole layout on the screen. I can get by with a black-and-white monitor for a while, but I can't do without a screen large enough to show a whole spread."

Project your needs over a couple of years. What else might you be doing on computer and what will you need to do it? Ask yourself these questions:

◆ What new tasks could I do on the computer?
◆ What would make it easier to do the work I now do?
◆ Will I be hiring someone to work for me?
◆ When will I need to upgrade the quality of my output?
◆ What can I afford?
◆ How much and how often can I increase the memory?

Be realistic about your plans and needs. It's fun to have dozens of fonts around, but how many will you use regularly? Then work on costs. Compare equipment, programs and prices. For example, Photoshop is primarily an image editing program, but it can be used as a paint program, too. If you definitely need an image editing program but would use a paint program only occasionally, it might make more sense to buy only Photoshop and then get a paint program when you have more need for it.

Next do some research. Find out what your friends and competitors are using. Ask your friends if you can "test drive" their hardware and software to see whether you like it. Consider what your clients want, both the type of work and the quality of presentation you need to be competitive. Also consider the kind of equipment your clients use; you need to make sure that you can at least easily translate word processing files they give you into

Leasing Equipment

Leasing is a great option if you don't have the ready cash to buy equipment or can't get a loan on good terms. Unlike banks, leasing companies are happy to use the equipment itself to secure the lease. Another advantage to leasing, especially if you're going through a dealer or manufacturer, is the option to upgrade the equipment during the lease. (This is a real plus with computer equipment, since the technology is changing so rapidly.)

There are two types of leases – financial and operating. A financial lease is actually a form of installment loan, and you can buy the equipment for a specific amount of money at the end of the lease. You must depreciate a financial lease, with a portion deducted in each of five or seven years. With an operating lease, you agree to make a certain number of monthly payments for a set period of time. At the end of that time, you can buy the equipment at fair market value. You can deduct the payments on an operating lease from your income as an expense item. (If you buy your equipment outright, you depreciate it over a number of years; with a loan, you deduct the interest charges.)

There are some disadvantages to leasing. You'll probably pay top dollar for the equipment rather than being able to bargain the seller's price down. If you have a problem with the equipment, you can't just stop making payments and give it back to the leasing company, and unless you bought a service contract, you're responsible for repairs. But, all things considered, if you're just starting out, leasing very expensive equipment is an excellent alternative to buying outright.

something your computer can use.

If you're just starting out or aren't technically savvy or mechanically inclined, see a reputable computer sales and service company for recommendations on the kind of hardware and software that's best for you. Make an appointment with a sales representative so they can spend more time with you and acquaint you with all the different options and prices. Bring a list of what you would like a computer to do for you. As a designer, you want a computer that can run graphics programs so you can produce layouts, comps, typesetting, illustrations, etc. As a businessperson, you want one that can handle accounting programs and word processing. Get the hardware and software that will help you do both. Ask to see a demonstration of any software, sample output from printers and sample input from scanners. Specify what you want to see them do.

 Then work out what you can afford. The final step is to investigate your financing options; you may get a better break if you lease. Often lease payments are tax deductible — and may give you a better tax break than buying outright and depreciating the cost — and arranging for hardware upgrades is easier than if you bought outright. Check with your accountant before choosing to lease or buy. You want to go with the option that will give you the best tax breaks and costs over the long term.

Murphy's Law and Computers

Once you've configured or expanded your computer setup, you will not automatically find yourself breezing through every project. Trying to do so guarantees you'll run smack into Murphy's Law — anything that can go wrong will go wrong. First, you have to learn how to use what you've got.

Allow for training time — and some lost productivity — when you're figuring up the costs of any new item. You'll need to allow time for making and correcting mistakes, too. Although finding — or hiring — someone to train you in the use of your new equipment will shorten your learning curve, it will also add to the start-up costs of your new system. Some computer stores do provide a little free training; ask about it when you are ready to buy your equipment. If lessons aren't normally included in the sale, try to negotiate a deal that will include instruction. Once you've agreed on the number of hours you'll receive, have the agreement written on your sales slip. Your local community college, college or university may offer classes, and other programs may be available in your area.

 Never, never, NEVER rely on using your new system or software package to complete a project at the last minute, or take on a project that requires you to use software you're not completely familiar with. You're invoking instant application of Murphy's Law if you do. In addition to simple human error, you can feel the effects of disk crash (the computer loses your file or locks up before you save a critical change), hardware failure (the computer dies as suddenly and mysteriously as a goldfish—a rare event but possible) or software failure (it works fine until you go to print at 4:00 A.M. and won't work again).

Always be prepared. Invest in an antivirus program that will detect incoming infected disks before they get to your computer. This is critical if you send disks to a service bureau; a good bureau uses antiviral software and takes all precautions, but accidents can still happen. Learn how to use drive recovery and file recovery utilities before you need them. It's twice as hard to learn anything when you're tired, frustrated or worried, and quick recovery can sometimes mean the difference between making and missing a deadline.

Guidelines for Getting It Together

You can start with very little and then add equipment or improve your work space as your finances permit. And many designers do. If you're starting out with a little money and some guaranteed work—you still don't want to blow your first year's budget on a lot of unnecessary stuff. On the other hand, you know you've got to be and stay competitive with other designers. That means having the same equipment, furniture, etc., while not wasting money on unnecessary extras. (And those of you starting out with the basics and little more probably didn't get there by throwing money around either—and aren't about to start.)

Your basic start-up will cost more now than when all a designer needed was a drawing board, a chair and some art materials. Now you can start a studio without a computer but won't stay in business for long without one. If you don't have the savings to buy a computer in the beginning, check into leasing. At the least, set up your own savings plan with a target of getting a computer within your first year in business.

How do you know what equipment is enough or when to add more? You begin with a little planning and an honest evaluation of your needs and capabilities. Look at the work you're doing now and determine what you ob-

viously must have to do it; what you could use to do it faster; and what you will need to grow your business in the future. To give you some help setting up and equipping your business, I've outlined some sample business-building strategies. Although they're based on descriptions of designers at three different career stages with certain types of work, you should find enough information to create your own guidelines even if your business isn't a perfect match for one of these. For example, if you're just starting out but anticipate getting a fair amount of income from sign design or logos, your needs will probably be closer to Strategy Two: Off and Running than to the strategy described for the start-up. So, read through these guidelines, then grab up those ideas that fit you and start writing your own Guidelines for Getting It Together.

Strategy One: Starting up Your Business

You: have just gotten out of school, are freelancing on the side, or have left a studio, agency or other company to go out on your own.

Work: Primarily one- or two-color flyers, brochures, newsletters, newspaper ads for small-scale clients.

Must Haves:
- A drawing board and/or flat work surface
- A chair
- Basic studio equipment for creating comps, roughs and mechanicals
- Process and flat color charts
- An attachable swing arm lamp
- A telephone and answering machine
- Shelving and storage
- Typewriter
- Computer with 40 megabyte hard drive, 1 megabyte RAM
- Expanded keyboard
- Two-page screen, black-and-white monitor
- A 300-600 dpi laser printer, preferably PostScript or compatible
- A page layout program
- A draw program
- Fonts
- Antiviral software and a file recovery utility

♦ Word processing program
♦ File translation utility if one didn't come with your computer
♦ As many diskettes as you can afford; 20 to 40 is good for a start
♦ A waxer

Beyond the Basics:

♦ A 60-100 megabyte hard disk with 2.5 megabytes RAM
♦ Conference table and chairs
♦ Reference books
♦ Photocopier with enlarging and reducing capabilities
♦ A desk
♦ A scanner
♦ A modem either as part of or added to your hard drive
♦ One SyQuest type drive with one 44 megabyte cartridge for removable and portable storage
♦ A paint program
♦ A special effects font program
♦ A set of picture fonts (optional, but very handy)

Comments: Even if you have a computer in your start-up, you should still have all the basic drawing and drafting tools as backup, because computers still don't trim paper, mount presentations on boards, or many other things you'll have or want to do by hand. The same applies to a typewriter. Even if you have a computer, it's still good to have one as a backup in case your computer goes down. Carbonless and many multipart forms won't work with a laser printer if you want to use them.

Remember that you can never have enough memory when it comes to a computer. Buy twice as much as you think you'll need in the first year. Then plan on buying more soon. Before you upgrade to the latest version of your favorite software, make sure your hard drive still has enough memory to store it and leave enough room for working files. Often developers add new features or make modifications that increase the amount of memory needed to run that software. Never cut corners on your printers or monitors, either. It can prove to be more expensive in the end.

PostScript printers are essential for design-

ers since PostScript is the language used by most Mac-based graphics programs and nearly all service bureaus. PostScript offers the widest variety of fonts and the highest resolution print quality. Fortunately, these printers are actually getting less expensive for higher resolution quality over time. (For DOS and Windows systems TrueType fonts and laserjet printers are the standard, but many service bureaus don't work with TrueType fonts.)

As you move into more complex graphics such as illustrations, photographs and font creating programs, be wary of printers with imaging models other than true PostScript. Salespeople may try to talk you into non-PostScript printers by telling you that you can get software interpreters that translate PostScript commands. They work as far as the translation goes, but what they probably won't tell you is that they print at unbelievably slow rates — a real killer when you're on a deadline.

I tried to work with a small monitor, the kind the earlier Macs had, but it's next to impossible to do graphic page layouts on one. You can't see the whole area you're trying to work with. The initial cost of a monitor large enough to show at least one whole or a two-page spread is offset by the time you save scrolling around the job.

With a draw program you can combine type and images to create mastheads and logos, even some graphics for letterheads. Adding a paint program and a type manipulation program when you can afford them will expand your logo and graphics creation capabilities, but you can get started without them.

There are many good draw and paint programs on the market. If you have experience working on a computer at school or on the job, it's probably a good idea to stick to the programs you know and like when you go out on your own. This is especially true of page layout programs. It takes time and effort to learn how to get the most out of one, so you will probably stick with the first one you buy for many years and upgrade as needed. If you're buying a type of program you're not familiar with or think you might want a change from the one you know, check it out thoroughly be-

fore you decide to buy.

Scanners and modems may or may not be a necessity depending on your and your clients' needs. An image scanner is great if you work with a lot of photos or illustrations that you will incorporate into a layout. But you can always use a photocopier to size photos and illustrations and paste them into position on your layout. A modem can save time you would spend taking files to the service bureau, but it, too, is not a necessity unless you're racking up large numbers of delivery charges (or parking tickets).

A removable SyQuest type drive that takes 44 megabyte cartridges lets you remove large files from your computer and take them to another computer or the service bureau. You can also store large projects, such as annual reports, on one removable disk. Removable cartridges are great for mass-storage backups, too.

Strategy Two: Off and Running

You: have developed a reliable client base or are moving from being a part-time freelancer to a full-time, self-employed designer.

Work: Flyers, brochures and newsletters, advertisements, catalogs, complex graphic designs, illustrations, logos; roughly half your projects involve at least some four-color work.

Must Haves:
- ◆ Basic studio equipment and furniture
- ◆ Flat files for storing art materials, artwork and client project storage, and shelves for supplies
- ◆ Conference table and chairs
- ◆ A telephone and answering machine
- ◆ A sheet-fed waxer
- ◆ Typewriter (even if you have a computer, it's still good to have one)
- ◆ Photocopier that enlarges and reduces
- ◆ Process and flat color charts
- ◆ Computer with 60-100 megabyte hard disk drive, 2-4 megabyte RAM, at least 16 megahertz clock speed
- ◆ Modem, either as part of or added to computer
- ◆ One or two SyQuest type drives with several 44 megabyte removable cartridges

- ◆ Two-page screen, color monitor
- ◆ An 8-bit color board
- ◆ A 300-600 dpi laser printer, preferably PostScript (would not recommend a compatible)
- ◆ A grayscale scanner
- ◆ A page layout program
- ◆ A draw program
- ◆ A paint program
- ◆ A font manipulation program
- ◆ A library of fonts
- ◆ Antiviral software and a file recovery utility
- ◆ Word processing program
- ◆ File translation utility if one didn't come with your computer
- ◆ Spreadsheet, accounting/bookkeeping or studio management program
- ◆ As many diskettes as you can afford

Beyond the Basics:
- ◆ A color PostScript printer
- ◆ A 24-bit color board
- ◆ A drawing tablet (optional, but very handy)
- ◆ A fax machine
- ◆ Slide projector and trays
- ◆ Film recorder if you are working with transparencies or color slides
- ◆ An image manipulation program
- ◆ A color management system
- ◆ A color calibration system
- ◆ Clip art programs (optional, but very handy)
- ◆ A set of picture fonts (optional, but very handy)
- ◆ A font management utility
- ◆ A color scanner or a slide scanner if you work with many transparencies

Comments: If you're working with an associate, partner or employee(s), you'll need more than one computer in your studio. In that case, you'll need to add at least low-end networking capabilities so you can swap files from computer to computer, and all units can use one printer.

If your work requires computer capabilities such as math processing or the ability to achieve certain color depths from your color monitor, be sure your computer and monitor provide you with the hardware to handle those demands. This is why it's so important to know what your computer needs will be six months to a year from the time you buy your system. You don't want to invest all that money in something that can't keep pace with your business growth.

Your computer's capability to expand (using expansion slots) is essential as you upgrade. If you intend to do color design work, you will probably need 8 megabytes RAM on your computer. A computer's clock speed refers to how fast your system can process information. A clock speed of at least 16 megahertz is essential as you get into more complex tasks such as illustration, font manipulation, and image/photograph manipulation. Color work alone triples the amount of information your computer has to process, and that can slow down even the fastest of computers.

In addition to continuing to expand your computer memory and storage capacity, you may also need to add an accelerator card to keep up to processing speed. An accelerator card will quickly become a necessity if you use an image manipulation program often. Digital signal processor boards that accelerate specific functions in Adobe Photoshop and other image processing applications are essential if you use this software often.

Remember that as you add peripherals — memory chips, printers, accelerators, add-in RAM cards, etc. — they must all be compatible with your computer and with each other. Ask your dealer if the equipment you have now and the peripherals you want to add can talk to each other. If not, you can't use them. Watch out for bargain basement mail order companies who will offer supposedly compatible peripherals that aren't always what they claim to be. Try to stick with companies and dealers that you know and trust.

Sheet-fed grayscale scanners are quite inexpensive, but they tend to distort the images vertically. They're also rather awkward to use, because you can only put flat, printed pieces through them. If you can afford it, a flatbed scanner is a much better investment and rapidly becoming the industry standard. Desktop color scanners still don't give you reproduction quality comparable to drum scanners, so

they're a luxury item unless you have to create a lot of color comps for clients.

A color printer is highly recommended for its convenience in preparing comps, if you can afford it. It's not essential, however, unless you are doing many slide presentations.

A SyQuest type drive that takes 44 megabyte cartridges is a necessity for storage and for transferring large files from your computer to a service bureau.

Strategy Three: Bigger and Better

You: have a large, established client base; have associates, partners, employees or use freelance help; and handle complex or sophisticated projects.

Work: Advertisements, collateral pieces, catalogs, packaging, corporate identity, graphics, illustrations, publications, some specialty work such as signage or labels and tags, extensive four-color work.

Must Haves:

♦ Basic studio equipment and furniture for all design personnel
♦ Shelving and storage
♦ Office furniture and equipment for all non-designers
♦ Conference table and chairs, preferably in separate area
♦ Multiline telephone system
♦ An answering machine (and/or receptionist)
♦ A fax machine with its own phone line
♦ Photocopier(s)
♦ Slide projector and trays
♦ Computer for each designer with 100 megabyte hard disk drive, 8 megabyte RAM, and 25 megahertz clock speed
♦ Accelerators if you plan to work with color photos or illustrations
♦ Networking capabilities to connect office computers and printer(s)
♦ Computer for receptionist/clerical and any business personnel
♦ Modem, either as part of or added to at least one computer
♦ Removable SyQuest type drives with several 44 megabyte removable cartridges
♦ Two-page screen, color monitor for each designer

- A 24-bit or 32-bit color board for each design computer
- A 300-600 dpi laser and color PostScript printers
- Print spoolers
- A flatbed grayscale and color scanners
- A page layout program for each computer
- A draw program for each computer
- A paint program for at least one computer
- An image manipulation program for at least one computer
- A font manipulation program for at least one computer
- Fonts for each computer, plus extra fonts
- Antiviral software and a file recovery utility for each computer
- Word processing program for at least one design computer, for receptionist/clerical and any business personnel
- File translation utility (if one didn't come with the computer) for each computer
- Spreadsheet, accounting/bookkeeping or studio management program for partners/owner and business personnel
- As many diskettes and removable cartridges as you can afford

Beyond the Basics:
- 1000 dpi laser PostScript printers or controller boards for laser printers that increase resolution to 1000 dpi
- An optical drive or CD-ROM
- Film recorder if you are working with transparencies or color slides
- Reduction and enlargement copier
- Stat camera (optional; may be more cost effective than computer output, depending on studio's activities)
- Color copier
- Separate reception area and furnishings
- Employee lounge
- Large, central area for storage
- Large, centrally located flat cutting and mounting surface
- Proofing room or area with appropriate lighting
- Some wall surface with corkboard or other material for pinning up artwork for review
- Intercom system
- A color management system

- A color calibration system
- Multimedia creation capabilities (optional)

Comments: You can probably recycle older units for low-end work or as servers for outputting or data transfer. You should also be able to upgrade rather than replace some of your equipment. But how many computers are enough? There's no set rule of thumb, but you may need more computers if you're doing a lot of scanning, image manipulation or color separations in-house. All these operations eat up computer time, and you don't want to miss a deadline because someone couldn't get on a computer to finish it. Also allow one computer per in-house copywriter, secretary, production manager and number cruncher. When these people need a computer, they need it now and the nature of their jobs makes it difficult to precisely schedule computer time.

The more people and computers you have, the more complex file storage and retrieval become. Develop file naming conventions and a storage and retrieval system so anyone can find a file fast no matter where it's stored.

 You'll realize tremendous savings from archiving and reusing parts of previous projects whenever possible. Some designers save all their unused logos, symbols, graphic elements and other items, creating personal clip art collections to be used in future projects.

 If everyone in the studio is a heavy computer user, you may want to have a SyQuest type drive for each computer. Each user keeps her work on her own removable cartridge rather than cluttering up computer memory and tying someone to working on a single computer. Depending on your storage requirements you may need to move up to 88 megabyte removable cartridges, optical drives or even CD-ROM.

If you work with color slides or color transparencies, you will need a color image scanner. However, you can use a video scanner to scan transparencies if you already have one for scanning three-dimensional objects or other video work. If you don't have a color image scanner or a video scanner, and you do need to scan transparencies, you can get a backlight unit for a light box which will allow you to light a transparency from behind, and then it can be picked up by a grayscale scanner or photocopier.

Some studios have begun investing in imagesetters with 1270 or more dpi. Although they are expensive, they are a good investment if you run up heavy monthly bills for output on resin coated paper or film at the service bureau. Investigate costs and trade-offs carefully before you go this route.

Don't Bite Off More Than You Can Chew

I've heard a lot of designers say that they would move out of their home office/studios and into an outside office when they could afford to "do it right." That meant when they had enough money to pay for a fancy, high-priced office, great furniture and all the right equipment. One of two things happened to these people: They never got out of their home office/studio, or they moved out into a space they couldn't afford in order to "do it right."

The one step at a time slow growth policy offers a sound alternative to those two extremes. Start with what you absolutely need and gradually add or improve as you can afford it. For example, you don't need an office the size of a football field when you only have a dozen clients. You need a nice, *small* office. Then when your client list expands, move on to a larger space.

I learned the value of growing slowly the hard way myself. One year, my agency grew to double its size within two months when we added one extremely large account and two slightly smaller ones. That was more new business than my staff of five could handle. I hired four new people within two weeks. That's four salaries with payroll taxes and benefits plus desks, drawing boards and partitions for four new work spaces. I enlarged and redecorated my conference room to have an appropriate place to meet with the new high-ticket clients. Even worse, I was spending all my time supervising the new people instead of be-

ing creative myself. It was pure madness, not to mention incredibly expensive. It was an endless cycle—the more furniture or equipment I bought, the more I worried about bringing in enough work to cover the additional expense. The more work we brought in, the more people I had to hire and buy new furniture and equipment for. It took me two years to end this nightmare by choosing to downsize my agency. I was happier with fewer clients, only a handful of employees, and me at the drawing board. We phased out large but less profitable accounts and surplus personnel, and I took over again as art director. Peace returned to the agency.

"Don't bite off more than you can chew" is a trite but vital axiom for the small or growing business. Although we'll look more at controlled, healthy business growth and how to plan for it in chapters eight and nine, more designers get in over their heads with furniture, equipment and fixtures than anything else. Why? Because they aren't planning what they do and, even worse, don't distinguish between wants and needs.

Wants vs. Needs

We all do it. And every time we swear we'll never do it again. Then the next catalog comes, advertising the New! Improved! Bigger & Better Than Ever! With Even More Bells & Whistles! item we know we've absolutely *got* to have. We're positive that:

◆ Everyone else has it already
◆ We won't be competitive without it
◆ A client will want to know why we don't have it, too
◆ Our productivity will drop drastically
◆ We'll be a business failure without it
◆ We'll never be happy again if we don't have it

(Right.) Before we know what hit us, we'll have worked out a way to squeeze yet another item out of our budget for the year—an item we might not really *need* but one we know we *want*.

Let unnecessary, small purchases start to mount up, and you'll find yourself in a pretty uncomfortable financial situation. Investing in expensive and unnecessary furniture, decor or equipment can be extremely painful for—

and possibly even fatal to — the small but growing business. This is a particularly dangerous trap in the age of computerized design studios.

So plan your purchases based on your goals and resources. Look at all the options before you buy anything. Can you reuse or adapt something you already have? Are you getting the most out of what you have? Do you really need an expensively decorated conference room to impress that new corporate client? Don't rush through considering alternatives; you may unconsciously be trying to provide yourself with an excuse for doing what you want to do.

Weigh the trade-offs carefully. You may want to write out the pros and cons of major purchases. List the advantages of the purchase in one column and the disadvantages in another. If you see more cons than pros, or it looks like the cons are stronger than the pros, you should defer — or better yet, forget — that purchase. And, whatever you do, always keep the bottom line in mind. If you find yourself thinking, "If I bring in X dollars more new business, I can easily afford this," you're probably headed for trouble. Buying an item so you can go after a different type of business may also be a risky strategy. What if the new business doesn't materialize? You'll be stuck trying to squeeze the difference out of your existing billings. The wonderful, whiz-bang whatever-it-is won't look quite so good when you're putting in sleepless nights wondering how to pay for it.

CHAPTER

two

Taking
Care
of
Business

 t's an all-too-typical day for D. Designer. A client calls (for the third time, she points out) for a production schedule D.D. promised to have for her two weeks ago. When D.D. tries to explain that he just hasn't had the time to put it together and type it up, the client retorts that there are other designers who do have the time. While D.D. is trying to find all the information, the phone rings again.

Another client calls to confirm that the meeting to review the comps for his ad is still on for tomorrow. The comps aren't exactly finished, but the review's already been postponed once. D.D. swallows hard and promises to be there. The production schedule gets shoved to one side and out come the roughs for the ad comps. The phone rings again.

The stat house wants an overdue bill paid *now*. D.D. knows he doesn't have the money to pay, but he's never billed several clients for projects that were finished ages ago. His head aches at the thought of searching through drawers and file cabinets for those pieces of scrap paper that he kept track of his time on, and those old invoices for stats and printing. D.D. stalls the stat house, pushes his roughs onto the production schedule, and starts frantically rooting for his time and expense records. The phone rings again.

D.D. almost doesn't answer this time. It's a good thing he did, though, since it's the printer. The mechanicals that have to be prepped for press today haven't arrived. Where are they? D.D. finds them sitting by the door, where he left them a week ago. He grabs them and races to the printer, forgetting that the client hasn't proofed, approved and signed off on them. When D.D. remembers, he'll call and tell the client the mechanicals looked fine and are at the printers. Which is too bad, because there's a major mistake — the client's company name, logo, and address got left off — and the client will be really angry when the final printed pieces come in. And refuse to pay the $6,000 printing bill. Back in his studio, D.D. wonders why he ever wanted his own design business.

Designers who've closed up shop like to blame the competition or economy or climate toward design. But often the fault lies in the designer's own studio. Like our friend D.D., they admit they couldn't keep up with their billing, their record keeping, or even their projects. They overworked but underplanned. They may have been great designers, but that wasn't enough. It never is.

A Dirty Little Secret

At some point in our design careers, we all are entranced by the myth of creative freedom. To be truly creative, we've got to be free of all other cares and responsibilities. Then we'll be great designers; clients will be so swept away by our work that they'll accept whatever we give them, whenever they get it — and throw money at us on the spot. (Imagine Joe Duffy or David Carson filling out time sheets or writing out invoices: impossible!)

There are only three ways the fantasy of total freedom to create can come true. You can plan to always work in someone else's studio so that person and/or staff will handle all the ugly details. You have a partner willing to do it for you. Or you can afford to hire your own full-time business and clerical staff to do it.

The dirty little secret of creative freedom is that it can't survive without control. Control doesn't mean piles of forms to be filled out in triplicate or time clocks to be punched. It does mean that *someone* knows what is going on in and with your business. If you're the only someone available, then you've got to take control of it.

The good news is that the more control you have of your business, the more time you'll have to be creative. Honest! Once you've set up systems to take control of your work life, staying in control takes less and less time. And all the time you used to spend fixing mistakes and coping with crises is now yours to spend on being creative. With less hassle, *all* the work goes faster, too. Sound good to you? Then let's create those systems that will let your design business know who's boss.

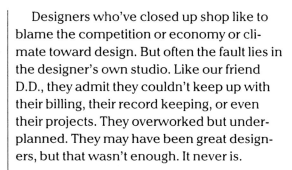

What Are Systems and How Do They Work?

Systems are methods of following procedures. Procedures are business guidelines translated into step-by-step ways of working. Business guidelines are what determine the way your business operates. Okay, enough of the anklebone-connected-to-the-shinbone approach. Let's take it from the top, beginning with how to develop basic guidelines for running your design business.

Guidelines are the keys to business success. Once you've established guidelines — decided what you want to do — you're ready to put them to work for you. (We'll look at choosing your own path to success and setting goals in more depth later in chapter nine, "Planning Your Future.") Although everyone has different criteria for success, there are two things no design business can do without: clients and profits. So, your first two guidelines would be: I have to find new clients while keeping current ones, and I must take in more money than I spend.

Procedures translate your guidelines into everyday practices. This means working out what steps you always need to take to get the job done. Setting up routine ways of handling activities now will actually save you time later, eliminating guesswork and reducing the risk of mistakes. And fewer mistakes means less work for more money. For example, to do quality work on time and at a reasonable cost to the client you must:

◆ Determine what the client wants from this project
◆ Set a deadline that works for you and the client
◆ Work out approximately how many hours you'll spend on a project
◆ Get costs from outside services such as printers
◆ Schedule the various steps of each project
◆ Coordinate project schedules
◆ Meet deadlines and always know where each project stands
◆ Keep clients informed of progress
◆ Get client approval of your work

Before you start feeling overwhelmed by all this, let's create a procedure for getting client approval of your work. It might go like this:

1. Get client's authorization in writing before starting project with all specs and budget clearly spelled out
2. Get signed agreement from client
3. Make note of all points at which client must sign off
4. Keep client updated on progress of project
5. Keep record of all changes and corrections
6. Keep record of all client approvals
7. Keep record all of client changes to project specifications

You may already do some or all of these steps automatically on each job. But if you're not doing them the same way (or nearly so) each time, you may skip something important. If someone is working for you or with you, the chances of a mistake go up even more when you don't have a set, consistent procedure for each step.

Systems are procedures in action. Once you've decided what you need to do, you work out the most effective way to do it. What information do you need to keep together? In what order? You'll need forms so you get the same information down the same way each time. What kind of forms? What should be on them? When will you use them? What will you use them for? One system for using our sample procedure would be:

1. When client gives verbal go-ahead on project, pull client authorization form from drawer. Fill it in and check it.

2. Pull agreement form from drawer. Fill it in and check it.

3. Take form to client by a set deadline.

4. Make up folder for project. Put in materials you've prepared. Indicate on the folder the points at which the client must sign off on the project and those in-between points when you'll provide an update.

5. When client returns form, place copy in folder.

6. Send/take approval form to client as needed. File approval. File all changed copy, boards, etc. in folder.

Organizing Electronic Files

Are you spending more time opening and closing computer folders, looking for project files and their revisions, than you spend working on the material once you find it? If so, you need a system for organizing your electronic files. Creating and setting up an organized file system will require an investment of time on your part, but it will be well worth the effort. It will not only save you search time in the future, but it will expand your present storage capacity by helping you sort out and trash those unnecessary files containing artwork and documents you'll never use again.

7. If the client changes project specifications, fill out and have him sign a change request form. File change request form in project folder. Change other forms, mark artwork where you need to.

8. Send mechanicals to client for final approval with form to sign. File form in folder with all other materials.

The rest of this chapter describes a system that has worked very well for me and adapted easily to different situations as my business changed and grew. Feel free to use or modify my system and the forms I've used for your own business. For your convenience in using them, you'll find the forms reprinted here full size with spaces provided for you to plug in your own logo and the name, address and phone number of your own studio.

Many of these forms, such as the Printing Bid Request, can be stored blank on your hard drive. When you need a copy, call the file up, rename it with the project name and number, fill it in and print it out.

Project Procedures

In this chapter, we'll cover only the system basics. Beneath each step on this list, I've listed the form or forms you'll need at that point. On the following pages you'll find a sample of each with an explanation of how it fits into the system, how to fill it out, and some suggestions for how to use it most effectively. Chapter four, "Work Smarter, Not Harder," will walk you through a sample project to show how all the systems and procedures can come together to make your life easier. Chapter three, "Money Talks," will cover pricing, billing and collecting money from clients.

1. Get project goals, specs and background information from client
Form: Client Information Sheet (pages 40-41)
Form: Agreement of Terms and Conditions (pages 51-53)

2. Set up a tentative production schedule
Form: Production Schedule (pages 48-49)

3. Contact all subcontractors needed (e.g., copywriter or printer)
Form: Printing Bid Request (if needed) (pages 42-43)

4. Put together pricing information
Form: Price Estimate Work Sheet (pages 44-45)
Form: Price Quote Estimate (pages 46-47)

5. Prepare production schedule
Form: Production Schedule (pages 48-50)

6. Meet with client to review prices, schedule and general ideas/concepts
Form: Price Quote Estimate (pages 46-47)
Form: Production Order (pages 54-55)
Form: Agreement of Terms and Conditions (pages 51-53)
Form: Production Schedule (copy) (pages 48-50)

7. Begin work on project
Form: Project Time Sheet (pages 58-59)
Form: Work In Progress (pages 56-57)

8. Set up project review meeting(s) with copywriter, photographer, etc.
Form: Production Schedule (copies for each) (pages 48-50)

9. Client meeting to approve preliminary layouts (colors, paper) and draft copy
Form: Client Change Request (pages 62-63)

10. Continue work on project
Form: Project Summary (to client at appropriate intervals) (pages 60-61)
Form: Project Time Sheet (pages 58-59)
Form: Work In Progress (pages 56-57)

11. If needed, supervise photo shoot/taping session
Form: Photo/Video/Audio Release (if needed) (pages 64-65)

12. Complete mechanicals
Form: Proofing Approval Checklist (pages 70-71)

13. Client meeting to approve mechanicals
Form: Proofing Approval Checklist (pages 70-71)
Form: Client Change Request (pages 62-63)

14. Revise mechanicals, as needed
Form: Proofing Approval Checklist (pages 70-71)

15. Client meeting to approve mechanicals
Form: Proofing Approval Checklist (pages 70-71)

16. Deliver electronic mechanicals to service bureau or printer
Deliver mechanicals to printer
Form: Service Bureau Instructions (page 66-67)
Form: Printing Instructions (pages 68-69)

17. Client meeting to approve blueline
Form: Client Change Request (pages 62-63)

18. Press approval
Form: None needed

19. Billing
Form: Project Expenses Tracking Sheet (pages 72-73)
Form: Project Billing Work Sheet (pages 74-75)
Form: Invoice (pages 76-77)

20. Bookkeeping
Form: Accounts Payable Record Sheet (pages 80-81)
Form: Accounts Receivable Record Sheet (pages 82-83)
Form: Monthly Client Statement (pages 78-79)
Ledger: See chapter three, "Money Talks" (pages 92-93)

Filing Is Critical

Once you've established systems and procedures and developed the forms to implement them consistently, you need some way to keep track of all those forms. That means determining what materials and documents you need to keep together and how you can store them so you can get what you need. You'll need file folders and holders and eventually filing cabinets.

For now, however, let's just concentrate on what you want to keep together. All materials for each project should be kept together and separate from materials for all other projects. The easiest way to do that is to set up a Client Project File for each client. While you'll actually store mechanicals and oversized pieces in flat files or something similar, one copy of the rest of the documents for a project should go into a single file folder in a filing cabinet. Keep copies of the following in that client project file:

◆ Client Information Sheet
◆ Notes taken during client meetings

◆ Price Estimate Work Sheet
◆ Price Quote Estimate
◆ Signed Production Order
◆ Project Summaries
◆ Signed copy of the Agreement of Terms and Conditions or client contract
◆ Photo/Video/Audio Release forms
◆ Proofing Approval Checklist
◆ Signed Client Change Request forms
◆ Signed Printing Instructions form
◆ Photocopies of all materials marked up for changes
◆ Sketches, layouts or other items critical to the project and small enough to be stored in a file folder

Organize the projects by client name and number, setting up the files alphabetically in the cabinet. Under "A," for example, you might have Alpha, Inc., Project #901101; Alpha, Inc., Project #901102; Amesbury Oil, Project #891201; and so on.

I kept a second copy of each signed Production Order, Photo/Video/Audio Release and Agreement of Terms and Conditions or client contract in a separate filing cabinet—a very sturdy, fire-resistant metal one. And although I cleaned out my Client Project files fairly regularly (but not as often as I should), I never threw out a single file from that second cabinet. Every one of them was vital in case of possible legal disputes over a project later. (See below under each individual form for its legal significance.)

I kept my accounting/bookkeeping documents in a separate place. I kept my Active Accounts Payable and Active Accounts Receivable file folders in a stand-up holder on or near my desk, because I used them constantly. Every item I needed for billing—Project Expenses Tracking Sheet, Work In Progress sheet, Project Time Sheets, copy of the Price Estimate Work Sheet, copies of any Client Change Request forms, and the Project Billing Work Sheet—was stashed in my billing book. I logged invoices to clients and bills I received on the Accounts Receivable or Accounts Payable Record Sheets and popped them into the appropriate file folder until paid. (And filed them in the right cabinet once paid.)

Automated Management

A number of software programs can take the anxiety out of project management.

ACT! 1.1, a Mac program, manages a client database linked to a calendar interface for scheduling and tracking meetings, calls and correspondence. Symantec, 10201 Torre Ave., Cupertino CA 95014, (800) 441-7234; $399.

REMEMBER? 2.1.1 is an electronic To Do list for the Mac, with a built-in calendar and an alarm to warn you when something important is coming up. David Warker, 1330 W. North St., Egg Harbor NJ 08215-1763; $20.

MacSchedule 3.0 can create schedules quickly and easily to monitor client budgets and compare them to actual project expenditures to date. You can even figure out how much more a project will cost if it gets behind schedule. Mainstay, 591-A Constitution Ave., Camarillo CA 93012, (805) 484-9400; $295.

TimeWise, which is Mac and DOS compatible, offers unlimited job tracking and scheduling capabilities that record project time, develop and maintain schedules, track vendor costs, and produce estimates, client invoices and purchase orders. David Berman Developments, Inc., (613) 235-9433; $895.

TimeView contains a DOS-based calendar that lets you schedule meetings, functions and events. If you overschedule or make an error, it will find and reschedule the conflict. Timeslips Corp., (508) 768-6100; $299.95 (single user), $599.95 (ten users).

For More Information

On using Client Information Sheets and a completed form, see page 117.

Client Information Sheet

Commentary

Before you can begin work on a client's project, you need to know more than just what type of project it is and its budget. To do your best work, you also need to know something about the client's business, who its competitors are, and the *personal* business goals of the person actually hiring you. It helps to know whether the client has worked with a designer before and what her experiences with that person were like.

The Form: Step by Step

1. Client Name: The person(s) you will actually work with.

2. Company Represented, Address, Telephone/Fax: Try to get your client's direct line and fax whenever possible. If you have easy access to a fax machine, you can fax changes to your clients. Then they simply initial and date it for approval or mark additional changes and fax it back.

3. What is the nature of the client's business? What type of product or service? Are they retail or mail order? What is the market?

4. How long has the company been in business? If the company has been in business for several years, you can safely assume that they will provide you with sound marketing information. If it's a young company or they're launching a new product, don't take anything for granted. Ask about their market research and/or sales results to date.

5. Who are its competitors? Try to get beyond company names — to get at the market and how the competition goes after it. What does the client like/dislike about the competitors' promotional or advertising materials?

6. What does the client expect from you? What is the company's goal for the project? Try to find out how the client wants to work with you. Does he want to have a lot of input? Does he have a strong mental image of how the piece(s) will look?

7. Has the client worked with designers before? And if so, in what capacity? What was the project? How does the client feel about that designer and the project now? If the client has never worked with a designer before, plan to spend more time educating the client about what you can and can't do. Also, be prepared to spend more time explaining the production process.

8. What type of project does this client want to do? Flyers? Brochures? Direct mail? If you're doing a presentation and no specific job is involved, try to discover what the client might need in the near future.

9. What would the client like to accomplish with this project? Try to capture the specific results — open a new market, reposition the product, or launch a new service?

10. What are the client's personal goals? Try to learn what the client personally wants from the project: make a big impression on the boss, carve out some turf, or move ahead in the company. If you understand why the client is coming on like a control freak or acting like none of it really matters (just to cover the extremes), it helps you frame your approaches to, and get what you need from, him or her.

11. Project Description: Write down as much detailed information as you can about the budget and specs. Note any issues still to be resolved, such as number of photos or colors.

Special Tips

◆ If you didn't meet to discuss a specific project, add the information to your file of prospective clients. Refer to it when preparing self-promotion materials and for follow-ups. Update the information or replace the sheet as you get new or more information or when beginning work on a specific project.

◆ If you used this form at a preliminary meeting on a project, make a folder for the job and put this in it with any other notes you took. This information will guide you through the early proposal stages, helping you focus your presentation and other discussions with the client. When you get a project, you can add any new information and the project description.

Client Information Sheet

Client Name: _____

Company Represented: _____

Address: _____

City/State/Zip: _____

Telephone/Fax: _____

What is the nature of the client's business? _____
_____
_____

How long has the company been in business? _____
_____

Who are its competitors? _____
_____

What does the client expect from you? _____
_____
_____

Has the client ever worked with designers before, and if so, in what capacity? _____
_____
_____

What type of graphics project does this client want to do? _____
_____
_____

What would the client like to accomplish with this project? _____
_____
_____

What are the client's personal goals in this business? _____
_____
_____

Project Description/Specifications: _____
_____
_____
_____

For More Information

On Printing Bid Requests and a completed form, see page 119.

On Price Quote Estimates, see pages 120-121.

On working with printers, see pages 142-143.

Printing Bid Request

Commentary

When a project involves printing, ask three printers to bid on it. This lets you compare the prices of competitive printers and select the shop that will best suit your client's needs. That shop is not necessarily the one that offers the lowest price, but the one that offers the best quality and service for the price. Sometimes, it may be better for the client to select the shop with a higher bid, if the printer is more accommodating to your deadlines, more reliable, or has quality that outranks the competition.

When you've compared bids and selected your printer, put a copy of the bid in the client's project folder and also in your billing book. This will serve as a quick reference when the project is complete and the printer's bill comes in. You want to be sure that the final bill reflects the quote given.

The Form: Step by Step

1. In addition to including the name and address, telephone and fax number of the printing company bidding on your project, indicate the contact person who will be responsible for handling the job.

2. The name of both your studio and the designer or production person responsible for the project should appear. If you're a one-person studio, this is obviously you — but it helps the printer to have your name, especially if your name isn't part of your studio's. If more than one person works in your studio, this helps the printer get the bid back to the right person.

3. List the specs given you by the client or those you've worked up based on the project's goals and budget. Make sure you've covered everything you'll need. Never just guesstimate your specs; that's asking for cost overruns sooner or later.

4. If you are delivering electronic disk files, be sure to indicate any specific information the printer may need. Always ask what is needed beforehand, so that you can label the files on your disk appropriately. For example, the printer may need to know the name of the specific file(s) to be printed, disk size and density, type of computer and system number used, program name and version your file was created in, names of any specific graphics used, the file they were placed in, and the format used to create them.

5. Mailing instructions apply only if the printed pieces will be direct mailed and the printing company has the facilities to handle that aspect of the project. If they don't, leave it blank. You'll then need to contact a direct mailing house to bid on that. There may be instances when you will prefer to use an outside mailing service even if the printer can do it, because that particular mailing service may have done it before or their prices are better. It pays to get competitive bids on this part of the project as well.

6. When filling out delivery instructions, be sure to include the exact address. If you don't want the delivery to come to your office, then indicate the name of your client's company. And be sure to include the name of the person who should be notified when the project is delivered.

7. Be specific as to the date of delivery and, if it's important, the time of day it needs to be delivered.

8. Keep a copy of your Printing Bid Request to check against the bids you receive from printers. If the printer overlooked something, you'll end up with an artificially low bid and cost overruns later.

9. If all the bids you receive exceed your budget, work with one of the printers who originally bid the job (one you know well and trust) on ways to reduce costs. You may achieve substantial savings without hurting the piece by changing paper or reducing the number of halftones. Get a revised quote from all three printers based on the changed specs. Unless you've changed all the specs extensively, call each printer and ask for an adjusted quote for the revised specs only. Note the changes on the bid sheets. You may want to send a copy of the chosen, revised bid for the printer to initial and return.

Special Tips

♦ Before you ask a printer to bid on a job, be sure to discuss the project details and your deadline with her before you send out the bid request form. Talking with a printer ahead of time also helps you to

Printing Bid Request

Printing Company: _____

Contact Person: _____

Address: _____

Telephone/Fax: _____

Designer's Name: _____ Date: _____

Project Description: _____ Project Number: _____

Printing Specifications

Quantities to Print: _____

Paper Stock: _____

# of Sides: _____ # of Colors: _____ PMS ink #s: _____

Delivered as Camera-Ready Film: _____

Delivered as Electronic Disk Files: _____

Prepress Service/Service Bureau: _____

Contact: _____ Telephone: _____

Stripping Required, See Specs Below: _____

Bleeds: _____ Screens: _____ Reverses: _____

Halftones: _____ Film: _____ Separations: _____

Proofs/Blueline: _____ Color Key: _____ Chromalin Proof: _____

Print Size: _____ Score: _____ Fold: _____

Finished Size: _____ Bindery: _____ Emboss: _____

Die Cut: _____ Perforations: _____ Drills: _____

Thermography: _____ Varnish: _____ Other: _____

Pack: _____ Mailing: _____

Mailing Instructions: _____

_____

_____

Delivery Instructions: _____

_____

_____

Date Due: _____

Please return bid by: _____

For More Information

On price estimates and a completed form, see pages 120-121.

On pricing your work, see pages 86-88.

On figuring markup, see page 88.

On choosing printers and subcontractors, see pages 138-143.

On Price Quote Estimates, see pages 120-121.

troubleshoot any unforeseen production or schedule problems. If the printing company has the press time to handle your project's requirements, tell the owner or sales rep that a bid form will be in the mail. Be specific about the date by which you need it returned. It takes time to put together a price quote, so in fairness to your printers, give them at least a week to prepare the bid.

◆ If you aren't already familiar with the shorthand lingo printers use for spec terminology (''#'' for pound, ''2/2'' for two sides), ask your printer for a quick lesson. They'll be happy to give it because it simplifies, for both of you, preparing and reading the bid specs.

Price Estimate Work Sheet

Commentary

Every client wants to know how much a project will cost before giving you the go-ahead. They'll ask you for a price quote to confirm that you can do the project within their proposed budget. To give them a realistic figure, you must estimate how much time you'll spend on a project to calculate your charges as well as costs for various services such as copywriting, typesetting and printing—and add on your markup.

Use this work sheet to arrive at a Price Quote Estimate for the client. You should *never* give a client a work sheet that shows your actual markup. A client who knows your markup may try to cut into your markup to force down your prices.

The Form: Step by Step

1. Enter the client's name and a brief description of the project (sales brochure, direct mail package, etc.) at the top of the form. Leave the space for Project Number blank until the project's been authorized and you've assigned it a number on the Work In Progress sheet.

2. Estimate the time to the nearest quarter hour that you think you'll take at each stage of production. Enter that figure in the column headed Time. Draw a line in the columns for any action not needed on this project

and write ''Sub-out'' in the Time column for anything you'll subcontract. Note that the first reference to typesetting is for in-house production; the second reference is for subbed-out typesetting.

3. For each action you will perform, multiply the hours in the time column by the amount you charge per hour to get the Total Production Cost.

4. Review the bids you've received from each printer, subcontractor or vendor. Select the ones you'll work with and enter their prices into the appropriate space in the Price column on the work sheet. Break out printing prices by the quantities your client requested.

 Sometimes it's impossible to estimate how much typesetting, stats, veloxes or screens will cost because there are too many production-related variables. If you don't know, don't guess! Enter ''Cannot be estimated at this time'' in the Price column. (You'll transfer this notation to the final Price Quote Estimate, too.) Also include an entry for ''Miscellaneous Materials'' under Other—a range of $100 to $150 generally covers you. This covers materials you may need to complete a project, such as special markers, Pantone papers and boards, that you can't more accurately estimate.

5. Figure your markup on the price from each subcontractor. For example, you have a bid of $3,000 from a printer and your markup is 20 percent. You would enter $600 in the Markup column.

6. Add the figure from the Price column to the figure in the Markup column for each subcontractor and the printer, and then enter the correct sum in the column for Client's Price.

7. Total all the entries under Total Production Cost and Client's Price to get the Total Project Cost. Make sure that this figure falls within the client's budget for the project.

Special Tips

◆ If you use a computer spreadsheet program, you can set up a price estimating spreadsheet with formulas for your hourly rates and markup built in. You enter your time and the subcontractors' and printer's prices for each job and the computer does the rest!

Price Estimate Work Sheet

Client: _____ Project Number: _____

Project Description: _____
_____

Production	Time	Cost/Hour	Total Production Cost
Client Meetings			
Research			
Concept Development			
Organization			
Layout/Design			
Art Direction			
Illustration			
Typesetting			
Mechanical Prep			
Consult with Vendors and Subcontractors			
Copywriting/Editing			
Proofing			
Press Approvals			
Acct. Administration			
Other —			

Printing Prices

Quantity	Price	Markup	Client's Price

Subcontractor/Vendor & Other Prices

Service	Price	Markup	Client's Price
Photography			
Typesetting			
Stats, veloxes, films			
Other			

Total Project Cost: _____

For More Information

On Price Estimate Work Sheets, see pages 44-45.

On Price Quote Estimates and a completed form, see pages 120-121.

On requests for multiple quotes, see pages 180-181.

On dealing with unworkable budgets, see page 180.

On Client Change Request form and client changes, see pages 62-63 and 126.

♦ Estimate your time for each phase of production as accurately as possible based on similar jobs. If you've never handled a project quite like this before, put down slightly more time than you think you'll need. For example, if you've never done a brochure, don't simply multiply the time it takes to do a flyer by the number of pages in a brochure.

♦ You don't have to charge the same hourly rate for everything you do. Client meetings, concept development and layout and design are extremely demanding activities and require special expertise. Price them at a higher rate than mechanical prep or proofing.

♦ You should get bids from at least two subcontractors and at least three printers on every job. Select your subcontractors and printers based on the price you were quoted, the quality of work you need, and their ability to meet your schedule.

Price Quote Estimate

Commentary

Clients want price quotes — and your firm commitment to them. *Don't do it!* Vendors may change their prices, the project may take longer than you anticipated, or you may discover you need special materials or services. Client changes in the project specifications can radically alter costs. And printers' quotes are only good for six months. If you've given a firm quote, any extra time or money automatically comes out of your pocket.

To calm client fears about accepting an estimate, I began calling my estimates Price Quote Estimates. I also added a disclaimer (which you can see at the bottom of the form on the facing page): "This is an estimate only. Billing will reflect the actual costs incurred. This estimate is valid only for six months. Client requested changes will be billed additionally. The client will be notified of any price changes."

The Form: Step by Step

1. Complete Price Estimate Work Sheet.

2. For the section headed Production, transfer the figures for your time, cost per hour, and total cost for each phase to the appropriate place on this form.

(Time becomes Estimated Time, for example.) Transfer all your Sub-out entries and draw a line through the boxes for time and costs for services you won't provide. Note that the first reference to typesetting is for in-house production; the second reference is for subbed-out typesetting.

3. For the section headed Printing Prices, transfer the quantities requested and the figure from the Client's Price column to this form.

4. Do the same for all subcontractor and vendor prices. Always make sure you pick up the figures from the Client's Price column, since that includes your markup. And remember to transfer all entries for "Cannot be estimated at this time," too. Finally, don't forget your charge for miscellaneous material, which should be written as "$100 to $150 for miscellaneous materials to be billed as needed."

5. Transfer the figure for Total Project Cost to the space for Total Estimated Project Cost on this form.

6. Review your Price Quote Estimate with the client. When it is approved, have him or her sign and date the form. Attach a copy to the Production Order form shown on page 55.

Special Tips

♦ This is another job that's easily done on a computer. You have your form set up in a computer spreadsheet program and copy the information from your estimating spreadsheet to this one.

♦ If the client quotes the budget for a project as a range, always try to bring the costs for the project in at the low end of that range. Clients will feel better about any extra costs when they see the project is still within their budget limits. But don't estimate so low that you *can't* hold to your original figure. In fact, you shouldn't exceed your estimate unless it's absolutely unavoidable — with the client's written agreement to the change.

♦ Some designers who do their own typesetting on a computer include that time under layout/design rather than break it out separately. They feel this reduces the chance that clients who think it should take minutes to push a button and set type will complain about how long it takes and how much it costs.

Price Quote Estimate

Date: _____ Project Number: _____

Client Name: _____

Designer Name: _____

Project Description: _____

Production	Estimated Time	Cost/Hour	Est. Production Cost
Client Meetings			
Research			
Concept Development			
Organization			
Layout/Design			
Art Direction			
Illustration			
Typesetting			
Mechanical Prep			
Consult with Vendors and Subcontractors			
Copywriting/Editing			
Proofing			
Press Approvals			
Acct. Administration			
Other—			

Printing Prices

Quantity	Price

Subcontractor/Vendor & Other Prices

Service	Price
Photography	
Typesetting	
Stats, veloxes, films	
Vendors	
Other Expenses	

Please Note:
This is an estimate only. Billing will reflect the actual costs incurred. This estimate is valid only for 6 months. Client requested changes will be billed additionally. The client will be notified of any price changes.

Total Estimated Project Cost _____

Client Approval: _____ Date: _____

For More Information

On Production Schedules and a completed form, see page 120.

On the second client meeting, see pages 121-122.

On contacting subcontractors, see page 119.

On working with vendors and subcontractors, see pages 138-143.

Production Schedule

Commentary

Use the Production Schedule to plan out and set target dates for each phase of a project — and to monitor your progress. A Production Schedule also helps the client understand how the project will come together and how much time each step takes. It also tells your subcontractors where they fit into the project and when to block off time to work on it.

The Form: Step by Step

1. Break the project down into phases and write out a list of everything you have to do in order.

2. Estimate the time needed for each and mark that next to each phase listed. Working backward from the Delivery-to-Client date, pencil in tentative due dates for each, making sure you've allowed a realistic amount of time for each. Check production schedules (or your master schedule/calendar) to make sure there are no conflicts with other projects.

3. Discuss the proposed schedule with each subcontractor or vendor involved. Then get confirmed schedules and delivery dates. Adjust the tentative schedule as needed.

4. If printing is involved, determine the date you need it completed and get boards-to-printer dates with your printing bids.

5. Now transfer your tentative schedule to the Production Schedule form. Using a calendar and working backward from the Delivery-to-Client date, fill in that date and continue working up the production schedule to the beginning of the project. Include both start and finish dates when appropriate; for example, "Layout: 3/6-3/10." Work the rest of the production schedule around the dates and time frames your subcontractors and printers gave you. Always build in an extra day or two with a false deadline for yourself and anyone else involved in the project (including the client). This reduces the chances that you'll be facing a major last-minute crunch toward the end of the project.

6. Prepare copies of the form for everyone involved in the project — including the client. Highlight the places where the printer's, client's and each subcontractor's commitments appear on the schedule so they can see at a glance exactly where they fit into the schedule.

7. Have the client verify that he will be available when you need him and get approval of the whole schedule.

Special Tips

◆ Call all subcontractors working on the project when the client approves the schedule and again a week before you need them, to confirm their availability.

◆ Keep the production schedules for all projects you're actively working on in a file called Current Production. (You want to use a Master Production Schedule or a calendar instead of or in addition to this file.) Check this file each day as you make up your To Do list or as you work on the project. That way you'll see if you're starting to fall behind.

◆ Update both your Production Schedule and Work In Progress sheets regularly (preferably at the same time). When you complete a stage, note it on both sheets. On the Production Schedule, write DONE and the date completed above the due date for each phase.

Production Schedule — Page 1

Project: _____ Project Number: _____

Name/Description: _____

_____

_____

Phase 1 — Concept

Client Meetings .... Due Date _____

Concept Development .... Due Date _____

Contact Subs/Vendors .... Due Date _____

Estimates from Subcontractors .... Due Date_____

Project Estimate .... Due Date_____

Design .... Due Date_____

Copy .... Due Date_____

Editing .... Due Date_____

Revisions .... Due Date_____

Client Approval .... Due Date_____

Phase 2 — Production

Layout .... Due Date_____

Client Approval .... Due Date_____

Comprehensive .... Due Date_____

Client Approval .... Due Date_____

Copy Revisions .... Due Date_____

Client Approval .... Due Date_____

Type Ordered .... Due Date_____

Type Proofed .... Due Date_____

Other Sub Work .... Due Date_____

Client Approval .... Due Date_____

Production Schedule — Page 2

Phase 2 — Production (continued)

Mechanical .... Due Date_____

Client Approval .... Due Date_____

Boards to Printer .... Due Date_____

Proofs .... Due Date_____

Corrections .... Due Date_____

Client Approval .... Due Date_____

Color Separations .... Due Date_____

Proofs .... Due Date_____

Client Approval .... Due Date_____

Phase 3 — Printing

Camera-Ready Work to Printer .... Due Date_____

Blueline/Color Proof .... Due Date_____

Delivery to Client .... Due Date_____

Revisions .... Due Date_____

Client Approval .... Due Date_____

Press Approval .... Due Date_____

Delivery to Client .... Due Date_____

Client Signature: _____ Date: _____
Please sign both copies. Retain one for your file and return the other to the above address.

Agreement of Terms and Conditions

Commentary

When a client gives you the go-ahead for a project, have her sign the Agreement of Terms and Conditions. This form is your proof, in writing, that the client has agreed to your price estimate and understands that all expenses incurred during this project are her responsibility. It is a contractual agreement between you and the client that clearly names the project, identifies the client, designates the responsibilities of both the designer and client, and outlines your terms for payment without the complicated terminology and lengthy discourse of most legal contracts. However, if you feel you need a more specific contractual agreement, rather than using the Agreement of Terms and Conditions included in this book, you may want to have your attorney draw up a contract created especially for your business. Or, you can contact the Graphic Artists Guild, 30 E. Twentieth St., New York NY 10016 to order copies of their Standard Contract for Artists and Designers.

A client contract, like the Agreement of Terms and Conditions, confirms that your client understands and agrees to your procedures, policies, billing and payment terms, as well as to other conditions such as ownership of art and design work, what happens if the project is canceled, provisions for changes in the project's specifications, arbitration if disputes arise, etc. But client contracts usually go a step further in that they may specify things like geographic and time limitations on the client's use of your work. They may also address the issue of releasing the designer from all claims and expenses which could result from the client's use or misuse of the design or artwork, if such use went beyond the stipulations in the contract. If you or a subcontractor, such as an illustrator or photographer, want to have a credit line identifying the work in a client's ad or publication, that should be addressed in the contract. It can be included in the Agreement of Terms and Conditions provided for your use here, if you reproduce the form in your computer or have it typeset.

Some designers use something similar to this form that also includes a complete description of what the client will receive for the money spent (e.g., "The fee quoted includes 8 preliminary sketches at $35 ea.; each additional sketch or design will cost $50").

You may feel this kind of detail is necessary with certain clients who are hard to please, specifically those clients who tend to demand that you continue working on ideas and concept layouts when you've already presented more than a reasonable number of preliminary sketches. Although this agreement form doesn't get into that kind of detail, you can spell out exactly what they will get in the way of layouts, comps, revisions, mechanicals, etc. in your Production Order (coming up on pages 54-55).

The Form: Step by Step

1. Plug in your name or company logo and address above the heading: Agreement of Terms and Conditions.

2. Type in the client's name and the company he represents in the space provided at the top of the form. Include the company address, the telephone and fax numbers, the project's name and a brief description.

3. On Line #1, enter the total estimated cost for the project. Be sure to attach a Price Quote Estimate for reference. Line #2 establishes the client's legal responsibility for the project's expenses.

4. Line #3 describes the usage rights you're granting the client in exchange for and upon receipt of full payment for the project. Specify those illustrations and/or photographs that remain the property of the creator. If the client wants exclusive rights or a work-for-hire, negotiate with the client a separate fee beyond the costs outlined on Line #1 for those rights.

5. Line #4 states the terms for payment. This extremely important section is where you will specify the billing policy you wish to use with each new client and when you expect payment. With some clients you may require that one-third of the total project estimate be paid as an advance on signing, another third as an advance paid midway, and the final payment due upon completion.

For More Information

On Agreements of Terms and Conditions and a completed form, see pages 121-122.

On Production Orders, see pages 54-55.

On billing and payment terms, see pages 90-91.

On pricing your work, see pages 86-88.

On working effectively with clients, see pages 178-183.

This form of payment is particularly desirable with new clients who haven't established a credit record with you yet. However, when new clients have long-term projects, it's advisable to get anywhere from one-quarter to one-third of the total project cost up front as a deposit, and then put them on a monthly payment schedule.

For other clients, particularly those whose ability to pay has been established or new clients with long-term projects stretching out over several months, you may prefer to bill them monthly. If a client is placed on a monthly billing cycle, but the project demands up-front expenses that can place a burden on your cash flow, you may need to specify that these expenses be paid in advance or billed directly to the client. This is the place to address such requirements.

On Line #5, you should indicate whether you expect payment of invoices to be made upon receipt of invoice, within ten days or within thirty days. If you're billing a client in thirds, always make the terms upon receipt of invoice and don't do any more work until you get paid. This is your best protection against slow-paying and nonpaying clients, because the only hold you have over them is delivery of the finished project.

6. In Line #6, you should write in the additional hourly fee that you will charge for overtime.

7. Lines #7 through #10 establish that the cost cited in Line #1 is an estimate only, not a firm quotation, that will be affected by certain client changes; that you will, however, obtain client approval before exceeding the budget limits; and that the cost cited in Line #1 is only good for thirty days (after thirty days, it might go up). Line #11 establishes both your and the client's responsibility for meeting deadlines. Line #12 establishes that if the client cancels the project, he or she is still responsible for all expenses incurred up to that point. Line #13 sets client responsibility for legal fees.

8. Have the client sign and date the agreement only after she has read it thoroughly. The client may request changes in the contract to reflect special concerns or to obtain more favorable terms from you. Ne-

gotiation over contract terms is standard; just know what your bottom line is on each issue. In other words, don't refuse to negotiate points important to the client, but don't give away the store to get the job either. Cross out or type in any changes; don't redo the whole contract. Both of you should initial each change.

Special Tips

◆ Never begin work on a project without having the client sign this agreement form or a client contract unless the client has established a solid payment record and satisfactory relationship with you. Then you need only have the client sign a production order for each new project.

◆ Keep all signed Agreements of Terms and Conditions and client contracts in a safe place separate from the other materials (signed price quotes, copies of layouts, logos, etc.) filed during the project. I recommend a fire-resistant metal filing cabinet with a folder used only for Agreement of Terms and Conditions forms or client contracts, Production Orders and Photo/Video/Audio Releases. These are your most important documents!

◆ Keep all agreements and contracts for one year following the completion of a project. You never know when a client or her company may question something about a project long after it's over, leading to a dispute or legal action. The signed contract or agreement form may be your only defense.

◆ Notice that on this agreement and other forms presented in this chapter, you write in the name of *both* the client and the company she represents. That's because, legally, if the client is only an employee of the company (not an owner), the company may claim that it will assume no responsibility for an employee's actions or agreements unless the company's name is also entered on the contract.

◆ If you are using subcontractors, such as an illustrator or copywriter, you may want to have that stated in the agreement. When the client will pay subcontractors directly, you should include that information and the agreed fee (and any extra charges such as rush charges) in your agreement.

Agreement of Terms and Conditions

Client Name: _____

Company the Client Represents: _____

Company Address: _____

City/State/Zip: _____

Telephone/Fax Number: _____

Project Name: _____

Project Description: _____

1. The total cost for this project is estimated at: _____ (See attached estimate)
2. All expenses incurred to complete this order shall be the responsibility of the Client.
3. Upon receipt of full payment, Designer grants to the Client the following rights in the designs: _____
   _____
   _____

   All rights not expressly granted in this agreement remain the exclusive property of the Designer. Unless otherwise specified, Designer retains ownership of all original artwork, whether preliminary or final, and Client shall return such artwork within sixty (60) days after use.
4. Payment for this project will be made according to the following schedule:
   _____
   _____

5. Payment for all invoices is due: _____
6. Designer fees quoted apply only to regular working hours—9 A.M. to 5 P.M., Monday through Friday. If the Client requests that project work be performed at times other than the stipulated office hours, additional overtime fees of _____ per hour will be charged, except for corrections made necessary by the Designer.
7. All costs are estimates only. Any alterations by the Client of project specifications may result in price changes.
8. All additional costs that exceed the original estimate will be quoted to the Client, in writing, before the costs are incurred.
9. The Designer/design company does not have the authority to exceed this estimate without Client approval.
10. The terms and conditions of this agreement are valid for only thirty (30) days.
11. The Designer/design company's ability to meet the requirements of the Production Order and Production Schedule (see attached) is totally dependent on the Client's delivery at the time specified on the Production Schedule (see attached) of any and all materials needed to complete the project.
12. If the project is canceled at any time, the Client is responsible for all expenses incurred to that point.
13. If a dispute arises between the Designer/design company and the Client over any term or condition agreed to in this agreement, the Client will be subject to pay all reasonable attorney's fees if the dispute requires legal counsel.

I have agreed to the terms and conditions presented in this agreement as it applies to the project named and described above.

Client signature: _____ Date: _____

For More Information

On Production Orders and a completed form, see pages 121-122.

On Production Schedules, see page 120.

On Price Quote Estimates, see page 121.

On client's goals for project, see page 40.

On your second client meeting, see pages 121-122.

Production Order

Commentary

This form should be signed at the start of each new project. It outlines the project's specifications, the prices that you and your client have agreed to (attach a copy of your signed Price Quote Estimate), the Production Schedule, and any other special information that may require acknowledgement, such as the number of layouts that will be prepared for a presentation and the cost for additional ones.

I've always included a brief description of my understanding of the client's goals for the project on the Production Order. If I've misunderstood anything the client has said about his or her goals for the project or the expected results, I want to catch it now. Having an agreement on goals confirmed in writing on the production order protects you not only from misunderstandings now but also from arbitrary changes later. For example, you're hired to do a direct mail piece promoting Christmas gifts for teenagers to other teenagers. When you present your layouts (or even later), the client tells you that your work is completely off base because it doesn't appeal to teenagers *and* parents. If you have a goals statement on your production order, you can prove that you've delivered what the client requested — making it easier to get the money you deserve for reworking the project.

The Production Order authorizes you to begin work on a project. It covers the specific details of the project itself rather than payment terms and client/designer responsibilities. Always have a new client sign both an Agreement of Terms and Conditions and the Production Order before you do any creative or preliminary work. Clients who have established credit with you need only sign the Production Order.

The Form: Step by Step

1. Type in the client's name, the company he or she represents, the date and the project name. You'll have to make sure the company name is on there, too, in order to make this Production Order legally binding.

2. Describe the project very specifically (e.g., a four-color, eight-page capabilities brochure, containing ten black-and-white photographs).

3. The project objectives should address what the finished piece is intended to do — increase sales through distribution to potential customers, for example. Also, any other goals that the client would like to achieve, such as ''redefine the company's image to the targeted audience'' should be specified.

4. Write in the price estimate total from the Price Quote Estimate and attach the copy of the form that the client has signed and approved.

5. Due date: the date the client wants to receive the finished project.

6. Unless the project is very short and simple, you should have completed a Production Schedule for it. Simply write in, ''See Production Schedule attached'' and make sure you attach a copy. If not all of the job will be delivered to the same place at once, you should note that in the space for Schedule on the Production Order. For example, the client may want to approve a sample before the piece goes to the mailing house.

Special Tips

◆ Never begin even the preliminary idea stage of a project without having the client sign this form unless you have agreed to do the creative on spec or you are making a presentation as a means of acquiring the project. In either case, the Production Order will have to wait until you are officially awarded the assignment.

◆ Keep a copy of this signed form in your project folder. But file the client-signed original in your file folder designated for signed Agreement of Terms and Conditions forms, or client contracts and Production Orders. Always use a metal filing cabinet.

◆ Keep the project name brief, but include enough description to help you distinguish it from other projects — especially if you file your work by project name or have more than one ongoing project for the same client. For example, ''Sales Brochure'' isn't as distinctive as ''Special Sales Brochure'' or ''Christmas Craft Brochure.'' (Also remember that the client *will* see the name and should be able to read it without either of you blushing.)

Production Order

Client: _____

Company Represented: _____

Date: _____

Project Name: _____

Project Description:

_____
_____
_____
_____
_____
_____

Project Objectives:

_____
_____
_____
_____
_____
_____
_____

Price Estimate Total: (See attached Price Quote Estimate for breakdown)

_____

Due Date: _____

Schedule: _____

Special Information: _____

_____
_____
_____
_____

Client Authorization Signature to Begin Work:

_____ Date: _____

For More Information

On Work In Progress Sheets and a completed form, see page 125.

On Project Time Sheets, see page 122.

On billing, see pages 90-91.

Work In Progress

Commentary

When a client has approved a new project, fill out a Work In Progress sheet for it. Assign the project a number and place it in your billing book as the first page of that project's information sheets. File it according to project name or number, depending on how your billing book is organized (see pages 90-91 for setting up your billing book). Update the sheet weekly, checking off each project phase as it's completed and noting the date, so you can tell at a glance when it's time to bill the client or how much. If you're only billing at the end of a project, you bill when all steps are completed. If you've asked for payment of your fee in thirds (two advances and one final payment), you can use this form to trigger those payments. If you bill monthly, you can quickly tell what you need to include on the next invoice.

The Form: Step by Step

1. Enter the date the project was ordered.

2. The project name goes on the second line.

3. Assign a project number to each new job. Enter in the space next to the project name. Use this number for cross-referencing project records: Price Estimate Work Sheet, Price Quote Estimate, Project Time Sheets, etc. Before you do any more work on this form, pull all the records for this project and make sure each has the correct project number!

4. When billing a project monthly or in thirds write "Monthly Billing," or the appropriate dates based on the Production Schedule, in the space under Project Billing Dates. Otherwise, write "End of Project."

5. Write in a brief description of the project on the next lines.

6. Then write in the due date, meaning delivery to the client.

7. Working from the Production Schedule, highlight each production category that's part of this project on the sheet so you can see at a glance what has to be done.

8. As each phase of production is completed, write in the date finished. When all the highlighted areas are dated as complete, it's time to send the final (if not the only) bill.

Special Tips

◆ The project number is a critical part of your filing system, especially if you're using a computer spreadsheet program to track all the project information for billing purposes. The project number is the most accurate way for the computer — or you — to search your files.

◆ Here's a suggestion for numbering your projects. Set up a six-digit number for each project. The first two digits will be the year, the second two a code to designate the client, and the last two the number of projects you've done with that client. For example, you're assigning a project number to the third project you've done for client code #12 (Alpha, Inc.) in 1990. The number would then be: 901203. This numbering system also helps you identify quickly which clients are generating the most business for you. Simply flip through your most recent Work In Progress sheets and note the client and project numbers. The higher the last two digits, the more work that client's giving you.

◆ If you have an employee who's responsible for all the studio's billing, the Work In Progress sheets are an excellent way to alert him or her that it's time to bill a particular client. They're also a good way to alert a secretary responsible for transcribing Project Time Sheets that it's time to get all the data for one stage together.

Work In Progress

Date Ordered: _____

Project Name: _____ Project Number: _____

Project Billing Dates: _____

Project Description: _____

_____

_____

_____ Due Date: _____

Production Phase	Date Completed	Production Phase	Date Completed
Concept _____		Color Separations _____	
Copy _____		Revisions _____	
Editing _____		Pre-press _____	
Layout _____		Blueline/Color Proofs _____	
Revisions _____		Approvals _____	
Art/Illustration _____		Revisions _____	
Mechanical _____		Press _____	
Photography _____		Other _____	
Halftones _____		Delivery _____	

Special Notes or Instructions: _____

_____

_____

_____

_____

_____

_____

_____

_____

_____

_____

_____

_____

For More Information

On Project Time Sheets and a completed form, see pages 122-123.

On business expenses, see pages 37-38.

Project Time Sheet

Commentary

You can't run a profitable business without time sheets. They are the only way you have of knowing exactly how much time you or an employee actually spent on a project. Make it a requirement for everyone to log in each time they begin work on a project, and log out with a time when finished.

The Project Time Sheet on the facing page was designed to keep your recording efforts to a minimum. The function codes eliminate writing in a description of activities or services each time you log in. These same function

 codes are also used with the Work In Progress sheet, Project Summary, and Project Billing Work Sheet. See pages 56, 60, and 74 to see how to translate your time directly from the time sheet to these other forms.

Keep all your time sheets on a clipboard next to your drawing board or desk. When you fill in a time sheet or when you finish a project, put that sheet into your billing book. When it's time to bill, a record of all the time will be there for the invoice. If you log time sheets on the computer, update all files weekly so your info is always current.

The Form: Step by Step

1. When you're ready to begin work on a new project, get a blank time sheet and write in your name at the top unless you work alone. Require an employee to write his or her name on each new time sheet so you'll know how long it takes to perform a given job.

2. Look over the function codes to see which ones apply to the specific job activity. Next to numbers 17, 18, 19, 20 and 21 write in any activities that are not already listed. Proposal and preparation time, if billable to the project, is part of the Concept Development time (function code 03). Pricing/scheduling, pick up/delivery and clerical belong under function code 14, and printing supervision falls under function code 13 (Press Approvals) on your time sheet. Use code 04 if you're doing typesetting on your computer and then sending a disk to the service bureau.

3. Enter the client's name, the project name and the project number. To make it easier to find the right sheet, arrange them on your clipboard in alphabetical order by either client name or project name. Because

 you'll sometimes have more than one ongoing project for the same client, it's probably better to organize by project name. That way, you won't have to dig through several sheets for the same client to find one. Enter the project number from the Work In Progress sheet.

4. Enter the date you begin work in the first column.

5. Write in the function code number for the job activity you're starting.

6. Log your starting and stopping times, giving hour and minutes (4:53 P.M.) for both—including breaks.

 Every designer in your studio should also log in and out for breaks or if they're interrupted to pick up another project. A five-minute pause for a telephone call or question can magically turn into a half hour or more. This helps reduce lost time and keep track of each employee's productivity.

7. At the end of each day, add up the total number of hours spent to the nearest quarter hour and write that into the last column on each line.

Special Tips

♦ While you may not be able to bill every hour spent if you quoted lower, you'll at least know the next time you quote a similar job that you may need more time to complete it. You can also tell if you're losing money on a job because certain job activities are taking longer than they should. If you feel, for example, that you're taking too long on mechanicals, you may decide that it's more profitable to farm them out.

♦ Keep all time sheets in a master file for at least six months in case a client or the client's auditors ask for justification of the time you charged on a certain project.

♦ Always make up a time sheet when you work on a proposal. If you later get the job, continue using the same time sheet. Your proposal costs will appear as part of your Total Hours for Concept Development (03). Include that proposal preparation time

Project Time Sheet

Employee Name: _____

FUNCTION CODES		
01 Consultation/Meetings	08 Typesetting	15 Revisions
02 Research	09 Mechanical Prep	16 Client Changes
03 Concept Development	10 Consult Vendors/Subs	17 Other—
04 Organization	11 Copywriting/Editing	18 Other—
05 Layout/Design	12 Proofing	19 Other—
06 Art Direction	13 Press Approvals	20 Other—
07 Illustration	14 Acct. Administration	21 Other—

Client: _____

Project Name: _____ **Project Number:** _____

Date	Function Code	Time Began	Time Ended	Total Hours

For More Information

On Project Summaries and a completed form, see pages 123-124.

On working effectively with clients, see pages 178-183.

on your Price Estimate Work Sheet, too. If you don't get the job, file those costs with your business expenses as marketing expenses.

Project Summary

Commentary

Prepare a Project Summary at least once during the course of a project and more frequently if the project takes more than a month. It lets the client know exactly what's been done on the project, what's left, and how many hours have been clocked in so far. It also lets the client know, in writing, if there's any special information she should be aware of—for example, if some part of the project is on hold because you're waiting for the client to get back to you with copy or photographs. It warns the client of any problems that could develop and makes clear whether they should contact you or not.

This procedure can be done with minimal effort by using the Project Summary form. Each project phase is already listed, although some may not apply to every project.

The Form: Step by Step

1. Write in the date you're preparing it.

2. The client's name goes on the second line, the company represented by that client on the third, and the company's address in the space that follows.

3. Write in a brief description of the project. If you're doing more than one project for this client, you may need to be specific in your project description so that the client doesn't mistake this summary for that of another project.

4. Use a yellow marker to highlight the phases that apply to this particular project. Don't assume clients will remember what appeared on the Production Schedule and call their attention only to items that apply to them.

5. Check the appropriate box for complete or incomplete, as it applies at the time the summary is being sent.

6. Take the figures for the Hours to Date from your Project Time Sheets using the function codes to transfer the entries correctly. Use function codes 18 through 21 as needed to pick up information from your time sheet. Use the letters N/A for not applicable in any project code spaces, such as subcontracted services, that you won't bill the client for. Enter the total number of hours worked to date.

7. If portions of the project are on hold, say why.

8. If you're waiting for a client approval, be sure to indicate when you need it. Build in a false deadline of a day or two. Mark the space for the client to contact you so you can confirm that date.

9. If problems could develop, explain why and always offer a solution if possible. If you have entered anything in this space, check the space for the client to call you immediately. (This is especially important if you have no solution ready!)

Special Tips

◆ Sending your client a Project Summary is more courtesy than necessity. It is, in fact, an extra little bother for you, but clients appreciate it because it makes them feel involved and valued. They're also less apt to be continually checking to be sure the project is moving along.

◆ If a project has a short turnaround time—a few weeks—a project summary isn't necessary. But if it takes at least a month, then I advise preparing it—it doesn't take long. Depending on the project, you can send one weekly or monthly.

◆ Keep a copy of every summary that you send in the project folder, so you know what you've previously told the client (especially handy if they call with questions). If you have a secretary, partner, associate or employee, the copy helps him or her work with a client in your absence.

◆ What if your project hours exceed your estimate? You have a decision to make. Bill the client for the additional hours? Risky. Although the estimate is not a final confirmation of costs, clients still expect you to stay within it. If the project begins to run over cost, it's your responsibility to inform the client before, not after, the overrun occurs. With early warning, you and the client can decide together

Project Summary

Date: _____

Client: _____

Company Name: _____

Address: _____

City/State/Zip: _____

Project Description: _____

Code	Project Phase	Complete	Incomplete	Hours to Date
02	Research			
03	Concept			
05	Layout			
05	Comp Prep			
11	Copy			
11	Copyediting			
01	Client Meetings			
07	Art/Illustration			
09	Mechanical			
08	Typesetting			
—	Photography			
—	Videography			
12	Proofing			
15	Revisions			
13	Press Approval			
—	Outside Typesetting			

Total Hours to Date: _____

Aspects of the project that are on hold: _____

We are waiting for client approval on: _____

Recommended changes: _____

Problems that could develop: _____

_____

Contact us immediately: Yes _____ Not necessary _____

Designer Signature: _____ Date: _____

For More Information

On Client Change Requests and a completed form, see pages 126-127.

On client approvals, see pages 126.

On working effectively with clients, see pages 178-184.

what to do about it. If the hours are mounting because of your inexperience, that's not the client's problem. You're far better off to bill the client only for the hours quoted in the estimate. While you may be losing money, at least you aren't losing a client. The important thing to understand is why your hours were on the heavy side. Then you can try to keep that from happening again or quote higher the next time a similar project comes along.

Client Change Request

Commentary

A client should sign a Client Change Request form when she has asked for any changes that may alter the original project specifications, and therefore affect the project's schedule or price. This doesn't apply to changes that occur during the early stages of layout and copy approval when revisions are standard fare. This form is for those alterations requested by the client after she has initially approved all facets of the project.

Your client needs to know, from the beginning, that when you have made a mistake, either in concept or execution, you'll take care of it without additional charges and you'll work overtime to stay on schedule. However, if the client makes preference changes, she is responsible for the additional costs to make those changes, which may include your fees, as well as cost increases in printing or subcontractors' fees. The client also needs to understand that any changes may seriously affect her deadline.

This Client Change Request form will help your clients understand the full impact of the changes they so often think can be made with a wave of the designer's magic wand. When clients not only *hear* you say that these changes will cost money and alter deadlines but have to commit *in writing* to accepting full responsibility for the additional charges and delays, this is often enough to discourage them. If not, at least you know they can't come back and say that you never informed them that their changes would impact the final bill or delivery date.

The Form: Step by Step

1. Fill in the client's name, date, the company name, project description and number.

2. Number and describe separately each change the client has requested in Section A. Be as specific as possible, and attach an extra sheet if necessary.

3. Have the client read through the change request form thoroughly, and then initial and date the form next to the description of the changes.

4. Do *not* fill in Section B until you've reviewed your production schedule and contacted any subcontractors or vendors whose work is involved to determine the impact of the changes on the project. Stipulate the changes to the original Price Quote Estimate, delivery date and Production Schedule in the spaces provided. Describe any delays in the Production Schedule or to the delivery date in terms of days or weeks ("will delay delivery of the finished project by three days") and attach a revised Production Schedule if several stages of production are affected. Highlight the affected stages on the schedule.

5. Section C is to be signed by the client and returned to you immediately.

Special Tips

◆ Always take a Client Change Request form along with you to every client approval meeting, even if you don't think you'll need it. It's better to be prepared. These change request forms have a greater impact if the client sees it as she is thinking about the changes rather than receiving it later in the mail.

◆ Do not, under any circumstances (even if the client tells you to go ahead and make changes to avoid delays) continue work on the project until you have Section C signed and in your possession. The client may say that it's in the mail, and it may be, but you should still wait to receive it before you do anything more on the project.

◆ You can fax this form to clients and have them return fax to save time. Remember to make a photocopy of the return fax for your files. This is legally binding, but get a signed original whenever possible.

Client Change Request

Client: _____ Date: _____

Company Name: _____

Project Description: _____ Project Number: _____

A. The following changes were requested by the client and considered to be additions or deletions from the original project specifications, time frame and/or price changes: (Use additional sheet if necessary.)

_____

_____

_____

_____

_____

I have requested the changes noted above, knowing that these alterations could affect the price quote estimate or time frame originally agreed to for this project.

Client signature: _____ **Date:** _____

B. This section is to be filled in by the design company/designer and returned to the client for final approval. This project will remain on hold until the client signs and returns Section C below indicating that he/she understands the changes that will occur in prices and/or scheduling and has accepted full responsibility for these changes.

1. The client change requests listed above will affect the original price estimate as follows: _____

_____

_____

2. The client change requests listed above will affect the delivery date as follows: _____

_____

_____

3. The client change requests listed above will affect the production schedule as follows: _____

_____

_____

C. I authorize the changes listed in Section A to be made and accept full responsibility for the resulting alterations indicated in Section B.

Client Approval Signature: _____ **Date:** _____

Photo/Video/Audio Release

Commentary

If you subcontract a photo or video shoot, or an audiotaping for a client project, it's your responsibility to provide releases for anyone who participates as a paid or unpaid model, as a bystander during the shoot, or as a voice for an audio recording. The release specifically identifies what the photos or audiotapes or videotapes will be used for. When participants sign it, they are allowing you and your client to use the photographs, videotapes or audiotapes for that specific purpose. In connection with that purpose, the release permits you and your client to alter the resulting photographs, video or audiotapes to better suit the project and use any or all of these in any related way. The release also protects you from any future liability that might result from the use of the signer's image or voice by your client or anyone else.

Always bring Photo/Video/Audio Releases to a shoot or taping session, and have them signed before it begins. If you wait and mail the forms after a session, and a participant objects to any aspect of the release, you may have to reshoot or retape the session.

When you distribute the forms, ask each participant to read it carefully and sign it. If you are photographing or taping minors, you will need to get a parent's signature. If you photograph someone's personal property, you must get the owner's signature. If you photograph a crowd of people at a stadium or on the street, releases are luckily unnecessary, because individuals can't be identified and they'd be practically impossible to get.

Professional models will bring their own contracts stipulating rights granted and fees. Read them carefully to make sure you get all the rights you need. Put one copy of the release in your Accounts Payable File if you'll cut a check for the model from it rather than receiving an invoice. (See pages 80-81 for more on accounts payable.)

If you don't get the rights you need from a model's contract, negotiate any desired changes *before* the shoot begins. Don't use any model on the shoot unless you can get all the rights you need at a price that falls within your budget. When using the release form provided here, cross out terms that you have agreed to eliminate or write in any additional stipulations. Both of you initial all such changes. If you can't reach acceptable terms with the participant, find someone else.

The Form: Step by Step

1. Fill in the project's description.

2. In the second space at the top, specifically identify what the photo, video or audio will be used for and where and how long it will be used by your client (for billboards, their locations and display time periods; for television commercials, stations and air dates, etc.).

3. This form shows in parentheses what is to be written in the blank spaces provided. Before you use the form, you will need to white out the directions inside the parentheses and photocopy the forms or delete the directions when you input the form into your computer.

4. Write the participant's name in the blank space on the first line of the first paragraph.

5. Write or type your client's company name in the blank space on the second line and your name or your company name on the third line.

6. If the participant is *not* a professional model, but you will be paying him or her a fee for the release, add a statement confirming the amount of the fee to the release form between the last paragraph and the signature. The following is typical wording: "In consideration of _____ dollars ($_____), receipt of which is acknowledged, I, _____ do hereby grant these rights to _____.''

7. In the second paragraph, write your name or company name on the first line. Then add your client's company name in the next space provided. Do the same on the third line of this paragraph and the second line of the next paragraph.

8. Have the participant sign and date the form in the signature/date spaces that follow, and write in the address and telephone number in the designated spaces.

Photo/Video/Audio Release

Project Description: _____

Photo/Video/Audio Use: _____

I, _____ , in consideration of your photographing, videotaping me, or otherwise recording me, my performance or voice for the above described project, hereby grant to _____(Client's Company Name)_____ and _____(Designer's Business Name)_____ the subcontractor, which term shall include not only yourselves, but your employees, agents, successors, licensees and assigns, the irrevocable right and license to use my likeness and/or voice on videotape or film, photograph or audiotape; to edit such videotape or film or audiotape or crop photographs at your discretion, to incorporate the same in the above production, and to use or authorize the use of such videotape or film, audiotape or photograph or any portion thereof in any manner or media at any time in perpetuity and to use my name, likeness, voice and biographical or other information concerning me in connection therewith, including promotion in all media.

I agree to hold _____(Designer's Business Name)_____ (hired by) _____(Client's Company Name)_____ harmless against any liability, loss or damage resulting from the use of my image and/or voice, and I hereby release and discharge _____(Designer's Business Name)_____ (hired by) _____(Client's Company Name)_____ from any and all claims whatsoever in connection with such use of my image and/or voice.

I am signing this release freely and voluntarily and in executing this release do not rely on any inducements, promises or representations made by _____(Designer's Business Name)_____ or _____(Client's Company Name)_____ .

Signature: _____ Date: _____

Address: _____

City/State/Zip: _____

Telephone: _____

Approval/Consent of Parent or Guardian

Minor's Name: _____

Parent's Signature: _____ Date: _____

Address: _____

City/State/Zip: _____

Telephone: _____

Service Bureau Instructions

Commentary

Always give your service bureau written instructions when submitting your files for imagesetting. Be sure to check with your service bureau representative to find out what specifics you need to indicate on this form. This information may vary from shop to shop.

Some service bureaus will carefully scrutinize each job's specifications to be certain they can handle it, and then carefully check the final work for any problems. Others won't bother. They will simply output whatever you tell them to, and send it off to you, errors and all. The more closely you communicate with your rep before the job, and the more exact you are in specifying all job-related details on this instruction form, the more likely you are to get good results. You will also be more likely to get a final price that is in line with the original job quote you received. So take the time necessary to provide as much information as your service bureau needs to ensure a quality job.

The Form: Step by Step

1. Write in your name or studio's name, not your client's name. You are the service bureau's customer.

2. Indicate the date that you delivered the files to the service bureau, not the date you filled out this form in your office.

3. Write in your name or the employee's name who is handling this project. It's also a good idea to include an after-hours phone number in addition to your office number just in case a problem comes up during a nighttime shift at the service bureau.

4. Include a brief project description and your studio's project number. Ask your service bureau rep to use that number when billing you for the job. This makes it easier to track incoming invoices.

5. Write in the service bureau's name, the name of your contact person, and your telephone/fax number.

6. Always ask beforehand how much rush charges are and what circumstances will necessitate a rush charge.

7. When filling out the Submission Format section, be as specific as possible. Service bureaus need to know the following: disk size and density and type of computer used to create the files. This same information applies whether you are submitting by modem, floppy, optical, tape or cartridge. They need to know the type of SCSI device, and for WORM optical drives, specify size, capacity and format. Always indicate the exact software program the files were created in and the version you used. XPress Data Files only need to be indicated if you are using an older version of Quark-XPress. Always specify font names and libraries used. All graphics must be named and the format indicated.

8. Under output specifications, indicate the exact file name that needs to be imaged since there are often many files on a disk. Also include the number of pages, the final output size, the resolution in number of dots per inch, and the linescreen you need. Indicate if you want film, paper, negatives or positives. Specify the kind of separations you require and the type of proof you want. Since service bureaus often have a number of different types of copiers, be sure to specify which you want used.

9. Special instructions might include things like crop marks, images centered on pages or any special packaging preparation, such as Federal Express packaging.

10. Be sure to keep a copy of this instructions sheet in your office in the client's project file for reference if a problem or question comes up.

Special Tips

◆ The work produced by service bureaus ranges from bad to good. The people who work in them aren't necessarily experts when it comes to producing quality or spotting potential problems with the images before they go to press. It's always wise to shop around for a service bureau willing to take the time to work with you and even consult with your printer to ensure that the job is being done correctly. So be wary of selecting a service bureau based on price alone. Service is crucial here.

◆ Interview your service bureau representative carefully before you send in a job. Find out what kind of equipment they have, what their output capabilities are, how much they charge, and how much experi-

Service Bureau Instructions

Designer Studio: _____ Date: _____

For Questions Call: _____

Billing Address: _____

Deliver To: _____

PO #: _____ Project Number: _____

Project Description: _____

Service Bureau: _____

Contact: _____ Telephone/Fax: _____

Date Needed: _____ Time: _____ Rush Charges Okay: _____

Submission Format

☐ Floppy ☐ Modem ☐ Optical ☐ Tape ☐ Cartridge ☐ SCSI Device ☐ WORM

Page Layout Program: _____ Version: _____ XPress Data Files: _____

Font(s) Used in Document

Name: _____ Manufacturer: _____

Name: _____ Manufacturer: _____

Name: _____ Manufacturer: _____

Placed Graphics

Graphic Name: _____ Format: _____

Graphic Name: _____ Format: _____

Graphic Name: _____ Format: _____

Graphic Name: _____ Format: _____

Output Specifications

File Name to Image: _____

Number of Pages: _____ Output Size Excluding Trim Zone: _____

Resolution: _____ dpi Screen: _____ lpi

Film: _____ Paper: _____ Negative: _____ Positive: _____

Separations: Spot: _____ Screen Color: _____ Illustrations: _____ Process Color: _____

Proof: Matchprint: _____ Cromalin: _____ Color Keys: _____

Mac-driven Color Copier: _____ Other (specify): _____

Special Instructions: _____

_____

For More Information

On Printing Instructions and a completed form, see pages 127-128.

On client changes, see page 126.

ence they've had in color work. Ask to see printed samples. You also need to know what programs, operating systems, file formats and font libraries they use. If you're having trouble finding or selecting a service bureau, ask your printer for a referral to the one best suited to your specific job.

◆ Watch out for extra charges with service bureaus. Their initial quote will not include additional charges tacked on when problems develop along the way. For example, if a service bureau's equipment, programs or systems are not compatible with yours, and informed them at the time they quote a job, they will charge you for whatever it takes to compensate for the incompatibilities.

◆ To avoid image errors, always use the most current version of your software when the files are going out for imagesetting. If you have an outdated version of a software program be sure to inform the service bureau ahead of time so that necessary conversion arrangements can be made.

Printing Instructions

Commentary

For your protection, always give the printer written instructions when you deliver mechanicals. This may save your neck more than once. Although you may have explained in great detail every nuance of the mechanical and printing specs to your contact person at the printing company, he may not remember everything you said. And when his version of your instructions is passed on to the pressroom foreman, there's no telling what the foreman will hear or how he'll interpret the specifications. With presses roaring in the background, 5,000 brochures can sound like 50,000. That's a big difference, and you'll have to pay for it if you don't have written instructions to back up your word. Marking instructions on the tissue over your mechanical helps, but that only goes so far. And the tissue is easily torn and smudged.

The Form: Step by Step

1. Write in your name or business name, since you're the printer's client. *Never* enter your client's company name here. You don't want some well-intentioned person at the printing company to contact the client di-

Billing the Client

I included a space on this form for the printer to bill the client directly. Most of the time, you'll get the printing bill, add your markup and bill your client. On very large or expensive jobs, you may prefer to have the client pay directly to avoid having to pay a hefty printing bill before the client pays you.

rectly if there are questions or something goes wrong.

2. Indicate the date that you delivered the mechanicals or electronic files to the printer, not the date you filled in the form at your studio.

3. For Questions Call: Write in your name or the name of your employee who is handling this project and a phone number. You may want to include a nighttime number if the printing company has evening shifts running presses and doing preprint production.

4. Write in a brief project description, and be sure to include the project number. Ask the printer to use that when invoicing you for the job. This makes it easier for you to track your incoming invoices.

5. Write in the printing company's name, your contact person, and the telephone and fax numbers.

6. Indicate the number of items sent or delivered with the job, such as 2 mechanicals, 10 halftones, etc.

7. Enter all printing, paper, bindery and other job-related specifications. Double-check your specs against the quote the printer sent to be sure that the final specifications you and the client decided on are the same as quoted in the original specs. If not, you or the client may have made a change without checking to see if it would affect the price.

If you have changed the specs, ask the printer for a revised quote for the job. If the new price will push the job beyond the original quote, call the client immediately, explain the effect of the change, and ask for approval either of the new amount or a return to the original specs (don't let work continue on the job until you've gotten approval). For small changes like this, phone approval is acceptable; follow up by sending a Client Change Request form for signature.

8. If you are delivering electronic disk files, be sure to indicate any specific information the printer may need. Always ask what is needed beforehand, so that you can label the files on your disk appropriately. For example, the printer may need to know the name of the specific file(s) to be printed, disk size and density, type of computer and system number used, program name and version your file was created in, names of any specific graphics used, the file they were placed in and the format used to create them.

Printing Instructions

Designer/Studio: _____ Date: _____

For Questions Call: _____

Project Description: _____ Project Number: _____

_____

Printer: _____

Contact: _____ Telephone/Fax: _____

Materials Sent

_____

_____

Printing Specifications

Paper Stock: _____ Quantity to Print: _____

# of Sides: _____ # of Colors: _____ PMS Ink #s: _____

Delivered as Camera-Ready Film: _____

Delivered as Electronic Disk Files: _____

Prepress Service/Service Bureau: _____

Contact: _____ Telephone: _____

Stripping Required, See Specs Below: _____

Bleeds: _____	Screens: _____	Reverses: _____
Halftones: _____	Film: _____	Separations: _____
Proofs/Blueline: _____	Color Key: _____	Chromalin Proof: _____
Print Size: _____	Score: _____	Fold: _____
Finished Size: _____	Bindery: _____	Emboss: _____
Die Cut: _____	Drills: _____	Perforations: _____
Thermography: _____		Other: _____
Mailing: _____		Pack: _____

Delivery Instructions _____

_____

Date Due: _____

Shipping Costs: _____

Billing: _____

Other Instructions: _____

Printer's Signature: _____ Date: _____

9. Give specific instructions for when — date and time — and where you want it delivered. Include directions if necessary and a contact person and phone number should the delivery person run into a problem. Attach a map or use an extra sheet of paper to make your directions as complete as possible.

10. Include quoted shipping costs, if any.

11. Write in your name or company name if you are to get the bill. If it's billed directly to your client, include your client's company name and to whose attention the bill should be sent.

12. Other Instructions might include something like asking the printer to deliver twenty-five samples directly to your office before the client receives his shipment.

13. Although you've carefully marked the mechanicals and attached printing instructions to one of the boards, you still must review the mechanicals and instructions with the printer when you deliver the boards. This is your last chance to correct any errors and to head off potential misunderstandings without expensive changes.

14. In addition to taping the form to the mechanicals, leave a copy of the instructions with the printer and keep one for yourself. Make sure that your contact at the printing company signs *your* copy of the form and dates it. His signature protects you if something goes wrong or is misunderstood; it's your leverage if you have to insist the printer reprints the project at his expense. The date is your proof of when you delivered the job in case it runs longer than promised.

Proofing Approval Checklist

Commentary

When proofing the mechanical, bluelines, color proofs or color separations, use a Proofing Approval Checklist to be sure you've gone over every possible detail. At this stage of the project, you're not just looking for typos and misspelled words; you want to be certain your measurements are correct, all overlays have been completed, registration marks applied, and halftones sized and cropped, etc. A

For More Information

On proofing mechanicals, Proofing Approval Checklists and a completed form, see page 127.

On Client Change Requests, see page 126.

proofing checklist can help you remember things you might otherwise overlook.

Bring your completed proofing checklist with you when you deliver the mechanicals, bluelines or color proofs to your client for her review and approval. This shows the client exactly what you checked when proofing and also helps her double-check the same areas.

The Form: Step by Step

1. For each applicable proofing stage, check off those items listed under that heading that were reviewed and are correct. Write in N/A for any that aren't applicable to this project. Before you pass the mechanicals and form to either a client or an employee for review, write in the number of mechanicals, halftones, line art, etc. that need to be approved next to the item.

2. Under Other, you can write in any special requirements that weren't covered above on the checklist.

3. Special Notes or Instructions might include a reminder to the client to check for recent changes in the mechanical or printing specifications.

4. When you have proofed and completed the checklist, sign it at the bottom and attach it to the mechanical(s) for the client to see and review when proofing for changes or final approval.

5. When the client proofs and approves the board(s), ask her to sign and date the checklist in the appropriate space at the bottom of the form. Be sure also to get a signed Client Change Request form if she makes any changes that alter the project's schedule or specs.

Special Tips

◆ Try hard to allow the client at least twenty-four hours to thoroughly proof and review the mechanical boards. If you hurry him through the process, you may both miss something that will spell disaster later.

◆ If you have an employee, ask her to proof the mechanical, too. Because you've been so close to the project, you may overlook things that an objective eye will easily notice. A mechanical can't be reviewed too many times because it's so easy to forget things like logos, phone numbers, prices and other small details.

Proofing Approval Checklist

Project Name: _____ Project Number: _____

Client Name: _____ Company: _____

✔ Place a check mark next to items listed below that were proofed and approved.
NO Use this to indicate items that were missing or incorrect.
N/A Use this for those that don't apply to the mechanical or proof.

Mechanical

☐ Page Content   ☐ Numbers   ☐ Headlines/Subheads
☐ Captions/Quotes   ☐ Color   ☐ Call Outs
☐ Graphic Treatments   ☐ Type Proofed   ☐ Phone Numbers
☐ Logos   ☐ Layout/Design   ☐ Crop/Fold/Trim Marks
☐ Folds, Perforations   ☐ Trims, Bleeds   ☐ Registration Tabs
☐ Halftones: Cropped, Sized   ☐ Screens   ☐ Paper Stock, Weight
☐ Postal Indicia/Codes/Permits   ☐ Other: Indicate

Other: Indicate Special Requirements: _____

_____

_____

Blueline/Color Proof

☐ Trim   ☐ Registration   ☐ Diecut/Perforate/Punch
☐ Reverses   ☐ Fold   ☐ Placement of Text
☐ Hickies/Marks   ☐ Proofed   ☐ Placement of Graphics
☐ Color: Placement   ☐ Clarity of Type   ☐ Clarity of Rules
☐ Clarity of Graphics   ☐ Halftones/Screens   ☐ Halftones: Position
☐ Screens: Position   ☐ Halftones: Labeled   ☐ Screens: Labeled
☐ PMS Labeled   ☐ Other: Indicate   ☐ Other: Indicate

Color Separations

☐ Color Quality   ☐ Changes   ☐ Clarity
☐ Quantity   ☐ Size   ☐ Other: Indicate

Other: Special Requirements

☐ _____ ☐ _____ ☐ _____
☐ _____ ☐ _____ ☐ _____

Special Notes or Instruction: _____

_____

_____

This is to verify that I, the above-named client, representing the above-named company, have thoroughly reviewed and approved the project materials described above. I understand that this is my last opportunity to request changes due to mistakes or preferences. I further acknowledge that any mistakes or preference changes that were not discovered or specified at this time are not the responsibility of the designers/design company named above. I accept full responsibility for this final approval and with it hereby authorize the designer to take the approved materials listed above to the printer for the final phase of the project—the printed pieces.

Designer Approval Signature: _____ Date: _____

Client approval Signature: _____ Date: _____

For More Information

〰〰〰

On Project Expenses Tracking Sheets and a completed form, see page 129.

On Price Estimate Work Sheets, see pages 44-45 and 120-121.

On Invoices, see pages 76-77 and 130.

On Project Billing Work Sheets, see pages 74-75 and 129.

On working with vendors and subcontractors, see pages 138-143.

On Accounts Payable, see pages 80-81 and 95-96.

◆ Each of the various types of proofing methods differs more or less from the final output. Know those differences well before making changes. This is especially important with digital proofing methods.

◆ If you don't have in-depth technical knowledge of reproduction, it's better to state the result required rather than tell the color separation house how to achieve it. But you must indicate in what way you think the proof differs from the original. It's not enough to say, "Needs color correction — see original," and unless you know a great deal about reproduction, "Make green darker, increase cyan" is probably too much. (It might be better to reduce the yellow.) "Make this green darker — see original" is the simplest and clearest direction to give.

◆ Realize that the printing process can't ever be perfect. If a proof or blueline is very nearly right, don't correct it.

◆ When color is critical, insist that the client attend the press check if at all possible. If compromises must be made — for example, the corporate colors can't be precisely matched in four-color printing — the problem and the need to compromise can be explained more easily then than after the event.

◆ A signed proof constitutes a contract that makes you legally responsible for paying for a job printed to those specifications. Make careful, detailed notes on proofs before signing them to avoid problems later.

◆ Proof all business cards and reply envelopes especially carefully. Postal regulations must be followed to a T. A mistake can cause your client to be charged extra for postage or even to get less than the hoped-for response.

◆ If you are having your electronic files imageset, you need to take extra precautions in the proofing stage to be certain that the final film output is of the highest quality. These tipes will help you avoid potential problems.

1. Add crop marks, file name, date and time.

2. When scanning consider the final scale of the image at the time you actually do the scan, since images lose quality as their size increases. Scan images at 100 percent.

3. Use the gray-scale mode when you are printing color proofs.

4. Indicate the number of colors on each black-and-white laser print.

5. Use gray values to distinguish layered tints.

6. Note For Position Only (FPO) or LIVE artwork.

7. Note special effects.

8. Be sure to account for your printer's nonprintable borders.

9. Always get hard copies of all files to be used.

10. Output at 100 percent to ensure that you get good detail.

Project Expenses Tracking Sheet

Commentary

Put a Project Expenses Tracking Sheet into your billing book for each new project. When you receive a bill for any expense related to that project, log it on the tracking sheet. You can quickly check whether the project is staying on budget by comparing this sheet to the original Price Estimate Work Sheet. You'll also have ready all the information to complete the expenses portions of the Project Billing Work Sheet and Invoice.

The Form: Step by Step

1. At the top of the sheet, write the project's number, the project's name or description and the client's name.

2. As you receive each invoice for a project-related expense, enter the date you received it in the first column, the name of the person or company who sent it in the second, and the invoice number in the third.

3. Check each invoiced price against your Price Estimate Work Sheet for the project before you enter it. Make sure the invoiced price matches the one you were quoted. If it does, enter it into that column. If not, review the actual original bid to see if you've picked up the amount correctly. When the amount differs from their original quote, contact that person or company

Project Expenses Tracking Sheet

Project Number: _____

Project Name: _____

Client: _____

Date Rec'd	Company Name	Inv. #	Inv. Price

For More Information

~~~~~~~~

On Project Expenses Tracking Sheets, see page 129.

On Project Billing Work Sheets and a completed form, see pages 129.

On Project Time Sheets, see page 122.

On Invoices, see pages 76-77.

On what expenses are chargeable to a project, see page 86.

and determine the reason for the discrepancy. If it's their error, request a corrected invoice, which you'll enter instead. When it's your mistake, whether you gave incorrect specs or simply wrote down the wrong amount, you can't bill the client for the difference. Note the actual amount on the tracking sheet in parentheses and write the cost you'll charge the client from the Price Estimate Work Sheet.

Special Tips

◆ Always enter invoices on the project tracking sheet as soon as they're received. It's too easy to forget one that's been filed in the Accounts Payable File.

◆ *Never* pass on the costs of your mistakes, even honest ones, to the client. It's one sure way to lose clients. I understand how painful it can be to eat the difference between an estimate and an actual bill (I've done it myself), but the short-term pain is really a small price to pay for a reputation as a reliable designer.

Project Billing Work Sheet

Commentary

Prepare a Project Billing Work Sheet for each new project. Use this to pull together all the information from the Project Expenses Tracking Sheets and the Project Time Sheets and prepare Invoice(s) for the client.

This form is especially useful if you have someone else add up the time from various Project Time Sheets or work up your invoices. You can then review the sheet before the final invoice is prepared and sent.

TIME SAVER

The Form: Step by Step

1. Write in the client's name and company name, along with the date the project began or was authorized, and the project number.

2. When you complete a project, collect all the Project Time Sheets for it. Look at the first column on your Project Billing Work Sheet. This contains a listing of work descriptions and a number opposite each description that corresponds to the function codes on your Project Time Sheets. Using a calculator, look

through each Project Time Sheet and add up, as you go through, the total number of hours you recorded for each of the function codes.

3. Enter the total number of hours you've added up from your time sheets into the Time column opposite the appropriate Work Description and function code.

4. Refer to your Price Estimate Work Sheet to determine the amount per hour you quoted for your time, which may be the same price for all job functions or varying rates for different activities (see pages 86-87 for more on varying hourly rates). Enter your cost per hour for each Work Description category for which you recorded time totals.

5. Multiply your Cost/Hour in Column 2 by the total number of hours recorded on each line in Column 1. This will give you the dollar amount to enter into Column 4, representing the Total Time Cost for each work description that was a part of this project. Check this against your original figures on the Price Estimate Work Sheet. You should have caught most problems, such as having spent much longer than you expected on layout, by reviewing your time sheets for Project Summaries and taken steps to correct the situation. However, problems that arose at the mechanical and proofing stages that didn't result from client changes must be adjusted now. Determine if there were client changes that should be reflected in higher costs for your time. If so, bill accordingly. If the charges are due solely to your taking longer than you anticipated to complete the project, adjust the hours and costs for the overtime stages to match the original estimate.

6. The Time total listed in Column 2 and the Total Time Cost in Column 4 can be directly transferred to a client invoice when you are ready to bill the project.

7. Transfer the amounts for each expense from the Project Expenses Tracking Sheet(s), entering Subcontractor, Vendor, Other Project-Related Expenses and Miscellaneous Expenses in the appropriate sections. Check the markup you gave each item on your Project Estimate Work Sheet to get the correct one for each. Although you'll generally use the same markup for all items, you may vary this occasionally to accommodate a client with a modest budget.

8. Add together the invoice price and the markup to

Project Billing Work Sheet

Client: _____

Date: _____ Project Number: _____

Work Description	Time	Cost/Hour	Total Time Cost
01 Consultation/Meetings			
02 Research			
03 Concept Development			
04 Organization			
05 Layout/Design			
06 Art Direction			
07 Illustration			
08 Typesetting			
09 Mechanical Prep			
10 Consult Vendors/Subs			
11 Copywriting/Editing			
12 Proofing			
13 Press Approvals			
14 Acct. Administration			
15 Revisions			
16 Client Changes			
17 Other —			
18 Other —			
19 Other —			

Subcontractor	Price	Markup	Client's Price

Vendor	Price	Markup	Client's Price

Other Project-Related Expenses	Price	Markup	Client's Price

Miscellaneous Expenses	Price	Markup	Client's Price

Total Project Cost: _____

get the client's price for each item. Double-check this amount against your Price Estimate Work Sheet to make sure your final client price also reflects the quoted price. If it doesn't, there is an error on your estimate or in the transcription of figures from the invoice or the original vendor's or subcontractor's bid. Locate the error and correct your records, but don't charge the client a higher amount than on the original estimate. (Once you've entered and verified all expenses for a final invoice, you can discard the tracking sheets.)

9. When it comes time to bill a client project, you will need only this work sheet to prepare the Invoice.

10. If you're billing a client on a monthly basis, start a new Project Billing Work Sheet each month. Include only your charges for time and expenses in that period. Staple each sheet on top of the previous one. When the project is finished, pull all the totals together on a final sheet for that last invoice.

Invoice

Commentary

The bill or invoice you send to a client consists of basically two things: 1. The number of hours, to the nearest quarter hour, that you spent working on that project. 2. The cost for all expenses incurred to complete the project. These expenses include bills from vendors, such as art supply stores and paper companies, or subcontractors such as printers, photographers, typesetters, copywriters, etc.

Clients should be invoiced according to the terms of the signed Agreement of Terms and Conditions or client contract. That may mean once on completion; once a month and on completion, for long-term projects; or a system of payment in thirds (one advance on signing the agreement, another halfway through the project, and the rest on completion) for new clients.

When you have completed an invoice, send a copy to the client, keep a copy in your Accounts Receivable File, and a copy in your Sales Tax File, whether you charged sales tax or not.

The Form: Step by Step

1. When you're ready to bill a job, assign a sequential invoice number (starting from 0001 for your first invoice). Enter your address, the client's name, the date you are preparing the invoice, the company name, its address, and the project number onto the blank invoice.

2. If you're invoicing for advances (payment in thirds), skip down to Step 9 of these directions.

3. Go to your billing book and open it to the Project Billing Work Sheet for the project you're invoicing to get the recorded totals for all the project time incurred, the costs for that time and the costs for all project-related expenses. If you haven't brought this billing work sheet up to date, do so before you begin to prepare the invoice. When you're billing for a project monthly, pick up on the Project Billing Work Sheet for that month.

4. Using the Project Billing Work Sheet, transfer all totals in the Time column and Total Time Costs to the Time and Amount columns on the invoice. Use the function codes that accompany each item under Services Rendered to match up the appropriate time for the various Work Descriptions listed on the billing work sheet.

5. Copy the entries under Client's Price for all Subcontractor, Vendor costs and Other Project-Related Expenses, as well as Miscellaneous Expenses from the Project Billing Work Sheet into the designated spaces at the bottom of the invoice. Add all the costs together to get the amount for the Total Project Costs.

6. If you've billed monthly or in thirds, enter all amounts previously paid in the space marked Less Previous Payments. Subtract this amount from the Total Project Costs to get the Final Project Costs. If this is the sole invoice for the project, simply mark N/A for Less Previous Payments and Final Project Costs.

7. Since sales tax doesn't apply to every phase of a project, you need to know what is taxable in your state. Place an asterisk next to the cost of any taxable service or expense, then total those taxable costs and multiply the total by the percentage of sales tax charged by your state. When billing monthly, add the applicable sales tax then. Then on the last invoice, add the applicable sales tax only on the last month's total.

Invoice

Number: _____ Date: _____ Project #: _____

Your Address: _____

Client: _____ Company Name: _____

Address/City/State/Zip: _____

Services Rendered	**Time**	**Amount**
01 Client Consultations/Meetings		
02 Research		
03 Concept		
04 Organization		
05 Layout/Design		
06 Art Direction		
07 Illustration		
08 Typesetting		
09 Mechanical Prep		
10 Consultations with Vendors and Subcontractors		
11 Copywriting/Editing		
12 Proofing		
13 Press Approvals		
14 Acct. Administration		
15 Revisions		
16 Client Changes		
17 Other—		
18 Other—		
19 Other—		

Subcontractor	**Costs**
Copywriting/Editing	
Printing	
Typesetting	
Photography	
Stats, Veloxes, Films	

Vendor	**Costs**

Other Expenses	**Costs**

Total Project Costs: _____

Less Previous Payments: _____

Final Project Costs: _____

Sales Tax: _____

Total Amount Due: _____

Payments not received within 30 days will be subject to an interest rate of 1½% per month or a fraction thereof from date of invoice. Client subject to reasonable collection fees.

For More Information

On Invoices and a completed form, see page 130.

On billing, see pages 90-91.

On sales tax, see page 94.

On Project Billing Work Sheets, see pages 74-75 and 129.

On Accounts Receivable File, see pages 82-83 and 94.

8. Finally, add the Total Project Costs or the Final Project Costs and the Sales Tax cost together. That will give you the Total Amount Due from the client.

9. If you're billing by thirds, with two advances against the Total Project Costs, use the space for Other Expenses to bill the two advances. This could read, "Advance against final cost of the project" followed by the amount.

10. When you deliver the final invoice for the project, follow Steps 3–6 above then go to Step 11 below.

11. Because the first two payments are characterized as advances, you'll charge sales tax only on the final invoice. Compute this on the total taxable costs for the project, following the instructions for determining those given in Step 7 above.

12. Follow Step 8 above to finish your invoice.

Monthly Client Statement

Commentary

Every month, you will send out a statement to those clients who have not paid their previous month's bill or any other outstanding bills. This is a gentle reminder for them, and also allows you to attach the monthly interest or finance charge of 1½ percent to each outstanding balance. The resulting new balance will be due in thirty days. If this balance or any remaining portion is still not paid by that time, you'll send another monthly statement with interest charges computed on and added to the previous month's balance.

Schedule two invoicing sessions a month: one in the middle of the month and another at either the beginning or end of the month. Assign each client to a session, based on the date of the first invoice you have, then always do his statement at that time. Your Accounts Receivable Record Sheet reminds you when you sent the invoice (see pages 82-83).

The Form: Step by Step

1. Assign a statement number, using a sequential system beginning at 001. You may want to using the year as part of the number; for example, on a 1994 statement you'd use 94001 (94-001).

2. Enter the date the statement is prepared, the client's name, company name, address, telephone and fax number and your name next to Remit To. Then include your business name, address, etc.

3. Check your Accounts Receivable Record Sheet for outstanding, unpaid invoices. If you find any for previous months, pull that Monthly Client Statement, too. Type in the past-due date of each invoice or balance. Include invoice number, project number, description of services rendered or project name, and amount due to be paid. If you need additional space, use another statement form as a second page.

4. Total all outstanding payments due and enter that amount in the space labeled Balance Due.

5. Calculate the interest charges for each balance that goes over thirty days and add all interest charges together for a total that will be entered on the line labeled Interest Due on Unpaid Balance. For example, you send Alpha, Inc. an invoice for a project at the end of January. In February, you do another small project and send them another invoice. When you prepare Alpha's Monthly Client Statement at the end of February, you discover they still owe you for January's invoice. So, on the February statement, you'll bill them for the January invoice plus 1½ percent interest on that January invoice plus the amount of the February invoice. If they've still not paid you for January or February at the end of March, you'll bill them for the amount of the February statement, including the interest for January, plus an additional 1½ percent interest charge on the Total Amount Due now.

6. Then total the Interest Due and Balance Due amounts together and enter that amount on the line labeled Total Amount Due.

7. Keep a copy of this in your Active Accounts Receivable File (see page 94).

Special Tips

◆ If a balance or any portion of it goes unpaid for more than 120 days, you have a collection problem. Send another statement calling for payment due upon receipt of statement for all balances over 120 days. Print "PAYMENT DUE UPON RECEIPT OF STATEMENT" in red next to all balances over

For More Information

On Invoices, see pages 76-77 and 130.

On Accounts Receivable, see pages 82-83 and 94.

On effective collections, see page 110.

Monthly Client Statement

Statement Number: _____ Date: _____

Client: _____

Company Name: _____

Address: _____

City/State/Zip: _____

Telephone/Fax: _____

Remit To: _____

Your Business Name: _____

Address: _____

City/State/Zip: _____

Telephone/Fax: _____

Date	Invoice #	Project #	Description of Services	Amount

Balance Due: _____

Interest Due on Unpaid Balance: _____

Total Amount Due: _____

Terms: Net 30 Days
Payments not received within 30 days will be subject to an interest rate of 1½% per month or a fraction thereof from date of invoice.
Client subject to reasonable collection fees.

For More Information

On Accounts Payable, see page 95.

On Accounts Receivable, see pages 82-83 and 94.

120 days. You can also have a stamp made with that message. Somehow, this payment due message is more threatening when stamped in red than when it's handwritten. As an extra incentive, you can also add to the bottom of your monthly statement (handwritten is fine): "If you have a problem paying this bill, please contact us immediately." If you still receive no response, call the client. If that doesn't work, refer to pages 112-113 for more information about clients who refuse to pay a bill.

♦ Try to head off problems by intensifying your collection efforts when any balance has gone unpaid for sixty days. The longer a bill doesn't get paid, the less likely you are to ever collect it.

Accounts Payable Record Sheet

Commentary

On the Accounts Payable Record Sheet, you will record all the bills you receive, when each is due to be paid, and the amount due. This sheet makes it easy to quickly identify bills that belong to client projects and those that are for office/studio operating expenses.

Unfortunately, and there's no way around it, it does take a few minutes every day or as bills come in, to record the bills you put into your Accounts Payable File. It's essential to keep these sheets up to date as this is the only way you have of knowing how much money you owe at any given time. The Accounts Payable Record Sheet has space at the bottom to enter the weekly total of money you owe, including all amounts due and any remaining balances. By comparing your Accounts Payable Record Sheet(s) to the weekly totals on your Accounts Receivable Record Sheet(s) (coming up next on pages 82-83), you'll know if your receivables (money owed to you) are greater than your payables (money you owe). This is extremely important information and should be reviewed at the end of each week.

If your receivables begin to drop below your payables, it indicates you're spending more money than you're making. Trouble sign! It may mean that you've gotten behind in your billing, clients are paying slowly, or you're not bringing in enough work or charging enough money to meet your expenses.

(Some of the difference may be accounted for by partial payments that no longer appear on your Accounts Receivable Record Sheet.

The Form: Step by Step

1. There are two categories listed at the top of the Accounts Payable Record Sheet shown on the next page, below the main heading — Project Expenses and Business Expenses. You need a separate sheet for each category because project expenses are charged back to the client while business (office) expenses are carried by you as part of your overhead. Make a number of copies of this blank sheet and then white out one category or the other.

2. On the sheet for the appropriate category, write in Column 1 the name of the company from whom you received an invoice.

3. In Column 2, enter the letter "V" if it's from a vendor, "S" for subcontractor, and "M" for all other miscellaneous expenses such as postage. (You'll need to keep track of this for tax and other purposes.)

4. In Column 3, write in the invoice number. The date the invoice was received goes in Column 4. And the date the payment is due (thirty days after you receive it unless the bill specifies other terms) goes in Column 5. Enter the due date in pencil. When you make a partial payment, you can just erase the old due date and write in the new one based on the date of the partial payment.

5. If the invoice belongs to a client, you will need to write the project's number in Column 6.

6. Write the amount due for each invoice in Column 7.

7. When you or your bookkeeper pay a bill, write the amount paid into Column 8. If the bill was paid in full, use a colored marker to cross out the entire row. That will separate paid from unpaid bills. (Use a light-colored, transparent marker so that you can still see the information you crossed out. This helps if you have to find an unpaid invoice that you may have mistakenly crossed out as paid.)

If you pay only a portion of the bill, enter in pencil the amount paid in Column 8 and the balance still due in the last column. When the final balance has been paid, cross out the entire row with a colored marker.

Accounts Payable Record Sheet

Project Expenses

Business Expenses

Received From	S/V/M	Inv. #	Date Rec.	Date Due	Proj. #	Amt. Due	Amt. Paid	Bal. Owed

Weekly Totals Owed: _____

Date: _____

For More Information

On Accounts Receivable, see page 94.

On Accounts Payable, see pages 80-81 and 94-95.

On bookkeeping for your business, see pages 91-92.

Special Tips

♦ When an Accounts Payable Record Sheet is completely filled in and every bill or balance is paid, you can transfer it to a master file labeled Paid Accounts Payable. Your accountant will need these completed sheets as well as those you are still filling in to prepare your taxes. Store your master file in a metal file cabinet for safekeeping.

♦ Always wait the full thirty days to pay a bill so you can continue to earn interest on your money in the bank as long as possible.

Accounts Receivable Record Sheet

Commentary

When you send an invoice to a client, you record the amount of that invoice on an Accounts Receivable Record Sheet. You then keep a copy of that invoice in an Active Accounts Receivable File along with the Accounts Receivable Record Sheet, which you should place in the front of this folder. These invoice copies should be filed by invoice number, not job number. Keep this folder in the same stand-up file holder that contains your Active Accounts Payable folder.

The Accounts Receivable Record Sheet provides space for you to list the client invoices as you send them out. Until they are paid in full, these invoices are called outstanding invoices. By keeping an ongoing record of all outstanding invoices, you know exactly how much money is still owed you at any given time. This is the list you should compare to your Accounts Payable Record Sheet list each week to make sure the receivables are always greater (you hope) than the payables.

Again, if your receivables begin to drop below your payables, it may mean that you've gotten behind in your billing, clients are paying slowly, or you're not bringing in enough work or charging enough money to meet your expenses. Some of the difference may be accounted for by partial payments that no longer appear on your Accounts Receivable Record Sheet. Whatever it is, you need to know the cause and act immediately to reverse the situation.

The Form: Step by Step

1. Each time you prepare a client invoice, record the date the invoice was sent in the first column, the client's name in the second, the invoice number in the third, and the due date and the amount due in the fourth and fifth columns.

2. When a bill is paid, enter the amount paid in the sixth column. If the invoice is not paid in full, record the balance due in the seventh column. When an invoice is paid in full, use a colored marker to cross out the entire line on your list. Use a light-colored, transparent marker so that you can still see the information you crossed out, in case you need to refer to it later.

3. When an Accounts Receivable Record Sheet is full, or at more frequent intervals — I recommend once a week — you can total the outstanding amounts due and enter them in the space at the bottom labeled Total Amount Outstanding and then indicate the date on which you reviewed this sheet.

Special Tips

♦ When a client pays a bill, take the invoice out of the Active Accounts Receivable File. Mark the invoice paid, date it, and record the client's check number on it. Put the invoice into a folder labeled Accounts Receivable Paid File. Keep the invoices in numerical order. Store this folder for safekeeping in your fire-resistant metal file cabinet.

♦ When an Accounts Receivable Record Sheet is completely filled in and every bill or balance is paid, you can transfer it to a master file labeled Paid Accounts Receivable Record Sheets. Your accountant will need these completed sheets, as well as those you are still filling in, when it comes time to prepare your taxes. Store this master file in the metal file cabinet as well.

♦ When I ran my weekly totals on the Accounts Receivable and Accounts Payable Record Sheets, I used a calculator that printed out the totals on a slip of paper. After I'd entered the total for the week on the sheet, I clipped the tape from the calculator to the sheets so I'd have a record of the total amount *and* each individual amount that went into that total.

Accounts Receivable Record Sheet

Outstanding Invoices

Date	Client	Inv. #	Date Due	Amt. Due	Amt. Paid	Bal. Due

Total Amount Outstanding: _____

Date Reviewed: _____

CHAPTER
three

Money
Talks

What Supplies and Materials Are Overhead

Many designers have trouble deciding which items are overhead and which are billable. Here's how to determine that. You need certain tools and materials simply to operate your business, including pencils, markers, layout paper, tracing paper, vellum, sketch pads, rulers, wax, erasers, spray mount, etc. These items are part of your overhead expenses and aren't billable to clients.

Billable materials include any special item that was purchased for use on only one project – a gold marker or specific Pantone markers and papers or Letraset type. All the boards, acetate overlay sheets or rubylith used to produce a mechanical should be billed to the client under miscellaneous materials. If a project calls for more than ten photocopies, that should also be billed to the client under miscellaneous. Purchases of specific materials in large quantities, such as balsa wood for a model, or any single item that costs over $25, should be listed separately on the bill.

If you buy a special piece of equipment to complete a job, such as an opaque projector for a large-scale illustration, you can't bill the client for it unless the client has previously agreed to foot the bill. Otherwise consider it to be part of your overhead. (Always

borrow or rent equipment for one-time use if you can.)

esigners seem to be most uncomfortable when dealing with the financial end — pricing, billing, bookkeeping, collecting money and paying taxes — of their businesses. (So am I.) But you can eliminate a lot of the hassle and worry by applying simple common sense to money matters.

There's nothing wrong with being money conscious. In fact, if you want to stay in business you have to be, but feeling self-conscious about money can be financially fatal. I'm not saying that greed is good or anything like that; I'm talking about knowing the value of a dollar — and your work. You are entitled to get paid for your work. You're entitled to get good value for the money you spend, too. So check your humility at the door, along with a disdain for doing business.

Much of what goes into keeping your financial affairs running smoothly is rather boring when compared with designing. That's why it's to your benefit to set up systems to handle money matters as efficiently and effectively as possible. Spend a little time up front, save a lot of time later. Since I've never enjoyed it either, I'm glad I can pass along some ideas that took me a long time to discover.

Pricing Your Work

The most difficult decision for designers is how much to charge for their services. Finding that answer seems simple enough: Just learn what other designers charge and go with that. But when designers who are self-employed for the first time hear that others are getting $50, $60 or even $75 an hour, they cringe — not because they think that's peanuts, but because they think that's more than they're worth. So they decide to base their charges on what they made while working for somebody else. If they made $30,000 a year, a little calculator action quickly tells them that figure works out to $15 an hour. So when they figure they have to pay their own health insurance and taxes, $15 becomes $20 or $25 an hour.

Other designers get a budget from the client and know he or she is only willing to

spend a certain amount. They work backward, allocating production costs, design and production time, overhead and profit to match that amount. Let's say A. Designer has a budget of $1,200 for a poster. First she deducts the estimated cost of producing it (paper and printing), about $400. That leaves $800 for labor, overhead and profit. From that $800, she subtracts $80, which represents a 10 percent profit margin. The remaining $720 covers labor and overhead.

A. Designer has an overhead ratio of 40 percent, so she divides $720 by 1.4 (1 = 100 percent labor, plus .4 = 40 percent overhead) to get the amount left for labor. That's $514.29, which she rounds up to $514.30. When she divides that $514.30 by her hourly rate (cost of labor), $40, she learns that the maximum time she can spend on the project and still make her profit is 13 (actually 12.85) hours. That's fine as long as thirteen hours is enough to complete the job properly. If it isn't, A. Designer could end up eating into her profit or lose money altogether.

Neither method of pricing work is the best, most realistic one.

Because it's not a question of how much you, the designer, should charge; it's how much *your business* should charge in order to pay for its operation, which includes your salary, and make enough to put a little aside for a rainy day when bills pile up and every client you have seems to be on vacation. So before you do the humble pie routine as you shyly decide what to charge, take a good look at the big picture — the cost of being in business.

So, How Much Should You Charge?

You should charge at least enough to cover the cost of doing business. That's not some random figure pulled out of the air; it's based on real expenses called operating costs or overhead, which include: rent, utilities, leasing equipment such as a fax or copier, telephone, materials and supplies, insurance, taxes, payroll or personal draw (what you pay yourself if not incorporated), travel and entertainment, memberships, petty cash and postage.

To determine your operating costs, list a month's ongoing expenses. If you're already using a disbursement journal (see pages 92-93 for how to do this), take your totals directly from there. Otherwise, go back through your bills for the last few months to determine your average monthly expenses.

Next, if you've been in business for a year or less, you need to know how much you invested in things like equipment and furnishings, business cards, stationery, envelopes, self-promotional materials, a telephone, an answering machine, etc. You should include these start-up expenses in your overhead to recoup them over the next year.

A Formula for Determining Your Prices

Here's a pricing formula to determine your fees. I've used a set of figures for a typical designer working at home. This designer has budgeted a salary of $24,000 a year or $2,000 a month to cover living expenses. The overhead—expenses not related to a specific project—breaks down like this:

Home Office Rent	$ 250/mo.
Salary	2,000/mo.
Utilities	50/mo.
Taxes	400/mo.
Insurance	250/mo.
Equipment purchases	300/mo.
Equipment leases	175/mo.
Furniture purchases	100/mo.
Sick days/paid vacation	154/mo.
Self-promotion	35/mo.
Office supplies	60/mo.
Art supplies	60/mo.
Travel expenses	40/mo.
Business entertainment	40/mo.
Savings for retirement	167/mo.
Total Operating Costs	**$4,081/mo.**

Formula:

1. **Divide your total monthly operating costs by 4 to get your weekly overhead costs.**
   $4,081 / 4 = $1,020.25
2. **Divide the weekly total by 5 to get your daily operating costs.**
   $1,020.25 / 5 = $204.05

3. **Divide your daily operating costs by 6, the average number of billable hours most people can manage to squeeze out of an eight-hour day.**
   $204.05 / 6 = $34.00

This figure, rounded off to the nearest dollar, represents the *absolute minimum* amount you can charge per hour just to break even. And that's assuming you bring in enough design projects to bill six hours a day, five days a week, fifty weeks a year (and saving money each month so you can afford to take two weeks vacation a year). Since that may not always happen, especially when you're starting out, your hourly rate should actually be slightly higher than your break-even point to allow for that.

Working through this formula should make you think twice about the fees you should charge. We're not even talking about profits at this point, just survival. If you want to see any profits—that's money you can save toward new equipment, a nicer studio or improving your standard of living—you *must* increase that hourly rate by at least ten or fifteen dollars an hour. In our example above, that would mean charging between forty and fifty dollars an hour. But don't just pull a number out of your hat. Add a percentage for profit—at least 10 percent, but 15 to 20 percent is better—to your hourly fee.

Also remember that you can raise your hourly fee for certain kinds of clients or projects. Clients in large cities are accustomed to paying higher hourly rates than those in small cities or towns and should be quoted a corresponding rate. Projects of very high value to the client, such as an identity design, or ones where client expectations and standards are quite high, such as packaging design or a corporate annual report, should be charged an hourly rate that reflects the situation.

Variable Fee Scale

You can have a variable fee scale for different services. Most designers charge their highest hourly rate for concept development and design work, because these are the most demanding in terms of the designer's creativity,

You'll Never Get What You Deserve If You Don't Ask for It

You may feel perfectly justified in setting a certain hourly rate for your time, but then some creatives back down when they think a client doesn't have the money to spend. Don't fall into the trap I sat in many times, that is, making assumptions about a client's finances or budget based on appearances, hearsay or business status. You must first decide how much your time is worth, and then ask for it. You will never get it if you don't ask for it. If a client asks you to cut corners, shave production costs, not your fees. But when you do cut corners, always advise your clients that a certain degree (and be specific about what that is) of quality will be lost. Assure them that you are happy to do it as long as they know what they are sacrificing. If you do decide that a particular project has merit, either because it will increase your exposure or because the project represents something that's important to you, then reduce your fees. But only do it to the point where you are still certain you can cover your own operating expenses.

talent and skills. Client meetings may also be charged at that rate because these occur at the client's convenience and require high-level communication skills. Paste-up and clerical work are often priced about one-third below the rate for creative work. For example, at a fee of $60 per hour for creative work, that'd be $40 per hour for paste-up.

I strongly recommend that you use a variable rate for your time and your employees' time (see pages 44-45 and 120-121 for calculating and billing this). If you're worried that the client will question the difference, simply quote totals for your design time on your estimates and don't give an hourly fee for each. This is not being mercenary; you're simply charging a fee that reflects the value of the services you offer. It also helps you pay your employees or freelancers what they're worth.

When to Raise Your Fees

Expenses will increase as you add new clients, hire employees, buy new equipment, or expand your office space. Then you'll need to

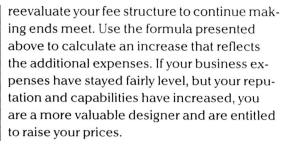

Are Retainers for You?

Working on retainer is becoming a more common practice for designers than it was several years ago. Some designers are now asking clients to commit to a six-month or one-year service contract called a retainer, with a specific sum of money paid to the designer on a monthly basis as a service binder. Future design and consultation services are billed against the retainer. The advantage to the client is that he or she will get a reduction of your hourly rates (usually 25 percent) in exchange for paying a monthly fee, and this contract gives them priority over per-project clients.

The advantages to you of working on retainer is the client's commitment to working with you in a partnership type of arrangement and the guarantee of a set monthly cash flow. The disadvantages include the client calling you with very minor questions and, sometimes, questioning whether or not he is getting what he's paying for.

Before you establish a retainer situation with a client, talk with other designers who are doing this or contact your lawyer or accountant, for whom working on retainer is a common practice. If you decide to establish retainer working relationships, don't do it with all clients. The best clients are those who have many projects to give you exclusively throughout a specified period of time and who will not pester you inappropriately.

reevaluate your fee structure to continue making ends meet. Use the formula presented above to calculate an increase that reflects the additional expenses. If your business expenses have stayed fairly level, but your reputation and capabilities have increased, you are a more valuable designer and are entitled to raise your prices.

When you decide to raise your fees, always inform your clients in writing ahead of time. Don't surprise them on the next bill. You don't have to go into any lengthy explanations. Send a short letter to each client stating that, "Due to an increase in operating expenses, we are forced to raise our fees effective as of (a specific date). We regret having to do so and have made every attempt to keep the increase as low as possible." Add to this blurb your new hourly fee or, if you do have a variable price scale, include a breakdown of services rendered for each new rate.

Markup

Most designers also add a markup, a standard percentage — usually 15 to 20 percent of the total — onto the costs of project materials and outside services. More experienced designers and larger design firms charge a higher markup than those just getting started. However, markup can go as high as 100 percent for projects that require overnight turnaround. This isn't an arbitrary fee; it's the standard industry charge to cover administrative handling and processing of the account and the use of your funds until the client reimburses you since you often must pay the vendor before the client pays you.

Although it's perfectly all right to charge a markup, you shouldn't tell clients what that percentage is. Just quote the total cost including markup on estimates and invoices (see pages 44-46 and 74-75 for how to do this). There may be times when you'll need to reduce your markup in order to make the numbers work on a project that's important to you but which has a very tight budget. But don't tell the clients you've done so, although you can make a point of letting them know that you spent a lot of time reworking the numbers to fit their budget.

When and How to Talk Money With a Client

Bring up the subject of money during your first meeting with a client. But the word to use is not money, it's budget. Once you've been fully briefed on the project, ask what kind of budget has been allocated for it. If the client stares at you blankly, explain that it's to their benefit to give you an idea how much they want to spend. That way, you can tell them if that amount is realistic for what they want to do and offer alternatives if it isn't. If the client maintains that he has no idea, come back within a day or two with a verbal ballpark figure (give them a range — for example, $12,000 to $14,000). If that's approved, then prepare a written price estimate.

When you bring up the issue of money, do it directly and matter-of-factly. Don't talk around it or leave it until the client raises the question of costs. You're in business, and people expect to pay businesses for the things they buy — including a designer's services. Therefore, we have to get over feeling awkward about the subject of money. In fact, discomfort about money may communicate to the client that *you* don't believe that your work is salable or valuable. So don't be reluctant to talk about money. Simply say, without cringing, "Let's discuss your budget for this project."

Once you've presented your written estimate, make sure the client understands what is and is not included in your arrangements. Don't depend on any client reading your estimate and all your terms carefully. Instead review with her how many concepts you'll be presenting and how many rounds of revisions are included. Many clients simply assume that you'll keep making changes to a project — for no extra charge — until they figure out what they want. Others think you'll bring them a dozen fully rendered comps so they can mix and match ideas. Also verify that the client understands what expenses will be billed separately as line items and how much you'll charge for overtime or rush work.

The practice of lowballing a job — finding out what the competition is bidding and then bidding lower — is considered unethical. When the economy goes into a slump, it can be tempting to lowball because you need the work and the clients want to lower costs. Regardless of the circumstances, I would caution you against lowballing. Sure, you can cut corners in production, but you still have to take the same amount of time for design or illustration. So, you are essentially agreeing to lower your income and devalue your talent. Also, once you get a reputation for lowballing, it's hard to get rid of it. Stick to your guns. Maintain a reputation for meeting deadlines and supplying good work. Clients who come to you for service and quality will stay if you deliver it. Those who come for your low prices will leave when a new kid has a better offer.

Working on Spec

Every designer will at some time be asked to do work on speculation (on spec, for short). That means that you'll do the creative work, and if the client likes it, then — maybe — she will give you the job. You're being asked to spend your time with no guarantee that you'll be paid for the work. You also have no guarantee that the client won't take your ideas and use them once you've been politely dismissed.

You may have to explain to some clients why no one should be asked to do spec work. They will probably respond best if you tell them why it's not good for *them* to ask for spec. Point out that spec designs seldom achieve the desired results — unlike designs based on detailed input from a client. Also mention that your creative thinking is your most valuable contribution to any project, so you can't spend much of it working up ideas that might not be used or paid for. Remind clients that they wouldn't appreciate a customer asking to try out their services or products and then paying only if they were satisfied. Show them a copy of the Graphic Artist's Guild's Code of Fair Practices as backup.

It's not unethical or totally unreasonable for a client to ask you to do a job on spec. Some clients have trouble making the leap from what you've shown to what they want.

Others think it's standard for designers to work up some sketches first. In this case, it may be better if you gently explain that you can't accept a project on spec. If you're fresh out of school and your portfolio only represents classroom projects, the client does have a right to be concerned about your capabilities. Until you get some real projects in your portfolio, you may have to work on spec to build a client base. But if you have a good portfolio that clearly shows experience with a variety of well-executed projects, there should be no reason a client can't make a decision to hire you based on seeing that work.

If you find yourself being asked to take a job on speculation, and you think it might be worth it "just this once," there are a few things to consider before you say yes. What's the client's time frame? Is it compatible with your present schedule of paying clients? Are other designers also doing this project on spec? If the answer to the last question is yes, I recommend you bow out gracefully. Your odds of getting the job drop significantly with other designers in the running.

One alternative to bowing out of a competitive presentation is to ask for compensation. Although only one designer will get the project, ask to be compensated for your presentation costs whether or not you get the job. Obviously you won't get a huge sum, but you could get enough to cover the time and expenses of putting the presentation together. You won't know how the client will react until you ask, so don't be shy. If the client rejects your request for compensation, then you can decide whether to present anyway, knowing you could lose your investment.

But if you feel that the client is honorable and sincerely does need to get a better sense of what you can do, then take the job. But keep your time commitment to no more than 10 percent of the time you estimate the entire job would take. Don't offer to do a presentation with fully developed comps.

Be sure the client understands up front that doing a job on spec means that you will only provide her with your creative ideas or concepts and some rough sketches. If this is not acceptable, be prepared to walk away. When you show your layouts or sketches to the client, put a hand-lettered or computer-generated © symbol and the date on every piece you bring in. Keep photocopies of all your work. This will help protect you if the client does intend to steal your designs.

Billing: It Doesn't Have to Be a Nightmare

Bill the client on a monthly basis for long-term projects, and within five days of the project's completion for projects that take less than a month. It's crucial to keep your client billing moving at a steady pace, because clients can take a full thirty days from the time they receive a bill to pay it.

If a project takes less than a month, and you bill it immediately, you should receive payment within a month. During the time you're waiting for payment from your client, you'll receive bills from the vendors involved in that client's project. You, too, have thirty days in which to pay them. The trick is to try to stay ahead of your vendors by getting your clients' bills out before you receive yours. That way, you can use the client's money to pay vendors, instead of dipping into your own business or personal savings. Projects that stretch out over several months can cause severe financial strain unless you bill your clients monthly for work done to date. Because you'll receive bills as soon as the work is done — often long before the project is finished — you'll find yourself in a cash flow crunch if you wait until the end of a project to bill. You need to have money coming in on a steady and predictable basis to keep operating with a positive cash flow.

In the signed Agreement of Terms and Conditions or client contract, specify your terms for payment so that clients understand what's expected of them and when. Once you've set a policy, you must establish credibility by consistently doing your billing on time.

Another reason to bill a job right away is that any discrepancies in your bill may cause a client to question it. That can take days or weeks to resolve. Once it's settled, a client will often ask for a revised bill. Most businesses, when issued a revised bill, take another thirty days before paying. That can create a logjam in your cash flow.

To keep your billing moving at a steady pace, you need an efficient billing system to help you organize project information. The following system is one I've used for several years. It may not be perfect, but it does work.

First, set up a billing book. A large three-ring binder works best because you can easily insert and remove your project recording sheets. To separate one project from another, use manila dividers with extending tabs. Label the extending tabs with the project name and file projects in alphabetical order. If you have clients with more than one project in the works at a time, set up your sections alphabetically by client and then by project. Each project section in the billing book should contain the following:

◆ Work In Progress Sheet
◆ Price Estimate Work Sheet
◆ Project Expenses Tracking Sheet
◆ Project Time Sheet
◆ Project Billing Work Sheet

The Work In Progress Sheet identifies the project by name, number and description. Update it on a weekly basis, checking off and dating each completed project phase. You'll also use it to tell you when to bill a project. (See pages 56-57 for more on this form.)

The Price Estimate Work Sheet gives you the figures you used to price the job—hourly rates and the markup on out-of-pocket expenses (you may change rates on some jobs; for example, charging less for nonprofits). When you prepare your bill, refer to the Total Project Cost quoted to be sure your final prices don't exceed it by more than 10 percent, which is generally acceptable. However, alert the client to the overrun in costs— even at 10 percent. When you do, they usually take it well. If not, you can negotiate, right then and there, how to settle the difference in a way that would satisfy both of you.

The Project Expenses Tracking Sheet is where you log each bill for a project-related expense that comes in from a vendor or subcontractor after checking it against the origi-

nal bid on the Price Estimate Work Sheet. (See pages 44-45 for how to fill in and more on how to use this sheet.) If you're billing in installments, this sheet tells you what the client owes you when, and you'll have the figures all in one place for the final bill.

Project Time Sheets go in that project's section of the billing book when each is completed. (See pages 58-59 for more on time sheets.) When it's time to bill, add up your hours and compare them to the hours estimated on your Price Estimate Work Sheet.

You'll use all the information in your billing book to prepare an invoice to send the client. This basically consists of the number of hours that you spent on that project and the cost for all expenses incurred for materials and services to complete it. You can use the Project Billing Work Sheet (see pages 74-75 for how to fill it out) to pull together all the information from your time sheets, Project Expenses Tracking Sheets, and the Price Estimate Work Sheet and prepare the invoice. (See pages 72-73 and 45-46 for how to fill out and use an invoice.)

When you've invoiced a client, keep one copy in your Accounts Receivable File and another in your sales tax file, whether you charged it or not (see pages 103-104 for more on sales tax). And remember that you have to account for each invoice by number for tax purposes at the end of the year, so keep all voided invoices, too.

Bookkeeping

While most people think bookkeeping's the most difficult part of owning a business, it's rather simple. You're keeping a record of all the money you take in (credits) and all the money you pay out (debits) just like you do with your personal checking account. Instead of writing your deposits and withdrawals on a little chart at the front of your checkbook, you use a ledger or disbursement journal. And you also have to enter the amount under a specific classification that tells what you spent it on, so you have a record of all tax-deductible business expenses. For example, if you write a check to a photographer for a

Using Preprinted Versus Customized Invoices

Many people use packaged preprinted invoices purchased in office supply stores. But typing in your services each time you prepare a bill takes time that could be better spent on other things. You're also losing the chance to display your design skills if you don't at least have your logo on the invoice. A unified system of stationery and forms looks more impressive and professional. (See pages 162-163 for more on how to use identity systems for self-promotion.)

Your Business Checking Account

You must have a separate checking account for your business to keep its money separate from your personal funds. Although it's cheaper to open another regular checking account, don't do it! It's worth every extra cent to invest in a business checking account so you can establish a *business* relationship with your bank or credit union. When you need a loan or line of credit to buy new equipment or make other investments in your business, you'll have established a track record with that banking institution.

Look for a bank or credit union that offers interest on checking accounts, but you should compare the interest paid to the monthly fees charged. You may need to maintain a high minimum balance to prevent paying fees that could offset any interest earnings.

job, you'd enter the amount of that check under the classification Outside Services because you hired a subcontractor to do a job for your business, which would constitute a business deduction.

Using a Ledger or Disbursement Journal

A ledger or journal has sheets of paper with both rows and columns printed on them. These provide spaces for entering every deposit into your account and every check written against it. Ledger sheets also make it easy to carry the amount of the check across the ledger to the row with the most appropriate classification for it.

You can special order business checkbooks that contain their own ledgers or disbursement sheets. This is called a one-write system, because you only write the information once — when you make out the check. The checks have a carbon strip across the back, so all the information for a ledger sheet — the amount, the check number, payee and the date — is transferred directly to the self-contained ledger sheet positioned beneath the checks as you write out each one. Then you enter the amount again under the proper classification. It's a time-saver that's worth the additional cost.

Setting Up and Using a Ledger or Disbursement Journal

Each time you write a check, use the ledger to record the information specified in the callouts. In the reduced version of a ledger sheet shown here, the first eleven columns call out the specific data to be entered into each. Use the wide row running across the top of the ledger to label each. The callouts for each column are listed below with a brief explanation of the information that goes into each column and what it means to you.

Numbers: Use this space to number each row, from the top of the ledger to the bottom, beginning with the number 1. There's another numbers column seven rows over; write the numbers there as well. These number columns serve as reference points to help you

stay in the correct row as you carry information about a check across the ledger to record it in other columns.

Date: Record the date of each check you write in this column.

Pay To The Order Of: Write in who you made the check out to.

Description: Enter your reason for writing the check.

Check #s: Record the number of each check you write.

✔: Every month when you reconcile your bank statement, place a check mark next to each check that cleared the bank during the previous month.

Check Amount: Enter the exact amount of each check you write.

Numbers: Explained above.

Bank Balance: Each time you write a check, subtract it from your balance to get the new one. Having an accurate, ongoing balance will keep you from bouncing checks.

Deposits: In the next two columns enter the date and amount of each deposit you make into your account. Add that amount into your bank balance in that column.

Columns 1-9: The remaining columns on this side of the ledger are numbered. These numbered columns can continue on the back side of the ledger. Number them 10 through however many columns you need or have available on your sheet. If you require more columns than your sheet provides, you can continue on a second sheet.

Label each numbered column with the name of a deductible expense. Each design business is a little different, so consult an accountant to learn what is and isn't deductible for your particular business. The following are examples of some classifications for the columns to show you how the system works.

Payroll and/or Draw: If your business is incorporated, you pay yourself and all employees a salary and would record the amount of the paychecks under the heading Payroll. If you have a sole proprietorship, you can't take a salary, but you can take a draw. That would be recorded in a column labeled Draw and employee paychecks under Payroll.

Office Expenses: Checks written for anything you use to keep your office in operation, including supplies, equipment, furnishings, rent, utilities, cleaning service, etc.

Petty Cash: Whenever you write a check for petty cash, enter the amount in this column. Keep all receipts for petty cash expenditures, as this is another area the IRS looks at closely. If you take $100 out for petty cash, you must show receipts amounting to $100 to match that expenditure. Receipts are required for every check you write, regardless of the classification.

Sales Tax: When you make your monthly sales tax payment, the amount of that check goes in this column.

Postage: Any business-related postage expense goes here.

Travel and Entertainment: Enter legitimate business expenses in this column. Keep accurate records stating what the expense was for, and what client or project it was related to.

Computers Can Help

Computers can make your business life much easier. Depending on the computer hardware and software you have, you can easily automate your bookkeeping system. There are a wide variety of general accounting software packages available for both MS-DOS–based and Macintosh computers. You can find packages with ledgers that can monitor and balance your checking account receipts and disbursements, keep track of accounts payable/receivable, and record billing information that can be transferred to an invoice.

There are also several software programs designed especially for the graphic arts industry. These include capabilities like estimating jobs, time sheet maintenance, calculating job profit and loss, production billing, time history on past jobs, as well as accounts receivable/payable and checkbook management.

You may want to use a simple spreadsheet program instead, or you can scan or input all the forms and work sheets shown in chapter two. For example, if you format a sample form or work sheet into your computer, then use a save command and retain it as a master blank (all the spaces for information are left

Keeping Up

You *must* keep up with billing and bookkeeping. And all your entries *must* be correct, because a mistake can be costly (think about IRS penalties for underpayment!). If you don't know anything about bookkeeping or have absolutely no head for arithmetic, the best investment you can make is to hire an accountant and bookkeeper right away. (You may also be able to work with an accounting program under your accountant's direction.) It seems hard to justify these extras when you're just starting out, but you'll be repaid the first time a bookkeeper finds an error.

You can hire a part-time bookkeeper who works once a week or so. You must have someone you can trust – someone who's both competent and honest – so put in the effort you need to find the right person. Ask your accountant or bank officer for recommendations. Get additional employer and personal references and check them out.

Depending on your studio size, you may want to hire an assistant to act as bookkeeper and handle other clerical chores for you. (Be sure to give anyone you hire a bookkeeping test to determine how good he or she is; you can find a model test, including answers, in most basic accounting books.) Some designers hire business managers (or find a partner, often a spouse) to handle not only bookkeeping but also pricing, contracts and other business functions. But any assistant or business manager will only be as good as the supervision you give them. That's why it's important to start out doing your own books – and to have in place complete billing and bookkeeping systems. This gives you and your employees a solid base for making the right decisions.

blank, just like the forms shown in this book), you can keyboard information for any form into the master and print it out. You can then save a copy of the final document in a computer file, make hard copies (cheapest on a photocopier) or both. Just don't accidentally save information on your master, and it'll be ready to use for the next project.

However, computers cannot operate by themselves. You still have to input the information *accurately* in order to make these programs work for you. While it is more efficient, in most cases, than doing it by hand, it does require a time commitment. (This is where an assistant can be extremely valuable.)

Here is a selection of software packages that will ease your business tasks.

Clients and Profits is a must for every serious designer. It requires a Mac and 2 megabytes of memory. The hefty price tag buys a lot of features: preparation of work orders, job tickets, cost estimates, production schedules, time estimates, client billing, cost tracking, assets and liabilities statement (usually your accountant's job). And it can be networked, which means any number of people in your office can use it. Three grades are available from Working Computer, The Triangle Building, 4755 Oceanside Blvd., Suite 200, Oceanside CA 92056; (619) 945-4334.

MACDesign Billing 1.0 is a lesser priced, easy-to-use alternative that runs on Claris FileMaker Pro 2.0 software and a Mac with 2 megabytes of memory, although 4 megabytes is recommended. You need at least a 6.0.5 system. The program lets you record and track job-related costs by standard categories (type, mechanicals, illustrations, etc.) or customize your own, in addition to preparing invoices and billing statements. Contact Desktop Graphic Services, 2265 Westwood Blvd., Suite 105, Los Angeles CA 90064; (310) 391-5275.

Colleague is easy to use and does it all, from tracking time and costs, to billing and even personal and project production schedules. It cranks out receivables and payables records and keeps a double-entry general ledger, payroll, checkbook and inventory. You need 3 megabytes of RAM and 4.5 megabytes of disk space. Call (512) 345-9964.

TimeSlips III and LapTrack offer an easy-to-use, efficient way to keep track of time and calculate expenses. TimeSlips also tracks billing and accounts receivable, while LapTrack keeps tab on expenses and time. Call (508) 768-6100.

Timekeeper is the simplest and least expensive program out there. It tracks time records for specific projects, calculates costs at varying hourly rates, and produces job sheets and daily activities reports. A demo version is available so you can try it out first. Contact The Timekeeper Company, 4907 Burke Ave., N., Seattle WA 98103; (206) 632-7089.

Set Up an Accounts Receivable File
When you send an invoice to a client, put a copy in this file. Keep the invoices in order by

invoice number, not job number.

Keep your Accounts Receivable Record Sheets in the front of your Accounts Receivable File. Each time you prepare an invoice, record the date it was sent, the client's name, the invoice number, the due date and amount due, as well as the amount paid if the invoice is not paid in full. When an invoice is paid in full, use a light-colored marker to cross it off your list. This way you know exactly how much money is still owed to you at any given time. Compare this list to your accounts payable list each week to make sure the receivables are always greater than the payables. If your receivables begin to drop below your payables, you're spending more than you're making and must act immediately to reverse the situation.

When a client pays a bill, take the invoice out of the Active Accounts Receivable File, mark it paid, date it, and record the client's check number on it. Put the invoice into a folder labeled Accounts Receivable–Paid File. Keep the invoices in numeric order.

Sales Tax File
Keep a copy of every client invoice in a file marked Sales Tax. Every month, on the day your state's sales tax report is due, go through the previous month's invoices to calculate your gross billings and resulting tax liability. Even if one or all of your bills are eligible for tax exemption (see pages 103-104 for what is exempt), you are still required to file a tax report and include tax-exempt billings with your other gross monthly earnings. You can then deduct the eligible total as an exemption in the space provided on your monthly return. When you file your report, attach a copy of the report to all invoices included in that filing month, and take them out of the Sales Tax File. Put them into another file called Paid Sales Tax.

Monthly Client Statement File
Every month, you will send out a statement to those clients who have not paid their previous month's bill and any other outstanding bills. This reminds the client of the outstanding amount to which you'll attach the monthly in-

Time Sheets: An Important Part of Pricing Cost-Effectiveness

What almost sent me over the edge of sanity when I was running a ten-person agency was discovering that employees weren't logging in real time on their timesheets. "It was too much trouble," they all protested. Too much trouble came down to fifteen seconds to jot down the time they began work on a project and another fifteen seconds to write in their finish time. Since I wasn't collecting and reviewing their time sheets daily, which was my mistake, they would wait until Friday afternoon when they were due to try and reconstruct the time they spent on each project during the entire week. As a result, they were always guesstimating their time. And, as I later discovered, those guesses were consistently on the low side. So I had no idea how much time projects were actually taking, and, consequently, when I used these projects as guidelines in pricing a new job, I lost money. Another problem that occurred was that I never really knew who my fastest production people were, since their time sheets weren't a true reflection of how long something took them. I needed to know that in order to assign low budget and quick turnaround projects to my most efficient workers. I also needed to know how much time my employees were spending on nonbillable tasks, and they weren't logging that in at all. That, too, was my fault, because I didn't insist on it.

The problem became history, however, when I instituted a policy of turning in daily time sheets. It also helped to explain exactly how those time sheets are used to prepare bills for each project, and when they are inaccurate, how that diminishes our year-end profits. I then explained how profits determine whether or not they will get a yearly raise. It may sound simplistic, but unless an employee is working with the billing, which most of them never do, they never understand how little things like time sheet accuracy, conserving on materials and working efficiently has any direct impact on them.

terest or finance charge of 1½ percent. This new balance will be due in thirty days. If it's still not paid by that time, another interest charge is added to the previous month's balance. If a balance goes unpaid for more than 120 days, you have a collection problem. (See the section on credit and collection, pages 110-113.)

Every time you bill a client for a project, take all the recording sheets for that project out of the billing book, including the manila divider you used to separate that project from the others. Staple a copy of the prepared bill or invoice to the work sheets and retire them to the Past Billing File. Use the manila divider as a cover sheet for that file. File it alphabetically by the first letter of the project's name. Taking project recording sheets out as soon as the client is billed will help keep your billing book from becoming overcrowded.

Set Up an Accounts Payable File

Keep this file with all the project-related invoices you receive as well as your business-related expenses—phone bills, electric bills, rent, etc.—in a stand-up file holder on or near your desk for easy access. When a bill comes in for a client project, check the price of the bill against the quote you recorded on the Price Estimate Work Sheet and enter it on the appropriate Project Expenses Tracking Sheet (see pages 72-73). Be sure to compare it to your price without the markup, not the client's price. Then record the invoice on an Accounts Payable Record Sheet (see below and pages 80-81), and put it into the Accounts Payable File.

To help you pay your bills on time, set up your Accounts Payable File with thirty file folders. Number the top of each folder consecutively from 1 to 30-31 to represent one day of the month. If an invoice comes in on the fifteenth, for example, put it in the folder marked 15. On the fifteenth of the following month, before you enter any new invoices for that day, take out all the old invoices from the previous month. Then pay those on that day and mail them.

UP THE LADDER OF SUCCESS

If you take just a few minutes every day to take out the bills from the previous month that have to be paid, paying bills will be a breeze. Not only will you avoid finance charges for late payments, but you can continue to earn bank interest on your money by waiting the full thirty days to pay a bill.

The Accounts Payable Record Sheet is where you record *all* the bills you receive, including due date and amount. You must keep separate sheets for project-related and business-related expenses, so you can keep track of your overhead. Keep the sheets clipped together in the front of your accounts payable file. To make it easy to distinguish paid from unpaid bills, mark through each

paid item with a light-colored marker.

It does take a few minutes every day, or as bills come in, to record the invoices you put into your Accounts Payable File. But this record of all incoming bills is the only way you have of knowing how much money you owe at any given time.

Each time you pay a bill, mark it paid, date it, and write the number of the check on it. Then file your copy alphabetically in your Accounts Payable–Paid File. If a portion of the invoice is to be torn off and sent back with the payment, do that, then file the remainder of the invoice, instead of a copy, in the accordion file.

Checking Your Studio's Financial Health

Having files and records doesn't help you if you don't keep them accurate and up-to-date and review them regularly. To understand how your studio is doing financially, you should check the following once a week:

- ◆ Cash on hand
- ◆ Bank Balance and General Ledger
- ◆ Totals for payments received from clients
- ◆ Records of cash and checks paid out
- ◆ Accounts Receivable File
- ◆ Accounts Payable File
- ◆ Payroll records
- ◆ Taxes collected and paid — sales and payroll

If you've entered information in your General Ledger and the appropriate files each time you paid out or received money, reviewing your records and checking for accuracy will take only about an hour.

When you hire an accountant, it is worth the money to have him or her check each item included in the list above and the list below on a quarterly basis. If you don't have an accountant, you need to do this yourself. The list below includes records and reports you should check monthly.

- ◆ Bank statement against your records
- ◆ Records of petty cash disbursement
- ◆ Proper payment of federal, state and local taxes
- ◆ Past-due client bills for further pursuit or write-off

- ◆ Cash flow (do at least once every three months)
- ◆ Monthly profit-and-loss
- ◆ Monthly balance sheet

The last three items in this list come under the heading of financial management rather than basic bookkeeping. This is how you discover if you're actually making money, barely breaking even or losing money.

You'll also need these three financial statements to persuade a bank to loan you money once your business is up and running. They tell the loan officer how good the odds are that you can pay back a loan. Sometimes your owner's equity (the difference between your total assets and total liabilities) can even be used as collateral for the business loan.

Your accountant or bookkeeper should prepare these statements for you. You should, however, understand how they are prepared, so that when your bookkeeper or accountant asks you to review them, you will know what you're looking at and you will know how healthy your business really is. If you are one of those rare designers who want to prepare these statements themselves, the information in this section will help you. Also, if you're using accounting software you need to know enough to avoid messing up your finances through operator error. That program is only as good as the data you feed it.

Cash Flow Statement

The Cash Flow Statement, prepared using information from your general ledger only, shows your studio's net increase or decrease in cash over a month, quarter or a year. This statement tells you where your cash is coming from and going, when and why. You'll see the impact of slow-paying clients here, especially if you're paying for printing, then billing your client. If you have to pay the printer in February, and the client doesn't pay you till March, you may have a temporary cash shortage in February. On the other hand, you can affect your cash flow in a positive way by taking a full thirty days to pay your vendors. When you do this, you are, in effect, getting a loan from your vendors that increases your available cash.

Accounts Receivable Aging Report

In addition to a Cash Flow Statement, you need an up-to-date weekly or monthly Accounts Receivable Aging Report, which helps you anticipate how healthy your future cash flow will be. It lists clients who owe you money and the amount and date the money is due, telling you at a glance if an account is overdue and how long it has been that way. To plan your cash flow you will need to compare an Accounts Receivable Aging Report to an Accounts Payable Aging Report (money you owe to others and when it's coming due).

To create this report, itemize clients by invoice number, payment due date, balances due and whether the balances are currently due or if they are overdue by how much. When a balance is paid off, the dollar amount is marked through with a line.

Accounts Payable Aging Report

This report is set up just like the Accounts Receivable Aging Report. It tells you how much money you owe to others, when it's due, and if it's overdue. It also can help you make payment decisions when your cash flow is tight and you may need more than thirty days to pay some of your own bills.

Aging reports take time to set up and maintain, so if you don't have the help of a secretary or an assistant, it may not be worth the time it will take you to keep one current. However, there are many computer programs that can assist you. Essentially, this report works like the Accounts Receivable Aging Report. You itemize companies that have billed you, the invoices, numbers, dollar amounts, discount amounts, balances due and their current status. (The discount column is where you indicate the percent that a company will discount your balance if you pay within a certain time period.)

Monthly Profit-and-Loss Statement

Your Profit-and-Loss Statement is the key to your being able to be an independent designer rather than working for someone else. It tracks your income, measuring expenses against revenues over a month to show the net profit (income) or loss for your studio dur-ing that period. In other words, revenues minus expenses equals net profit (income) or loss. It's also helpful to glimpse the bigger picture by looking at an entire quarter or year on one statement.

Making a profit does matter. It means money saved to invest in new computer equipment or to move your studio into a more attractive space. You don't need to make a profit every month or panic if you show an occasional month's loss. If you're consistently losing money or barely breaking even, then it's time to reevaluate your income and expenses to correct the situation.

The income statement, aka a profit-and-loss statement, is where you figure out what you're doing right or wrong. If you compare the line items in your monthly profit-and-loss statements, which convert dollar amounts into percentages, you will see very clearly which areas of income have increased and which areas of your expenditures are up or down. Also, if you compare the percentages for one month to the percentages for any past month, you can see where you are making money and where you may be losing it. For example, if you're taking in only 5 percent more from clients than you did in a previous month while your net profit (income) has increased by 8 percent, a check of each line item on the profit-and-loss statement will tell you how you did it. You might have cut the costs of art and office supplies when you switched to a different supplier. Or you might discover that hiring that freelancer let you take on more work and bring in more money while only slightly increasing your expenses.

As important as tracking your cash flow is, it won't tell you if you're making a profit or losing money. You can have a healthy supply of cash in any one month but still be losing money over the long haul. For example, let's say that one month you were paid for five projects and ended the month with a good amount of cash in hand. However, you cut your hourly rate to bring three of those jobs in on budget because you needed the work. The next month you discover you have actually lost money overall because you didn't earn enough to cover your overhead. You have to

Accounts Receivable Aging Report

(by Due Date)
As of: 2/28

CLIENT NAME	INV. #	DUE DATE	CURRENT	31-60	61-90	91-120	121 +	BALANCE
Fly-By-Night Real Estate	334-21	3/28	1,530.00					1,530.00
	157-10	1/15		1,735.00				1,735.00
	128-21	12/15			~~2,432.00~~			~~2,432.00~~
	Client Total		**1,530.00**	**1,735.00**	**~~2,432.00~~**	**0.00**	**0.00**	**3,265.00**
Carbon Steal	335-22	3/1	1,618.23					1,618.23
	Client Total		**1,618.23**	**0.00**	**0.00**	**0.00**	**0.00**	**1,618.23**
Transport Freight	067-41	10/1					8,795.40	8,795.40
	Client Total		**0.00**	**0.00**	**0.00**	**0.00**	**8,795.40**	**8,795.40**
Allstar Products	129-22	12/15			987.00			~~987.00~~
	Client Total		**0.00**	**0.00**	**987.00**	**0.00**	**0.00**	**~~987.00~~**

Report Totals *13,678.63*

Accounts Payable Aging Report

(by Due Date)   **Page 1**
As of: 2/28

CLIENT NAME	INV. #	DUE DATE	DISCOUNT	CURRENT	31-60	61-90	91-120	121+	BALANCE
Rainbow Printing	42606	2/28	2.00	165.00					~~161.70~~
	42290	2/28	2.00	18.25					~~17.89~~
	43738	2/28	2.00	921.50					921.50
	43736	3/24	2.00	22.10					22.10
	Vendor Total		**0.00**	**1127.55**	**0.00**	**0.00**	**0.00**	**0.00**	**943.60**
Ad Graphics	1576	3/1	0.00	620.00					620.00
	Client Total		**0.00**	**620.00**	**0.00**	**0.00**	**0.00**	**0.00**	**620.00**
Photolab	15239	2/12			195.40				195.40
	Client Total		**0.00**	**0.00**	**195.40**	**0.00**	**0.00**		**195.40**

Report Totals 2,702.60

January Profit & Loss

Account Description	Amount	%
Sales:		
Sales Taxable — RI	47,090.15	11.4
Sales Taxable — MA	25,722.15	6.2
Sales Taxable–CT	15,232.44	3.7
Sales Nontaxable — RI	56,577.99	13.7
Sales Nontaxable — MA	145,399.46	35.3
Sales Nontaxable — CT	9,688.50	2.4
Sales Nontaxable — Other	112,212.40	27.2
Total Sales:	411,923.09	100.0
Net Sales:	411,923.09	100.0
Cost of Goods Sold:		
Freight	1,776.01	0.4
Purchases	228,488.67	55.5
Supplies	133.24	0.0
Subcontractors	6,912.50	1.7
Total Cost of Goods Sold:	237.310.48	57.6
Gross Profit:	174,612.61	42.4
Expenses:		
Gross Payroll	57,878.71	14.1
Travel	1,918.01	0.5
Entertainment	155.76	0.0
Auto Expense	369.63	0.1
Advertising	7,155.60	1.7
Equipment Lease	1,192.54	0.3
Office Expenses	1,799.44	0.4
Telephone	3,758.75	0.9
Total Expenses:	74,228.44	18
Operating Profit:	100,384.17	24.4
Total Other Income & Expenses	0.00	0.0
Net Profit (Earnings Year-to-date):	100,384.17	24.4

cut back your own salary for the month to make ends meet.

To prepare a Profit-and-Loss Statement you must itemize your taxable and nontaxable sales by state and the cost to you of producing the final work. Total each category separately, then subtract costs from sales to get your gross profit. Then itemize the expenses associated with running your business and total these. Subtract this figure from your gross profit to get your operating profit. If you have additional income or expenses, such as savings interest or taxes due, add or subtract them from your operating profit to arrive at your net profit, or earnings-to-date.

The Balance Sheet

A Balance Sheet is a statement of your total assets, total liabilities and the net worth or owner's equity of your studio at a given point in time, usually the end of the month. Your studio's net worth is the difference between your total assets and your total liabilities. Net worth is a key to getting a business loan. Equally important, a Balance Sheet tracks in detail the value of assets other than cash—your computer, studio furniture, even software—and how much you owe to suppliers, banks, the tax people and others.

The Balance Sheet is where you can check the effectiveness of your investment in equipment against how much you owe for it. If you bought a new computer and made more money from clients than you had to pay out for the loan or lease, that will show up on the balance sheet (most likely at year-end). Even if your income has bounced between profit and loss all year, the snapshot of your studio's fortunes taken in the balance sheet at this one point in time tells you how you came out over the long haul.

As a tool to measure your net worth in relation to the amount of profit you've been making (as shown in the Profit-and-Loss Statement), it will be most effective when you are able to compare one year against another. Again, as with the previous two statements, your accountant or bookkeeper will most likely be the one preparing monthly or quarterly balance sheets for you, but you will still

need to know what the line items mean and how to read it.

The most important thing to remember is that your assets and liabilities are always listed in the following order: The cash assets (savings, investments, etc.) come first, and accounts receivable (money due you from clients) are listed before the fixed assets (furniture, computers, etc.). These figures are totaled. The liabilities (what you owe) come next in the order they are due. Listed last is permanent capital, which is the difference between your total assets and total liabilities. Capital is categorized by stocks, distribution to shareholders, retained earnings (money not distributed to shareholders) and earnings year-to-date (the final figure from your Profit-and-Loss Statement).

Taxes and You

When I was starting out, I bought materials for a project and paid the sales tax, never realizing my client should pay it instead. Then I received a letter from the state department of taxation asking why I was running a business they knew nothing about. They were auditing a company that had many bills from me for graphic design services, none of which even hinted that sales tax was included.

Confused, I called the tax office right away. "There must be some mistake," I said eagerly. "I'm not running a store. What could sales tax have to do with me? And I haven't registered my business because I'm only doing a little freelance work." I could tell, even over the phone, that I had just said something terribly wrong.

It was a painful, but important, lesson. I found an accountant, set up real books, and went to that state division of taxation to register my business. They taught me how to file my monthly sales tax return and how to decide which of my design services were taxable.

No matter what title you give yourself or how often you work, you must pay taxes. The legal structure of your business (see page 10), however, does determine how you calculate your taxes and which forms you use. Consult

Balance Sheet

January

Assets:

Current Assets:

Cash	34,974.26	
Accounts Receivable	+90,043.89	
Total Current Assets:		**125,018.15**

Fixed Assets:

Depreciable Assets	1,029.15	
Furniture & Fixtures	378.79	
Office Equipment	6,420.00	
Accumulated Depreciation	−535.00	
Total Fixed Assets:		**7,292.94**

Total Assets: 132,311.09

Liabilities:

Current Liabilities:

Accounts Payable	81,367.03	
Taxes Payable	889.00	
Sales Tax Payable	2,416.52	
Total Current Liabilities		**84,672.55**

Total Liabilities.. 84,672.55

Capital:

Capital Stock	3,000.00	
Distribution to Shareholder	−27,729.92	
Retained Earnings	6,459.30	
Earnings Year-to-date	67,909.16	

Total Capital 47,638.54

Total Liabilities & Capital 132,311.09

an accountant or contact your local IRS office and your state's division of taxation to find out what is required. Remember the old line, "Ignorance of the law is no excuse"? If you fail to file and pay sales tax, or fail to claim your earned income, sooner or later you will get caught and fined.

What Is and Isn't Subject to Sales Tax

If your state has a sales tax, then 90 percent of the work you do as a graphic designer is taxable. A few design services and work done for nonprofit organizations are tax exempt (because those organizations are), but that income still must be reported. Sales tax is a percentage of the sum total dollar amount that represents your taxable services and the materials and services you purchase to complete a job, such as art supplies, typesetting, printing, photography, etc. That percentage is then added to your clients' bills.

Each month you must file a sales tax report that states how much you billed in gross income and how much of that income is taxable. If you don't file, they fine you. No matter how part-time your freelance business is, the state office of taxation will eventually find you. Why? Because your clients will claim the work you do as a business expense, and that will send up an immediate red flag to the local tax collectors. Call your state division of taxation to learn how to register your business and what's taxable and what's not. The process usually involves filling out a form and paying a small fee. The state division of taxation will then issue you a *Permit to Make Sales at Retail.*

Designers, especially freelancers, tend to find that word retail confusing. We all seem to think of our work as a service rendered because our ideas and initial design concepts are simply services rendered to our clients. And that's true, as long as we give them an idea, a concept, a rough sketch or two *without producing a finished product.* This is categorized by most states (check your own state's regulations to be sure) as Services Rendered—For Resale. This means that your client is taking your ideas or sketches and using them to create her own brochure, stationery,

catalog or whatever is needed. Or your client is using your ideas to create an item or product to be resold to her customer; in that case your client will charge that customer for the end product. Charging for the end product—the actual catalog, brochure, stationery, logo, etc.—is considered a retail sale. An example of this would be the work you might do for an advertising agency—perhaps a layout for a magazine ad. Because you are providing ideas or preliminary work the service is tax exempt. The agency takes your layout and has its own designer or art director finish the ad. It is now the agency's responsibility to bill their client for the finished product—the ad—and the sales tax.

However, most of the work we do as graphic designers does end up as a finished product. That means a completed design such as a logo that the client can turn around and use or printed materials such as brochures, print ads and posters, are all considered to be retail products. Bingo—sales tax!

Sales Tax on the Materials and Vendors You Use

The materials you buy and the vendor services you use for your clients' work is tax exempt to you. When you go into an art supply or stationery store and purchase anything to use on a project, inform the clerk that these materials are for resale. You may be asked to fill out a resale tax-exempt form, on which you will need to include your sales tax permit number. However, you must be sure to bill your client for these materials (with a markup, of course) and charge sales tax on the total. Your bill can show either an itemized listing of these materials or just indicate miscellaneous materials with a cost total. You must keep all of your purchase receipts for these items in case of a tax audit. Do the same thing with all your vendors.

State and Federal Taxes

Everyone must pay federal income and social security taxes on all income. As of this writing, if you're single and earn more than $6,050 in gross income from any combination of sources—such as freelancing and teaching—

1099 Forms

If you bill any client more than $600 in a given tax year, at the end of the year he must issue you a 1099 form stating the total amount paid to you. Each form is attached to your income tax return. If you've earned less than that amount you must still report those earnings. While some people don't report that income, if they or the company they worked for is audited, they will be caught and penalized. If you use a freelancer for work that exceeds the $600 minimum, then *you* must issue a 1099.

or you're married with a combined gross income of more than $10,900, you must pay federal income taxes.

If you've registered your graphic design business as a sole proprietorship and not a corporation (see page 10 for the difference), then you're self-employed. If you have net earnings (income after expenses are paid and deductions are taken) of $400 or more, you are liable for federal income tax. (These figures can change from year to year.) You'll also pay self-employment (instead of social security), state and local taxes (if any). You can't pay yourself a salary and withhold taxes from your paycheck if you're self-employed. You can pay a lump sum against these taxes quarterly; ask your accountant or tax preparer how and why to do it.

But you won't pay the Federal Insurance Contributions Act tax (FICA) — federal unemployment insurance. This means you aren't eligible for unemployment benefits if your business goes under. Even if your state has a Temporary Disability Insurance (TDI) tax program, you can't use it because you don't pay into it. As soon as you can afford one, you should consider a personal disability insurance policy.

If your business is, or will soon be, incorporated, then you'll deal with a different set of tax regulations. When you incorporate, you're no longer self-employed but an employee of the corporation — it's a separate business entity. The corporation will be liable for separate taxes on both the state and federal levels. Each pay period, taxes will be withheld from your salary just as if you worked for someone else. Your business will pay separate taxes. Your accountant will set up a system for doing this. You absolutely must work regularly with an accountant when you incorporate because the regulations and liabilities become more complicated and are subject to frequent change.

Lowering Your Taxes
It's nearly impossible to stay current on the frequent changes in the tax laws — that's what you hire an accountant to do. But you do need a general sense of what the IRS considers de-

ductible expenses in running a business. This section covers most of the current regulations as of this writing, but they can change before the ink is even dry. Always check with your accountant before the beginning of each tax year to be aware of any new laws that may apply to your business structure, and to be sure you are properly documenting all deductible expenses.

You can reduce your tax liabilities by itemizing deductions for business and operating expenses — rent, utilities, supplies, travel and entertainment, work-related educational programs, subscriptions, insurance, and the purchase or leasing of equipment. Equipment and furniture can be depreciated over a period of years for additional tax credits.

Business-related travel and entertainment is 50 percent deductible. The IRS checks these items carefully, expecting to find fraud. Keep accurate records stating what the expense was for, what client or project it related to, and keep all of your receipts. Payments to accountants, financial planners, business consultants or advisers, and legal fees are all deductible. Even with these expenses, you will still need to keep all receipts in case you are ever audited. The health insurance deduction has been reduced to 25 percent for the self-employed. And pro bono work is *not* considered a charitable contribution.

Regulations have changed regarding the IRS's interpretation of a "home office," which now must be your "principal place of business." You can't deduct office expenses if you work full-time for someone else and use a home office to put in additional hours on your employer's projects or if you work full-time somewhere and do freelance work at home. The office space cannot be used for anything else. If your office space qualifies, you can deduct all of your business-related expenses, such as the installation and cost of a business phone or the cost of long-distance business calls, which must be documented with phone bills and a calling log. You can also deduct the cost and installation of a fax machine and usage fees. The cost of equipment and furnishings can be deducted and depreciated over a period of years. All supplies, educa-

tional expenses, and subscriptions are tax deductible. If you rent your home, you can deduct a percentage of your rent based on the square footage of your office. If you own your home, you can take a deduction based on a percentage of your mortgage interest but not your mortgage principal, and you can also deduct a percentage of your property taxes, water bills, trash collection, and other house maintenance expenses.

Regarding educational expenses, you can't deduct the cost of getting a degree or the basic training necessary to become a designer, but you can deduct the cost for additional training to further your areas of expertise or to learn a new but related skill. For example, a workshop to learn how to use some new software or market your design business counts, but a master's degree in scientific illustration when you have a bachelor's in graphic design doesn't.

Listed below are additional ways to cut your taxes; consult with your accountant to be sure you fit the specific qualifications, as they will take some advanced planning. If your accountant isn't up on all the ways you can defer income with retirement plans, tax-free investments and tax shelters, you may want to consult a financial planner.

- If you prepay by December 31 taxes, such as real estate, automobile, state and federal quarterly estimated taxes, that aren't scheduled to be paid until the following year, you can get a tax credit for the year in which the payments were made.
- You can deduct contributions to an IRA (Individual Retirement Account) or a Keogh Plan.
- If your business is incorporated, ask your accountant about SEP plans (Simplified Employee Pension), which allow for higher yearly contributions than IRAs and Keoghs.
- Cash-deferred annuities and life insurance plans can help you shelter some of your earnings while building a secure financial base for yourself and your family.
- You can also arrange for a private retirement fund to be set up between your business and your insurance company if you anticipate that your income will hit the $135,000 level. Such retirement plans are not subject to social security tax.

- If your interest earnings in CDs (Certificates of Deposit) are beginning to add up, you may want to check into the many types of mutual funds available, as well as stocks and bonds. The advantage is that these types of investments are taxed on a capital gains basis which can save you additional money.
- If you have an S corporation, look into the new laws regarding the lower tax rates paid by C corporations. You may want to ask your accountant if it would be worth it to convert your corporate status.
- Increasing your charitable contributions can help cut your tax bill, but remember to get receipts because canceled checks are no longer acceptable to the IRS.
- Invest your money in tax-free bonds that will save you some federal tax dollars. In addition, if you invest in municipal bonds, you may get a break on your state taxes as well.
- It may be a good time to buy that new computer system or the copier you've been wanting, because the new tax laws allow you to take an immediate depreciation deduction of up to $17,500 in equipment, rather than the previous limit of $10,000.
- You can now amortize over a fifteen-year period your business's goodwill and other intangible assets, which is essentially your business reputation and client base. Prior to 1993 these assets were not deductible. Your accountant can advise you on what's eligible and what's not.
- The cost of taking a spouse or relative on a business trip is deductible only if he or she is an official employee of your company.
- Try to pay as many of your office-related bills as possible before the end of the year; that will increase your cost of doing business deductions and reduce your tax liabilities.
- If you have a corporation and you operate on the accrual method of accounting (which means a transaction can appear in your books even though the money hasn't yet been paid out), you can deduct the entire year's cost of your employees' health insurance policies and defer payment until after the first of the following year. You can also take advantage of the accrual system with charitable contributions. Check with your accountant as to exactly how these contributions and deferred benefit payments work.
- Rather than paying out all that cash to buy equip-

Watch Out for Printer Overrun Charges

Early in my design career, I had my first experience with a major printing cost increase that came as a big surprise. We were doing an annual report and the printing bill alone involved a lot of money. The printer I selected was new to me. They were good, and their prices were up there, but the client wanted top quality and I knew this shop could provide it. All went well until the day I received the printer's bill. It was $2,700 more than the original quote. Of course, I had already billed the client based on the original quote, so this new price would have to come out of my profit pocket. When I questioned the printer's sales rep, he showed me the back side of the original price quote. There, in light grey ink and six point type were the words, "Add an additional 10% for print overruns." I knew printers always had to print overruns to account for misprints, but I didn't know that some (not most) printers charge for them.

I felt that even though it was stated in writing on the estimate, because it was on the back side of the quote and since the sales rep hadn't pointed it out, I had grounds for fighting it. And fight it I did. After a letter to the president of the company and a threat to never use their services again, along with a check for payment in full, less the $2,700, the charge was dropped. I never did use that printer again because they put up such a fight.

Always ask about overrun or any other costs that may be submerged in the fine print of a contract.

ment, check out a lease with an option to buy. You can take a deduction on the rental costs that may actually save you more money than the cost depreciation deduction.

♦ If you are going to sell some equipment, and the amount of the sale is sizable, it could affect your tax liability since you will have to claim it as income. You can reduce that liability by setting up the sale's transaction on an installment basis that can be prorated. Then the payments can be claimed during the period of time in which the equipment is being paid for.

♦ Finally, you can take a deduction for abandonment. No, that doesn't mean you can take a loss if a client leaves you for another designer. It means that if you have a piece of equipment or some old furniture that you no longer need or want, you can abandon it rather than store it, which allows you to take a loss on the remaining book value. The same principle applies if you work out of an in-home office in a house that you own, and you have to make a major repair to the house's structure. For example, if you have the whole house re-sided, but there was still some value to the siding that was replaced, your business can take a deduction on the depreciated value of the old siding. In addition, you can deduct the cost of removing the old siding.

Hiring Employees

If you hire an employee, you must have an Employer Identification Number from the IRS. You then must make payroll tax deposits on a monthly basis including your employee's federal withholdings for income, social security (FICA) and Medicare taxes, as well as state (including temporary disability insurance if applicable) and local taxes.

All the money you owe the government, including your studio's matching contribution for social security and Medicare taxes, must be deposited in a depository bank account (one solely for this purpose) by the specified date. You must also send the IRS a quarterly summary of payroll taxes withheld.

You'll want to provide benefits to your employees if you can. Large studios generally offer vacations, health insurance, life insurance, disability insurance and retirement (401K) plans. Although most small studios

can't afford this kind of package, nearly all provide employees with two weeks vacation, some paid holidays, and a reasonable number of paid sick days. Health insurance, the benefit employees want most, is expensive even though it's tax deductible. Research insurance and retirement plans carefully before choosing one for your design business. Work closely with your accountant to determine the best package you can afford. (When budgeting for payroll, add 20 to 25 percent to salaries as part of your labor costs.)

How to Choose an Accountant

To put off hiring an accountant is the biggest mistake many designers make when they first start out in business. I know, because I did it myself. For nearly a year, I convinced myself that I could save money by taking care of my own bookkeeping, billing and tax liabilities. But as April 15 drew closer, I panicked. I had no idea how to prepare my business income taxes. I grabbed the phone book, and selected an accountant based on only one qualification—nearest location to my studio. I ran off to dump my problems in his lap. He got my taxes filed on time, but he wasn't a business accountant. What I learned from that experience is that I had concerns and questions that he couldn't answer. That's when I began my search for an accountant who could not only answer my questions, but tell me what questions I should be asking. My search taught me some important lessons about what to look for when choosing an accountant.

An Accountant Is More Than a Tax Preparer

An accountant is your business adviser and the person who will set up the financial systems you will use to operate your business. Before you even take on your first freelance project, or get your business cards printed, hire an accountant. He or she will get you started on the right foot from the beginning. An accountant will set up your bookkeeping system and show you how to maintain it. He can help you decide what kind of business structure is best for you and when you may need to change it.

An accountant will also keep you informed about your tax liabilities as the laws change. This is especially important when it comes to sales tax regulations, which are always changing and are different for every state. Your accountant can also provide you with the forms necessary to file your monthly sales tax reports and your quarterly self-employment taxes. And if you decide that you need a loan, an accountant can prepare a financial statement (absolutely essential for a business loan) for your lending institution.

When it comes to choosing the right accountant, make sure he is willing to perform all of the services mentioned above. If he suggests that you only need to see each other at tax time, and takes little or no interest in setting up your record keeping system, then this is not the right accountant for you.

A Good Accountant Is Conscientious

A good accountant is not someone who can help you slip through loopholes in the tax laws, so you can get away with paying as little as possible. A good accountant knows the tax laws and is creative in working with them to help you retain as much of your hard-earned income as possible. A good accountant will not risk his or her own reputation by doing anything illegal.

See Your Accountant More Than Once a Year

Your accountant is also your financial planner. Meet with him or her at least every six months to review your financial operations and make sure that you are filing your tax reports properly and on time. An accountant can be especially helpful when you go through a slow income period. She can show you how to economize on your expenditures, cut overhead and review your billing to determine where you may be losing money on a project or undercharging for materials and outside services. Also, your accountant is the one to turn to when you are thinking about buying new equipment. She can tell you not only what you can afford, and what's the best way to pay for it, but what the amortization of the equipment over time will mean in tax ben-

efits. You should also ask your accountant's opinion when you are thinking about hiring a new employee. And if you are planning your future, she can steer you in the right direction with advice on retirement plans, tax shelters and insurance policies.

Don't Look for the Cheapest Prices

Accountants charge anywhere from $50 to $125 an hour. The best way to be sure that your accountant isn't overcharging you is to check with other designers in your area. Find out how much they pay their accountant a year and by the hour.

Be sure to ask, before you actually hire an accountant, how much he would charge you for your yearly tax preparation, a biannual or quarterly (whichever seems most appropriate based on your studio's size) review of your operations, and occasional phone questions that might arise.

Select Your Accountant Based on Referrals

I finally found the right accountant by asking the owners of other design studios who they used as an accountant. When I got several names, I called the State Board of Accountants to see if a complaint had ever been issued against any of them.

Ask Questions

When I met with each of my candidates for an initial interview, I had my questions ready. I had done enough asking around and reading up to know what to expect from an accountant. The first question I asked was if they could help me set up my business's financial system. Two of them hedged the question, giving me the definite impression that it wasn't their favorite thing to do. That ruled them out right away. The third person had two of my competitors as clients. During our first meeting, he told me who their clients were, what clients they were pitching, how much money they made last year, and which one was getting a divorce. Obviously, this was a person who couldn't be trusted with confidential information. The fourth interview turned golden. He was perfect—easy to talk

to, professional, precise in his speech and how he approached his work, experienced with small creative businesses. And he never once revealed anything about his other clients. He was patient as he explained what he would do for me and how he would do it. He didn't use all that accountant mumbo jumbo that makes me crazy. And he clearly explained what I could expect to pay for the services I needed.

It's a Matter of Chemistry

In the end, if it comes down to a choice between two or three accountants who do and say all the right things to impress you, choose the one with whom you feel the most chemistry. You have to be able to get along with this person, trust him, and just plain feel comfortable. This is a long-term relationship. If you feel dismissed every time you call your accountant with a question or put down when you don't understand something, this isn't the right accountant.

All Accountants Are Not the Same

♦ A CPA is a Certified Public Accountant who has taken a prescribed number of courses and passed a thorough and comprehensive state exam resulting in a license to practice. A CPA is also qualified to perform business audits. CPAs must conform to strict standards of professional ethics, and they must also continue to take courses during the time they are in practice to keep pace with tax changes and requirements. In addition, CPAs must go through an audit of their own business practices and procedures every three years.

I strongly recommend you hire a CPA. The training standards and reviews a CPA goes through are good indicators that he or she is not only qualified to prepare your taxes, but also has the expertise necessary to assist you with the financial planning and business management that's essential to running your business smoothly.

♦ A CMA is a Certified Management Accountant. This accountant is more specifically trained to work with larger companies, more often as an internal comptroller or business manager. The program a CMA goes through is

not as extensive as a CPAs, and they are not qualified to perform audits. They also do not have to submit to a personal business practice audit as CPAs do. Many of these accountants will moonlight doing taxes on a freelance basis.

♦ An Enrolled Agent is an accountant who has passed an audit given by the IRS verifying that she is capable of representing a client during an IRS audit. All CPAs must be enrolled agents, but not all accountants are enrolled agents. If you are ever audited, you will want your accountant to be an enrolled agent so that she can represent you.

♦ A Tax Preparer is anyone who is professionally offering his services to the public to prepare taxes. A tax preparer does not have to be an accountant. Many independent bookkeepers move into this arena as their clientele builds and they acquire enough experience to prepare tax returns. There are also a number of commercial tax preparation companies, such as H & R Block. They are fine for personal tax preparation but inappropriate for your business needs.

The Final Burden Rests on Your Record Keeping

Your accountant can only be as good as the records you keep. If you are haphazard or inaccurate, even the most brilliant accountant will have a tough time keeping you on course. So make a commitment to yourself to be faithful about following the systems and procedures your accountant sets up for you.

Freelance Help

If your work load fluctuates a great deal, you may want to use freelancers on a per project basis instead of hiring a part- or full-time employee. You won't have to pay employee taxes even if the freelancer sometimes works in your studio. However, you must be very careful to conduct and document the relationship so it will be clear to the IRS that the freelancer is not an employee.

The issue of hiring freelancers versus hiring employees has become a major concern for both designers and the IRS in the last several years. The IRS sees graphic design studios and advertising agencies as "misclassifying" independent contractors, that is, freelancers. According to the IRS, if a freelancer is working on a regular basis in a design studio's office, using their materials, abiding by their directive when to show up and leave, working only on that studio's clients while in-house and being paid on a regular (weekly or monthly) schedule rather than per project, that person is an employee. As such, the studio is responsible for paying their share of his or her tax withholdings, which include state and federal unemployment taxes, social security and workman's compensation. Numerous small design companies have been audited, sometimes years later, for freelancers the IRS now claims were really misclassified. These studios are responsible for all back taxes, plus accrued penalties. If the IRS feels that the misclassification was intentional, the firm can even be shut down. A number of designers have tried to fight the IRS, even in court, with little success. The one piece of good news amidst the witch hunt is that a moratorium has been called with the IRS regarding this "independent contractor" issue while congress reviews the law. Meanwhile, that moratorium does not apply on the state level, so the red flags are still waving around this issue in terms of state tax liabilities.

How do you protect yourself? There are twenty factors the IRS considers when an investigation occurs. You can call the IRS at (800) 424-3676, and they will send you the publication that clarifies employee/independent contractor classification under ruling 8741, 19871CB296. The highlights of this twenty factor litmus test are as follows:

◆ Does the independent (freelancer) have "ultimate control" (the key factor) over his time, work flow, profit and loss and work location?
◆ Does the independent operate under a business name, purchase the materials used in a project and bill by the project?
◆ Does the independent have an in-home or outside office/studio that is his main place of work, even though occasionally work may be done at a client's office or studio?
◆ Does the independent perform a service that the hiring company does not provide for itself?

The last two points are the sticklers that have been snagging most of the freelancers and the clients who use them. As a freelancer who wants to remain one, you can guard against reclassification by not accepting in-house jobs that last for more than a few weeks at a time. If you do, draw up a contract or have the company that hires you provide one (they have as much, in fact more, to risk financially) stating that:

◆ You are an independent contractor. You will provide your own materials, keep your own hours while working on the premises, bill by the project and provide a service not presently available within the company; call it anything that fits — typographic designer, illustrator, computer specialist, etc.
◆ Always use your business name, business letterhead and invoices for billing, and provide a written estimate for each project.
◆ Have other clients. Don't fall into the comfy, but dangerous trap of letting your time go to one or two clients.
◆ Set up real office space, not just a desk at home that doubles as a work station/drawing board.
◆ Get a business telephone and checking account under your business name.

If you are hiring freelancers, basically the same considerations apply. Provide a contract spelling out the circumstances. See your accountant for advice on how to set it up. You must provide these freelancers with a 1099 form in January and send a copy to the IRS. Insist on written estimates on the freelancer's business stationery, don't furnish materials, and don't be a control freak. Let them come and go at their discretion if they work in your office. If in real doubt, you can always call the IRS and ask for an SS-8 form to fill out, which will request a ruling on a particular situation you may have. But the material I've read warns that once the ruling is given there is no disputing it, and it may flag your company for further investigation for years to come.

The best advice, whether you're a freelancer, freelancer-to-be, or designer hiring freelancers — TALK TO YOUR ACCOUNTANT!

Credit and Collection

There's no 100 percent guaranteed way to avoid problems in collecting payments from clients. But as with many other things, your best defense is a good offense. Establish your payment and credit terms at your first client meeting on a project and stick to them. *Always* get the client's agreement to those terms *in writing* before you begin work.

Adopt policies for advance payment. Stipulate in writing that all new clients will pay as the project progresses, rather than letting them pay thirty or more days after it's done; payment of one-third of the total price estimate on signing the agreement, the next third at the project's midpoint, and the final third upon delivery of the finished project is standard. You may want to ask for 50 percent upfront with new clients. On longer projects you should go to monthly billing even with established clients. Require that both old and new clients pay individual expenses as they're incurred.

Another alternative is to have vendors and subcontractors bill the client directly for all materials and services. Many designers, especially those just getting started, prefer this method because it reduces their out-of-pocket expenses and improves cash flow. If you do this, you can't charge a markup, but it will save you from carrying a hefty bill if the client pays slowly or not at all. Even if you do pay all other out-of-pocket expenses yourself, you should consider billing the printing — your largest single expense — to the client.

Some designers act as print brokers for their clients, making arrangements and overseeing quality control but having the client pay the printer. These designer/print brokers then receive a commission from the printer for their services.

When it's time to bill the client, do so promptly. Keep careful records so you know when you have to follow up and can do so immediately. Be aggressive in your collection efforts. You're entitled to that money, so don't

feel or be apologetic about asking for it. On the other hand, being hostile and angry isn't going to help your cause. You improve your chances of collecting any bill if you can establish a direct, friendly relationship with the person who actually pays the client's bills — usually the company's accountant or bookkeeper. Some designers offer a 5 percent discount for payment on the day the project is due. They often protect themselves against clients who don't pay as stated but still take the discount by increasing their estimate by 5 percent.

Check Out a New Client's Credit History

When you acquire new clients, it's smart to check out their credit history. Even if you don't extend credit to new clients for the first project, always check on them before you do additional projects. Most clients with bad credit ratings will be on their best behavior early in the relationship with a creditor. Once the relationship has been established, payment gets gradually slower.

There are several ways to investigate a client's credit. Check the local credit bureaus for information. Some only give out reports to subscribing businesses, so you'll have to find those that will help you. Check out local clients through your contacts in the community. Call a few vendors, subcontractors or other designers who may have worked with this client before. You can also contact the Better Business Bureau or the state attorney general's office if you come up empty with your own contacts.

Ask for three credit references from all clients new to the area, from a local client with a big project, and when you're worried about a business's financial health. (Get personal credit references, too, on a sole proprietorship.) Of course, they'll only give you the names of contacts who'll give a good report. But you can ask each reference if they know anyone else who may have done business with this client. If you get a name that the client didn't give you, call that business, too. Ask each reference you call:

◆ How long has your client been a customer?

- What is the client's payment record?
- Does the client pay within the agreed time?
- Has there been any significant change in the client's payment habits in the last six months?

Be very wary of the client who gives you only one reference — that may be the only bill he or she pays regularly and on time. Although you want to get a reference from the client's bank, that shouldn't be the only reference you get. Even if they have money in the bank, they may not pay their bills. Get as much information as you can. Ask for the names and addresses of relatives, professional affiliations, the home office (if appropriate), and other information that will help you track down a nonpaying client.

When a Client Questions the Bill

A raging client calls — this is not at all what he expected to pay for this project. He hurls some nasty remarks, suggesting you're unethical, if not dishonest! What do you do now? No matter how many times this happens — and it does happen to all of us despite our best precautions — we're never prepared for it. Our first response will be fear or anger.

Most clients will be polite and professional when questioning a bill. But when one blows up, do your best to remain calm. Just listen to him or her without interrupting. Try to understand exactly what the problem is. Is it the entire bill or one specific area that is in question? Then acknowledge and express sympathy for his or her feelings. Don't discuss the bill until you have a copy of it and any other forms to substantiate the invoice, such as the price estimate, in front of you. Ask for time to review the client's file. This will give the client a chance to calm down before you discuss it further. Set a time to return the call. The nicer you are, the harder it will be for them to stay angry.

Once you have all the information in front of you, decide how to settle the problem. Either you made an error or she misunderstood some aspect of the price estimate, the payment terms or whatever. Explain calmly, and without accusation, where the misunder-

standing occurred. Offer to send copies of any forms to document the amount owed. If the bill was wrong, apologize and either have the client make the adjustment directly on the bill or issue a new bill.

If the client refuses to pay when the misunderstanding was clearly her fault, there may be another, hidden, problem. Try to remain sympathetic, but don't back down. Restate causes and circumstances of the miscommunication. If the client remains upset, ask if something other than the bill is the problem. Sometimes when a client is unhappy with something about the project, she may divert her displeasure toward the bill rather than tell you what's actually wrong. You may not want to hear it, but in the long run it's to your advantage to know if there really was another problem. Remember that word of mouth can be the most effective form of positive or negative advertising for your business. An unhappy client may turn countless others away from you. Try to solve the client's problem with the project. If you can't, offer them a discount of 10 or 15 percent on the next one. If nothing you suggest satisfies this client, be pleasant but insist on holding to the written agreement and the bill. Say goodbye, and get on with your work.

Collecting Late Payments

Far too much energy goes into dealing with late payers. But there are ways to get the client to pay without embarrassing him and preserve a good business relationship. Sometimes all it takes is working out a schedule of partial payments — smaller amounts over a longer period of time.

Check your accounts payable records twice a month. The sooner you go after someone who's late the better your chances of collecting. Begin your pursuit of a late paying client with a monthly statement that itemizes overdue balances. Add on the interest rate of 1½ percent for each remaining balance. Invest in two self-inking stamps that say: "Payment due upon receipt" and "Overdue." The first time you send out a client statement with interest, stamp "Overdue" next to each balance that is beyond thirty days, but under sixty. When a statement reflects a balance

Collection Notices

This system of stamping invoices as overdue and due upon receipt worked very well for me. Other people prefer to send separate letters or notices to delinquent accounts. These list only unpaid, overdue items and stress the need for prompt payment, with each notice making a stronger demand for payment. Each also asks the client to contact you with any problems. The standard sequence of collection letters or forms is a first, second and final notice – at which point you alert the client that nonpayment means you turn it over to a collection agency or lawyer.

When You Have to Pay a Vendor Before a Client Pays You

This shouldn't be a problem if you've planned carefully and managed your cash flow well. You should be collecting from clients promptly so you have that money available to handle incoming bills for work in progress. But in spite of your best efforts, there will be times when a bill is due to be paid and you won't have the money. What can you do?

Ask the vendor for more time. If you have a serious cash flow problem but a good relationship with your creditor, talk honestly with them. Explain that the client was billed and you expect the money anytime now. Ask if it would create a problem if you send the payment when you receive the client's money. But if you do this, tell your creditor that if you don't have the client's money within a certain time, you'll pay the bill yourself. That way, you are making it clear that you won't keep the vendor hanging on indefinitely. Or you can ask for an extended schedule of smaller payments over a period of time, perhaps with payment in full to arrive as soon as the client pays you. If you can make this kind of an arrangement with your vendors, they will usually hold off on charging you interest for payments made after thirty days.

You can take up to sixty days to pay. It's not unusual or unprofessional to take up to sixty days to pay a bill. Some businesses even go 120 days. Personally, I think that's taking advantage of your vendors. But in an emergency it may be better than withdrawing money from your personal savings or taking out a loan, when you have no idea when a client will pay her bill. Remember that you'll be charged interest, usually 1½ percent, or 18 percent annually, after thirty days.

that has gone past sixty days, stamp it payment due upon receipt. Make follow-up calls after the client has had time to receive the notice. It's easier to resolve problems when you catch them early. The problem may be only the lack of a purchase order or an invoice your client forgot to approve. Or it may be something big, but at least you'll know. Personal contact is often the best way to do that.

Stamp any balances that go into the 120-day category "Payment due upon receipt," but also write in red pen next to or below the stamp, "Please contact us if there is a problem paying this bill upon receipt. Otherwise, if payment is not received within five business days, this matter will be turned over to our attorney." Send any notice indicating that collection action is imminent in a way that requires the client to sign a receipt acknowledging delivery. That's your legal proof you properly notified him or her. Be sure that "Client subject to reasonable attorney's fees if collection is necessary" is on every invoice and client statement, because you can't legally charge interest or attorney's fees without this statement of policy.

Personal contact with a slow-paying client can often speed up the process. But sometimes it's hard to do yourself if you dread confrontation. Before I had a bookkeeper to handle this, I used a little gimmick to investigate discreetly. When I had a collection problem with a client, a fellow designer would call my client and, using the fictitious name Mary Whitmore, say that she was my business manager. She would then explain that she was checking on the status of payment for such and such an invoice. I would do the same for her. Our secret was never discovered, and it worked beautifully, because the fictitious Mary Whitmore was an impartial third person with whom the client could speak frankly about misunderstandings regarding the bill or could explain why making the payment was difficult without losing face with the designer.

If a client wants to continue working with you after you've had collection difficulties, consider restructuring the relationship. Notify the client calmly and objectively that it is your policy to require a client to establish a new credit rating when a payment problem occurs. Explain that for a three- or six-month period (whatever seems appropriate) no further credit can be extended. Then tell the client that it is standard policy that all such accounts (such phrases keep clients from feeling like they're being singled out) return to payment in thirds.

If a Client Refuses to Pay

When all your efforts to solicit a payment from a client have failed, you may be forced to turn the matter over to an attorney or a collection agency. Depending on the amount, you may be better off financially if you don't pursue payment and take a tax deduction for the loss. You may also lose 25 to 40 percent of the amount due since collection agencies operate on a contingency basis, taking part of the balance due as their payment if they collect. Many attorneys work the same way. An uncooperative client can cost you substantial money in legal fees to pursue the matter with no guarantee that they'll pay. You may find it more effective and affordable to pursue bills for less than $1,000 in Small Claims Court yourself.

If you want to make a last ditch attempt to resolve an unpaid bill before turning to a collections professional, there is a method that sometimes works. Write a letter to the president of the company—who may not be your contact. Explain clearly, but politely, your inability to collect payment. Attach copies of any items, such as contracts, production orders or price estimates, that support your position. Convey, in nonjudgmental language, your disappointment in the company and your regret that you will now be forced to turn this over to an attorney (a collection agency isn't as threatening) if payment isn't received in ten days and that copies of this letter and all attachments are being sent to the Better Business Bureau, the state attorney general's office, Dun & Bradstreet and professional groups they belong to.

This may be all it takes to solve the problem. But, this tactic works only with those clients who value their reputation in the community. And believe it or not, there are many who don't. It's sad but true that many businesspeople no longer see stiffing their creditors as being unethical. Since there's less social stigma to being in debt or even going bankrupt, these people think that not paying their debts is another tactic for business survival. Some will ignore your notice as an empty threat, so you have to be prepared to back it up with action. Or they'll fight you with their own attorney, finding some reason why your bill is invalid or in error. That's when signed agreements are worth their weight in gold.

CHAPTER

four

Work
Smarter,
Not
Harder

Breaking Appointments

Don't break an appointment unless you have no other choice. When you do reschedule a meeting, always try to do it at the other person's convenience. And never, never keep a client waiting. If you are running late, call ahead so that they can reschedule if they are now short on time or use the time until you arrive.

If you have to reschedule a client meeting, always do it in a professional manner. In other words, your explanation should have to do with business, not your personal life (even if it is because your child fell out of a tree).

e were raised to believe that if we worked harder, we'd get ahead faster. Today, those who work *smarter*, get ahead faster. Working smarter means making the most out of every working hour by finding the fastest, most effective way to get the job done.

Since how much you make as a designer depends on how much billable time you have, you must squeeze as many project-related hours as possible out of each workday. That means you've got to deal with other tasks in the most effective manner to give yourself more billable time. Reducing the number of your mistakes (can't bill the client for those!) increases your billable time, too. If you take less time per project, you can handle more projects and bring in more money. This doesn't require working at the speed of light every minute; all it requires is planning and organization.

It's not easy to train ourselves to plan before we work. We see those looming deadlines and decide we just can't spare the time to plan. So many times I've plunged into a project headfirst because I was in a hurry. After grunting and groaning my way through it, I'd discover that I'd made some big mistake and would have to start over. Why? Because I hadn't stopped to check the specs carefully or to make sure I could get that paper in time.

Planning does pay. In his book, *The Time Trap*, time management guru Alec Mackenzie assures us that "one minute of planning saves four minutes of wheel-spinning." For every hour you spend planning, you're saving four hours of potentially billable time. Multiply that by your hourly fee, and you're talking big bucks in savings. I'll show you how easy it is.

The process of project organization is similar to putting together a large picture puzzle. You spread the pieces out in front of you. You compare the end result, the picture, to the disconnected pieces on the table. Then one by one you can organize the individual pieces of the puzzle into sections that match up with the different areas of the picture. Working within those sections, you will begin to see the connections between the pieces.

You tackle a project the same way. You look at the big picture—the project's goals. Then you break the project down into its smallest pieces and arrange them in a logical sequence. With the sequence in place, you can easily move through each phase of the project. Let's walk through a sample project so you can see how the various systems and procedures we've discussed in the last two chapters can work for you.

A Sales Brochure for Taylor & Derne Electronics

Over a month ago you pitched a sales brochure to Richard Taylor, the president of Taylor & Derne Electronics, Inc. You haven't heard anything more and pretty much gave up on the project. But today there's a message on your answering machine to return his call ASAP. When you finally get to Mr. Taylor, he tells you they've decided to give you the project. Because of the delay in making their decision, Taylor would like to meet tomorrow. You pull out your master project schedule and thankfully discover that you can start right away.

Step One: Prepare for the First Client Meeting

It's important that your first meeting with the client goes well. It will set the tone and structure of the whole working relationship. If you are prepared when you enter the client's office, you can ask the right questions to get the information and the direction you need not only to see but also to understand the big picture—the project's goals. So you review what you know about this project and write out a meeting agenda.

You already know from your presentation what this client hopes to achieve: to reach a new and untapped market for their products—teenagers who are fascinated by electronic gadgetry. You have a general idea of his style and design preferences and the image his company has tried to portray through other printed pieces. Although you believe you understand his goals and objectives, you'll bring along a Client Information Sheet to fill in any missing pieces of information. You don't know why he decided to go with you. You need to ask him to explain his reasons, so you can deliver exactly what he wants and expects. Then you want to discuss his desired time frame and evaluate whether it's realistic. You also need to nail down the project's specifications and the budget.

Next, you'll explain about his reviewing and approving the price estimate and the production schedule. This is also the time to clearly state your policies regarding payment schedules and the terms and agreement form or contract you'll ask him to sign. Bring a

blank copy, so that he can read it through before you give him the real thing. This way if there are any problems, disagreements or confusions, they can be settled right away. You'll explain his role in reviewing and approving project materials and describe the project summaries he'll receive.

As you begin your work with a new client, it's important to clarify the areas of responsibility each of you has. *Your* responsibilities include: fair and ethical pricing, producing your best quality work, advising your clients when you know they want something that is wrong for them, keeping any confidential client information to yourself, and completing the project on time. *Client* responsibilities are: giving you information you need to do a good job, returning materials on time, making every effort to be available for meetings and approval sessions, and honoring your terms for payment.

Richard Taylor Meeting Agenda:

1. **Why did you hire me – what's expected from me?**
2. **Run through Client Information Sheet.**
3. **Discuss project's time frame. Is it doable?**
4. **Go through project specs.**
5. **Explain payment policy for new clients, terms and agreement form, price estimates, production schedules, project summaries, and client approvals at various stages.**
6. **Confirm date for a follow-up meeting on prices and schedule.**

You put your notepad, a blank Client Information Sheet and an Agreement of Terms and

Conditions form in your briefcase. Now you're ready to leave in the morning without having to fuss around at the last minute gathering up the things you need.

Step Two: First Client Meeting

Listen carefully, take notes, keep the meeting moving smoothly.

When you meet with Taylor, your enthusiasm continues as you both recap the presentation. While you're talking, you learn why he decided to go with you. He thought that you were the kind of thorough, detail-oriented person he wanted. (Great! Detail *is* your strong suit.) He also felt that you would allow him to participate creatively in the project. (Gulp! Is the guy a control freak?) This can get sticky, but you'll plan to send him *frequent* project summaries and to allow extra time for approval. You make a note to remind yourself to involve him in each stage of the project's development and encourage his ideas and participation.

Although you had planned to lead into your Client Information Sheet by asking when Taylor had worked with a designer before, he starts to talk about his role in founding the company. So you'll introduce the sheet by ask-

Client Information Sheet

YOUR BUSINESS LOGO

Client Name: Richard Taylor

Company Represented: Taylor & Derne Electronics, Inc.

Address: 57 Industrial Dr.

City/State/Zip: Center City, NS 99999

Telephone/Fax: PH: (999) 555-1234 FAX: (999) 555-2345

What is the nature of the client's business? mail order & direct sales of electronic leisure equipment; toys, games, radios, television attachments for family entertainment

How long has the company been in business? 5 years

Who are its competitors? Radio Shack and Impulse

What does the client expect from you? To develop a sales brochure for their retail outlets marketing electronic toys and games to the pre-teen and teen audience.
SPECIAL NOTE: Must make sure that Taylor feels he's actively involved with project

Has the client ever worked with designers before, and if so, in what capacity? yes; produced an image/identity package, direct mail pieces and sales brochures. from Taylor's concern about being involved, sounds like there may have been problems

What type of graphics project does this client want to do? occasional brochure like this one; mostly sales flyers, direct mail

What would the client like to accomplish with this project? to open a new market with 11-18-year-olds

What are the client's personal goals in this business? to make HIS company the number one nationwide manufacturer/distributor of electronic toys, games and leisure equipment. He's probably the creative, marketing ideas man; Derne probably financial, more conservative

Project Description/Specifications: sales brochure--quantity 30,000 (20,000 bulk mailed, 10,000 to client; printed size 12-1/2" x 10-1/2", fold size 10-1/2" x 6-1/4" with 1 fold; printed two sides, 3 colors (black + 2 PMS?); 4 panels; approx. 15 halftones. BUDGET = $10,000-$12,000

ing for more information on the company's products at the next clear break in the conversation.

Taylor begins to slow down as he answers—a signal to bring the meeting to an end. While you don't want to cut a client off during a discussion, try to sense when the meeting has run its natural course. To be certain that you have clearly understood what the client wants and needs in this project, you will finish the meeting by summarizing what you believe he has said. That gives him the opportunity to correct any mistaken impressions. You set a date for the next meeting—two weeks from today—and explain what he can expect to see then.

Step Three: Break the Project Down Into Phases

When you get back to your studio, you take a half hour to review your notes and set up a project file. Taylor's marketing director has spent a lot of time researching their target market because it's new for them. They gave you lots of information before the earlier presentation, so you started out on target. The additional materials Taylor gave you at your meeting appear to reinforce the direction you originally took. In fact, Taylor liked the concept you presented a month ago and has only requested some minor changes in approach. That saves you a lot of time, because you won't have to start out from scratch (or start over on) developing the concept.

Now you break the project down into specific phases. (This listing of phases and the production schedule used in this chapter follow traditional production methods, terms and schedules. I've done this for clarity and simplicity, since not all designers own computers or use them for the same production chores.)

Taylor & Derne Project Phases

1. Prepare the schedule, initial price estimate and terms and agreement form.
2. Select copywriter and photographer. Call for quotes and date confirmations based on specs.
3. Select three printers to bid on the job and

Schedule Snags

Not every project is this easy to schedule. You may suddenly discover you can't make a deadline because of other work. In that case, you may be able to farm out part of the work to a freelance designer. But if you can't find a good, realistic solution, be up front with your client. Give him or her the option of finding another designer. You might be able to work miracles and get it all done, but what suffers if you don't? At least one client's project and your reputation. It's better to give up a job than to blow it.

If the client has set an unreasonable deadline, you'll have to try to persuade him or her to change it. Or try to negotiate compromises on design elements such as eliminating four-color printing or photographs to reduce the amount of time needed for the job. Or try to get approval for a bigger budget, so you can hire extra help or pay premium rates for rush jobs.

Sometimes nothing works, and the client insists on having that exact project on that precise schedule at that set budget with top quality. At that point, you may have to tell the client that it's against your professional judgment to take responsibility for this project. This is usually enough to convince the client to back down. If it isn't, *walk away fast.* You're in a no-win situation if you go on: either you won't make the deadline and the client gets mad or you can't deliver the quality work needed and the client gets mad. Make every effort to resolve the situation, but know when to give up, too.

call for quotes based on specs.
4. Meet with client to review prices, schedule and general ideas.
5. Have project review and creative session with copywriter and photographer.
6. Lay out roughs.
7. Review copy.
8. Adapt copy to layouts—decide which ones will work best.
9. Prepare layout comps and copy samples to go to the client for approval.
10. Meet with client for approvals.
11. Call specialty type house about charges for setting headline in typeface you saw in catalog. Order if price is right.
12. Revise layout files; begin to set them up as mechanicals.
13. Photo shoot of products.
14. Contact sheets ready for client approval.
15. Photos delivered from photographer—send out for veloxes.
16. Meet with client to approve mechanicals.

17. Make changes.
18. Do final mechanical review.
19. Send files to service bureau for output on RC paper.
20. Deliver output to printer.
21. Have client approve blueline.
22. Press approval. Have client attend.

Step Four: Set Up a Tentative Production Schedule

Sketch out a rough production schedule based on your list of phases for the project. Although you can't determine a final schedule until you've gotten bids and dates from your subcontractors, you can estimate the time needed for each phase. Add that information to your list, allowing slightly more time than you think you'll really need. For example, it may only take the client one or two hours to review the blueline, but he may not get to it till late in the day. Budget one day for "Have client approve blueline."

Taylor wants to have this brochure ready to mail in six weeks. As you review the project phases you've listed, you feel the time frame is workable. You're ready to move ahead.

Step Five: Contact Subcontractors

You call a copywriter and a photographer that you work with on a regular basis to see if they are available for this project. They are, and you give them the specs over the phone. (If

something can be discussed with a phone meeting rather than in person, do it.) They promise to get back to you in a few days with written price quotes and schedule confirmation. Just as a backup, however, you send a written spec sheet to another copywriter and photographer you've worked with. You like to compare quotes, just to be sure you're being given competitive rates. And you never can tell what will happen in this business. If you are counting on one person, who suddenly can't come through on this project, it may be too late to find a replacement. Having a backup, until you receive a written confirmation of prices and schedules, will give you a safety cushion.

Step Six: Send Bid Request Forms to Three Printers

You now call three printers to see if they want to bid on the brochure. You explain your schedule requirements and find out if they have press time available when you need it. Talking with them ahead of time also helps you to troubleshoot any production or schedule problems that may not have occurred to you. All three feel they can handle the job on your schedule, so you tell them that you're sending the bid request forms out today. If you were going to output film from disk rather than have the printer make the film, you would also have checked on the film specs for the service bureau output. All three printers promise to return the forms within the week. (See pages 142-143 for more on working with printers.)

If you call printers and subcontractors all at the same time, it's easier to remember the project specifications and the questions that surface as you discuss the project with each of them.

YOUR BUSINESS LOGO

Printing Bid Request

Printing Company: _Sloan Printing_
Contact Person: _Dan Sloan_
Address: _25 S. Main St., Center City, NS 99999_
Telephone/Fax: _(999) 555-1212/(999) 555-1222_
Designer's Name: _Ima Designer_   Date: _1/15_
Project Description: _Sales Brochure_   Project Number: _911501_

Printing Specifications
Quantities to Print: _30,000_
Paper Stock: _L.O.E.--Gloss_
# of Sides: _2_   # of Colors: _3:BLK & 2 PMS_   PMS ink #s: _481 & 232_
Delivered as Camera-Ready Film: ____
Delivered as Electronic Disk Files: ____
Prepress Service/Service Bureau: _Hot Shots_
Contact: _Kelly Wade_   Telephone: _555-1223_
Stripping Required, See Specs Below: _Camera-ready line art, duotones to be created_
Bleeds: _yes-2 sides 20%_   Screens: _15-duotones_   Reverses: _yes-2_
Halftones: _15 duotones_   Film: _yes_   Separations: _no_
Proofs/Blueline: _yes_   Color Key: _no_   Chromalin Proof: _yes_
Print Size: _12-1/2 x 10-1/2_   Score: _yes_   Fold: _yes-1_
Finished Size: _10-1/2 x 6-1/4_   Bindery: _no_   Emboss: _no_
Die Cut: _no_   Perforations: _no_   Drills: _no_
Thermography: _no_   Varnish: _no_   Other: ____
Pack: _yes_   Mailing: _Yes, bulk mail-20,000_

Mailing Instructions: _Bulk mail-carrier sort-20,000_

Delivery Instructions: _Remaining 10,000 delivered to Taylor & Derne Electronics,_
57 Industrial Dr., Center City, before noon.

Date Due: _March 1_
Please return bid by: _1/19_

Step Seven: Fill Out a Production Schedule

You fill out a production schedule right after talking with the printers and subcontractors, while dates and other details are still fresh in your mind.

Using a calendar and working backward from the Delivery Date to Client, you fill in that date and continue working up the schedule to the beginning of the project. Work the schedule around the dates and time frames your subcontractors and printers gave you.

Production Schedule — Page 1 YOUR BUSINESS LOGO

Project: Taylor & Deme Sales Brochure Project Number: 911501
Name/Description: Teen Brochure

Phase 1 — Concept
Client Meetings	Due Date	1/15
Concept Development	Due Date	1/22
Contact Subs/Vendors	Due Date	1/15
Estimates from Subcontractors	Due Date	1/19
Project Estimate	Due Date	1/19 to client 1/20
Design	Due Date	1/24
Copy	Due Date	1/24
Editing	Due Date	1/26
Revisions	Due Date	—
Client Approval	Due Date	—

Phase 2 — Production
Layout	Due Date	—
Client Approval	Due Date	—
Comprehensive	Due Date	1/28
Client Approval	Due Date	1/29
Copy Revisions	Due Date	1/31
Client Approval	Due Date	—
Type Ordered	Due Date	1/27
Type Proofed	Due Date	1/28
Other Sub Work Photo Shoot	Due Date Shoot: 2/3, Photos: 2/7
Client Approval	Due Date	

Send copies of the completed schedule to each subcontractor and attach one with each Printing Bid Request form. Highlight the places where each subcontractor's date commitments appear on the schedule. This will help them see, at a glance, exactly where they fit into the project schedule. You also make a copy for your next meeting with the client.

Step Eight: When You Get the Quotes, Do a Price Quote Estimate

You fill out a Price Estimate Work Sheet, and then transfer those figures to a Price Quote Estimate form (double-checking everything, of course). Your budget for the project was

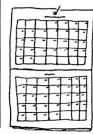

$10,000-$12,000, and you wanted to come in right around $10,000 on your quote. That way, you'll still be safely under the maximum limit if — despite your being careful — the project comes in higher than your initial estimate. Although you're never happy about having to explain that a project came in higher than you estimated, you've found that clients do take the news *much* better if you can point out that you're still within the budget range. So, you're especially pleased to discover that you're actually under $10,000 — at $9,797 in fact.

When you've completed it, you insert the Price Estimate Work Sheet into the billing book along with a Work In Progress form that you fill out at the same time. That way it's ready when you start work.

Before you're finished, you still need to make a copy of the Price Quote Estimate to take to your next client meeting. And while you're at it, you might as well fill out a Produc-

Can I Get Part of It Sooner?

What if a client asks you to design and produce 2,000 printed folders with coordinated insert sheets for an identity/capabilities package? He needs these in eight weeks for a national convention. That's workable. But two days into the project, he asks if he could have 100 of them for a special meeting next week that he just found out about.

Solution: Obviously, this is physically impossible to do — even with unlimited help and an unlimited budget. You'll have to tell him no, but do it carefully so you don't lose the whole job. Explain that it takes the same amount of time to design and produce 100 as it does 2,000, so you can't make up time due to that. And that this job with these specifications will take the entire eight weeks scheduled. (Be prepared to describe in detail why that's the case.) Once they understand the problems, many clients will accept the situation.

Depending on the client, you may want to offer an alternative. In this case, you could suggest using standard, solid color folders available from most printers for this one event. You, or someone else, will design and typeset inserts and have them laser printed. (This is especially easy to do if you're working on a computer.) Be sure he understands that such a rush job won't be the same quality as the piece he originally ordered and is willing to accept that. If he's willing, send a Client Change Order for his signature confirming the nature and quality of the rush job and the additional charges for it.

tion Order and an Agreement of Terms and Conditions form, so they will be ready to take to the meeting as well. (Samples of these completed forms appear on pages 120 and 122.)

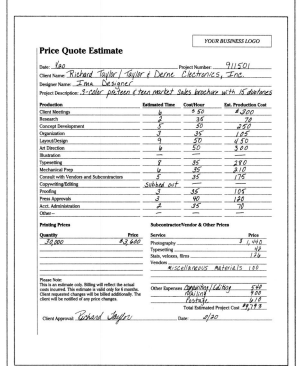

Price Estimate Work Sheet — YOUR BUSINESS LOGO

Client: Taylor & Derne Project Number: 911501
Project Description: Sales Brochure: 3-color, 15 duotones, printed both sides, 4 panels

Production	Time	Cost/Hour	Total Production Cost
Client Meetings	6	$50	$300
Research	2	35	70
Concept Development	5	50	250
Organization	3	35	105
Layout/Design	9	50	450
Art Direction	6	50	300
Illustration	—	—	—
Typesetting	8	35	280
Mechanical Prep	6	35	210
Consult with Vendors and Subcontractors	5	35	175
Copywriting/Editing	Subbed out	—	—
Proofing	3	35	105
Press Approvals	3	40	120
Acct. Administration	2	35	70
Other—	—	—	—

Printing Prices

Quantity	Price	Markup 20%	Client's Price
30,000	$3,000	$600	$3,600

Subcontractor/Vendor & Other Prices

Service	Price	Markup 20%	Client's Price
Photography	$1,200	$240	$1,440
Typesetting out of house	35	7	42
Stats, veloxes, films (Svc. Bureau)	105	21	126
Other Copy	450	90	540
Mailing & postage	750 + 610	150 + none	1,510 + 610
Misc. Materials	80	20	100

Total Project Cost: $9,793

Price Quote Estimate — YOUR BUSINESS LOGO

Date: 1/20 Project Number: 911501
Client Name: Richard Taylor / Taylor & Derne Electronics, Inc.
Designer Name: Ima Designer
Project Description: 3-color preteen & teen market sales brochure with 15 duotones

Production	Estimated Time	Cost/Hour	Est. Production Cost
Client Meetings	6	$50	$300
Research	2	35	70
Concept Development	5	50	250
Organization	3	35	105
Layout/Design	9	50	450
Art Direction	6	50	300
Illustration	—	—	—
Typesetting	8	35	280
Mechanical Prep	6	35	210
Consult with Vendors and Subcontractors	5	35	175
Copywriting/Editing	Subbed out	—	—
Proofing	3	35	105
Press Approvals	3	40	120
Acct. Administration	2	35	70
Other—	—	—	—

Printing Prices

Quantity	Price
30,000	$3,600

Subcontractor/Vendor & Other Prices

Service	Price
Photography	$1,440
Typesetting	42
Stats, veloxes, films	126
Vendors Miscellaneous Materials	100
Other Expenses Copywriting/Editing	540
Mailing	900
Postage	610

Total Estimated Project Cost $9,793

Please Note:
This is an estimate only. Billing will reflect the actual costs incurred. This estimate is valid only for 6 months. Client requested changes will be billed additionally. The client will be notified of any price changes.

Client Approval: Richard Taylor Date: 2/20

Step Nine: Begin Concept Development by Reviewing Your Client Notes

Now for the fun part—developing the concept! You review the client's information sheet and the notes you took during the meeting to be sure that you understand not only what Taylor wants graphically from the project, but what his goals for it are. When you're ready, you begin to sketch out some initial ideas that you can discuss with him during the next meeting.

Step Ten: The Second Client Meeting

The day before your next meeting with Taylor, you write up your meeting agenda. (If you use

TIME SAVER

an agenda for every client meeting, you can avoid having to schedule extra meetings—wasting the client's time and yours—to review something you forgot to do the last time.) You need to review prices, the production schedule and concept ideas with him. If these are approved, you need to get a signed Production Order and Agreement of Terms and Conditions. You'll then ask for a check for one-third of the total project price. With the agenda completed and copies of the Production Schedule, Price Quote Estimate, and Agreement of Terms and Conditions form made, you're ready.

As you expected, Taylor is delighted with the prices. (If he'd rejected them, you'd have either found where you could cut costs or negotiated a compromise with him.)

You've highlighted the client's copy of the schedule to clearly show the dates when he needs to be available to approve the various phases of the project. Fortunately, Taylor is anxious to have input and will make himself available then.

You only talk to Taylor about your ideas and get his reactions. You'll share the visuals after he approves the project and signs the Production Order. You learned the hard way not to take rough layout sketches into a client meeting before you had a signed contract. In fact, you once foolishly left some original sketches with the client without keeping copies for yourself. He said he wanted to think about your ideas, but you never heard from him again. Three months later, you saw a brochure for his company that strongly resembled your sketches. You'll never make that mistake again!

Taylor has a few suggestions. You make notes, so you'll remember exactly what he

wanted. He asks a few questions about your Agreement of Terms and Conditions form.

He's satisfied with your answers and signs. Because this is a short-term project, you agreed to one-third of the money on signing the agreement, one-third on mechanical approval, and one-third on delivery of the brochures. On a long-term project, you'd have arranged to bill him monthly, rather than at the end of the project because you get a better cash flow that way. You have him sign the Production Order at the same time. He even offered to get you a check while you were there! (If only they would all go this smoothly.)

Step Eleven: Return to Your Studio and Get Going

Back in your studio, you immediately fill out a Project Time Sheet for this brochure and put it on a clipboard. If you don't do this right away, you end up putting it off until you're halfway through the project. And if you keep the clipboard next to your drawing board, you always remember to record your time as you work on a project.

You call your photographer, printer and copywriter to let them know that the project is a go. You also confirm their work and dead-

---

Agreement of Terms and Conditions

YOUR BUSINESS LOGO

Client Name: Richard Taylor
Company the Client Represents: Taylor & Derne Electronics, Inc.
Company Address: 57 Industrial Dr.
City/State/Zip: Center City, NS 99999
Telephone/Fax Number: PH: (999) 555-1234 Fax: (999) 555-2345
Project Name: Sales Brochure
Project Description: 3-color brochure to introduce retail outlets to preteens and teens

1. The total cost for this project is estimated at: $9,797.00 (See attached estimate)
2. All expenses incurred to complete this order shall be the responsibility of the client.
3. Upon receipt of full payment, Designer grants to the Client the following rights in the designs: ownership of the mechanicals upon receipt of payment in full for the project

All rights not expressly granted in this agreement remain the exclusive property of the Designer. Unless otherwise specified, Designer retains ownership of all original artwork, whether preliminary or final, and Client shall return such artwork within sixty (60) days after use.

4. Payment for this project will be made according to the following schedule: One-third due on signing this agreement; one-third due on approval of the mechanicals; one-third due on delivery of brochures to the mail shop.
5. Payment for all invoices are due: on receipt. A 1½% monthly service charge is payable on overdue balances.
6. Designer fees quoted apply only to regular working hours—9 A.M. to 5 P.M., Monday through Friday. If the client requests that project work be performed at times other than the stipulated office hours, additional overtime fees of $5.00 per hour will be charged, except for corrections made necessary by the designer.
7. All costs are estimates only. Any alterations by the client of project specifications may result in price changes.
8. All additional costs that exceed the original estimate will be quoted to the client, in writing, before the costs are incurred.
9. The designer/design company does not have the authority to exceed this estimate without client approval.
10. The terms and conditions of this agreement are valid for only thirty (30) days.
11. The designer/design company's ability to meet the requirements of the Production Order and Production Schedule (see attached), is totally dependent on the client's delivery at the time specified on the production schedule (see attached) of any and all materials needed to complete the project.
12. If the project is cancelled at any time, the client is responsible for all expenses incurred to that point.
13. If a dispute arises between the designer/design company and the client over any term or condition agreed to in this agreement, the client will be subject to pay all reasonable attorney's fees if the dispute requires legal counsel.

I have agreed to the terms and conditions presented in this agreement as it applies to the project named and described above.

Client signature: Richard Taylor   Date: 1/20

Production Order

YOUR BUSINESS LOGO

Client: Richard Taylor
Company Represented: Taylor & Derne Electronics, Inc.
Date: 1/20
Project Name: Sales Brochure

Project Description:
Develop a brochure to be printed in a quantity of 30,000.
Printing specs: 3 colors- BLK & 2 PMS colors. Printed on 2 sides with approximately 15 duotones. Printed size: 12-1/2" x 10-1/2". Fold size: 10-1/2" x 6-1/4"--1 fold, 4 panels. 20,000 to be mailed. 10,000 delivered to client.

Project Objectives:
A brochure to target a new market--preteens & teenagers--introducing Taylor & Derne electronic toys & games sold in nationwide retail outlets.

Price Estimate Total: (See attached Price Quote Estimate for breakdown)
$9,793.00
Due Date: March 1
Schedule: attached

Special Information: Copywriting & editing to be subcontracted by designer.

Client Authorization Signature to Begin Work:
Richard Taylor   Date: 1/20

Project Time Sheet

YOUR BUSINESS LOGO

Employee Name: _____

FUNCTION CODES		
01 Consultation/Meetings	08 Typesetting	15 Revisions
02 Research	09 Mechanical Prep	16 Client Changes
03 Concept Development	10 Consult Vendors/Subs	17 Other—
04 Organization	11 Copywriting/Editing	18 Other—
05 Layout/Design	12 Proofing	19 Other—
06 Art Direction	13 Press Approvals	20 Other—
07 Illustration	14 Acct. Administration	21 Other—

Client: Taylor & Derne
Project Name: Teen Brochure   Project Number: 911501

Date	Function Code	Time Began	Time Ended	Total Hours
1/15	01	9:00	10:00	1
1/15	04	1:00	3:00	2
1/15	10	3:00	4:00	1
1/15	14	5:00	6:00	1
1/16	03	10:30	11:30	1
1/17	03	2:00	5:00	3
1/18	14	2:15	3:15	1
1/22	06	2:00	4:00	2
1/23	10	9:00	10:00	1
1/23	03	10:00	11:00	1
1/24	05	8:30	10:30	2
1/24	08	10:30	12:00	1.5
1/24	05	12:30	4:00	3.5
1/26	05	9:00	10:00	1
1/26	10	11:00	12:00	1
1/26	08	1:00	5:00	4
1/29	01	9:00	10:00	1
1/30	14	10:00	11:00	1
1/30	15	11:30	2:00	2.5
2/3	10 (photoshoot)	1:00	4:00	3

A Proofing Horror Story

As you can see from the detailed Proofing Approval Check-list I use (page 127), I'm a firm believer in Murphy's Law. But despite my best efforts, Murphy still manages to find me. When that happens, I have to take a deep breath, remind myself not to panic, and solve the resulting problems somehow. And that's the important part. Making every effort to prevent mistakes is your first line of defense against Murphy. (In other words, the best defense is a good offense.) If an error does get through, you've got to come right back with a plan of action that resolves the situation or lessens its impact.

My agency produced a full-color brochure for the New England Chiropractic Association's annual meeting. In all the rounds of proofing, one little typo got past me, my art director, the account executive, the typesetter and the client. When the brochures were delivered to the client, it wasn't such a little typo. There in big, bold type on the cover of the brochure "Chiropractic" had become "Chiropactic." Oops!

Now, there are sometimes ways of correcting problems such as this. If there's time and it won't be glaring, a label with matching colors and graphics can be printed and applied on top of the error. Sometimes you can overprint the mistake directly on the piece itself. Or the printer may have some other suggestions for fixing the problem.

This time, nothing would help. We couldn't put a label over it because "Chiropactic" was in the middle of other words and surrounded by a graphic texture. We couldn't overprint for the same reason. We couldn't even have all the brochures printed again because they had to be mailed that day. If we could have gone back to press, I'd have done it gladly – no matter what it cost me. (Notice I said "cost me"; even though the client missed the typo, too, this was still my mistake because I'm the professional and it was my responsibility.)

What did I do? Apologized profusely and offered to reduce the client's bill by 25 percent to compensate for our error. I offered the 25 percent reduction because I felt that 75 percent of the brochure was correct. The client was delighted. He felt he could live with a little embarrassment for that kind of savings. (And he did use my agency again.)

The moral of this story, of course, is don't make mistakes. But if you do, accept responsibility for the problem and find a solution acceptable to everyone concerned.

---

line dates. (The sooner you do this the better.) This way you've got time to find a replacement if someone backs out or a problem develops.

At a project review session with the photographer and copywriter, you fill them in on the client's objectives and discuss your concept ideas. They always have some interesting ideas and often spot potential problems you've overlooked. Plus, it heightens their involvement and interest in the final piece.

Step Twelve: Working on the Design and Layout

About three days later, the copywriter drops off a disk with five ideas for headlines and sample copy for each. At last you're ready to begin the layout sketches. As you do, you try to balance the client's requirements for the finished piece with the technical aspects of the brochure — size, number of colors, photos, etc. As you play around with ideas, you keep asking yourself: Can it be done? You have to know that your idea can actually be produced within the budget parameters you quoted. You learned your lesson the time you designed that gorgeous logo that both you and the client loved. You didn't know that it would cost you over $300 and negative and trapping work to reproduce it. You never quoted the client for anything like that. You wound up absorbing the extra costs yourself.

Two days later, your rough sketches are done. After taking a break from the project, you look at the sketches again. Although you can't always do this, you feel it helps you see which ones work best. When you review them, three of the twelve roughs jump out as not only good, clean design, but just what the client was looking for. So you begin to translate them into presentation comps on the computer for your next client meeting. After working with the three ideas for a while, you choose one for some additional experimentation. You quickly explore some variations and decide to present one of these to the client.

Step Thirteen: Third Client Meeting

As you write out your agenda, you also gather together everything you need to take to the meeting tomorrow. You need him to review the layouts, making changes and notes on the

Before It's Too Late . . .

It's difficult for designers because we must give out costs before we actually do the work. So, think each design through before you present it. When in doubt, check it out and get revised cost estimates if necessary *before* you present it to the client. When you fall in love with a more complex, expensive design, present it along with several simplified versions of it. Then if the client really wants the more complex design, you can explain that it will cost more to produce. That way if the client still decides to go with it, the problem becomes his, not yours.

photocopies. He has to review and approve the sample copy, PMS colors and paper.

Just in case there are any major changes that Taylor wants to make now that he has a chance to see some actual layouts, you bring along a blank copy of the Client Change Request form. You will only use this form if the changes could alter the schedule and Price Quote Estimate. This form protects you from a client trying to hold you to an original quote or denying that he requested certain changes. You always take a blank form to every client approval meeting, right up through the final mechanical approval.

When you meet with Taylor the next day, he approves everything without a hitch. Terrific! You have him sign the comp and copy he preferred. He did make a few minor changes in the copy, but nothing that will cause any problems. You had him indicate the changes himself right on a photocopy, then had him initial it. This was another school-of-hard-knocks lesson you learned when a client made numerous changes in copy and then later denied he'd asked for those changes. You got stuck with the additional typesetting costs. Before the meeting ends you make a note of the PMS color numbers and the paper stock he chose. You always write it down directly on the layout the client signs. That way you don't have to worry about losing your notes. Fortunately, the Client Change Request form wasn't necessary.

Step Fourteen: Prepare Electronic Mechanicals

You begin work on the mechanicals. You order a special display face from a typesetter because you're not sure you can use that face enough to justify buying the font. Although you plan to scan in the chosen photos for FPOs after the photo shoot, you don't feel up to handling the duotones and prefer to have the printer prepare film for those. Instead of sending film to the printer, you will have the service bureau output the layout to resin-coated paper and send that with the veloxes to the printer.

You call the printer to confirm press time and delivery. Then you set up your page lay-

		YOUR BUSINESS LOGO

Project Summary

Date: 2/1
Client: Richard Taylor
Company Name: Taylor & Derne
Address: 57 Industrial Dr.
City/State/Zip: Center City, NS 99999
Project Description: Sales Brochure

Code	Project Phase	Complete	Incomplete	Hours to Date
02	Research	Yes		2
03	Concept	Yes		5
05	Layout	Yes		7
05	Comp Prep	Yes		Included above
11	Copy	Yes		subbed out
11	Copyediting	Yes		subbed out
01	Client Meetings		Yes	2
07	Art/Illustration	None	—	—
09	Mechanical		In progress	2
08	Typesetting	Yes		6
—	Photography		Yes	subbed out
—	Videography	None	—	—
12	Proofing		Yes	
15	Revisions		Yes	
13	Press Approval		Yes	
—	Outside Typesetting	Yes		subbed out

Total Hours to Date: 24

Aspects of the project that are on hold: None
We are waiting for client approval on: Nothing at this point
Recommended changes: None
Problems that could develop: Nothing anticipated

Contact us immediately: Yes ___ Not necessary x
Designer Signature: *Ima Designer* Date: 2/1

outs with spaces for the photos that are roughly the size and orientation you think you'll need. You also set up the color palette with the chosen PMS colors and place the type. Before you break for the day, you send the client a Project Summary to let him know what's been accomplished and how much time you've spent on the project to date.

Step Fifteen: Supervise Photo Shoot

With the final layout selected and approved, you know exactly how many photographs you need and what mood they should convey. Now you're ready for the photo shoot. So off you go, layout in hand, to the photographer's studio to art direct the shoot. Remembering that Mr. Taylor likes to be part of the creative process, you invite him to the shoot. Most photographers hate getting directions from two people, so you know you'll have to handle this carefully. You need to make the client feel valued, but you also have to tactfully override him if he wants something that, in your professional opinion, is wrong for the brochure.

But, as it turned out, you didn't need to worry. In fact, it's lucky Mr. Taylor was there, because he noticed that two of the products had some critical facing parts missing. You had no way of knowing that.

You're also relieved that Taylor didn't suddenly decide he wanted to show models using the products. Fortunately, you've only had to deal with that once. But was that a headache! You ended up recruiting the children of everyone you knew and then standing over each parent to get your Photo/Video/Audio Release signed before shooting could start. Not to mention wrestling all those restless children and their star-struck parents!

Step Sixteen: Complete Mechanicals

The headline type and the photos are back, so you can finish the mechanical. When you're done, you print out a dummy for the client to review. The scanned FPOs clearly show how it all works. You also print out a version with cropmarks and all your notes. Reviewing a dummy is easier for many clients because the mechanicals can be very confusing. But you always show the client the mechanical as you review the dummy, to help him understand how the mechanical is put together. You use a Proofing Approval Checklist to help you remember everything you need to look for. It also shows the client that your proofing was thorough.

YOUR BUSINESS LOGO

Work In Progress

Date Ordered: _1/20_
Project Name: _Taylor & Lorne Sales Brochure_   Project Number: _911501_
Project Billing Dates: _Signing, approval of mechanicals (2/9) delivery_
Project Description: _Sales brochure targeting preteens & teens — new market for_
Client — introducing electronic toys & games sold in nationwide retail
outlets.

Due Date: _3/1_

Production Phase	Date Completed	Production Phase	Date Completed
Concept	1/22	Color Separations	
Copy	1/24	Revisions	
Editing	1/26	Pre-press	
Layout	1/24	Blueline/Color Proofs	
Revisions	1/31	Approvals	
Art/Illustration	none	Revisions	
Mechanical	2/8	Press	
Photography	2/3 & 2/7	Other	
Halftones	2/8	Delivery	

Special Notes or Instructions: _Need to scan in photos and run test page at_
service bureau before sending them whole job ASAP. Need to meet
with printer about duotones now that I have halftones.

Mechanical Tips and Time-Savers

1. It takes time and practice to master color corrections and trapping (creating an overlapping area between two colors to prevent misregistration). You may find it's faster and less expensive to have an experienced professional at your service bureau, prepress shop or printer do trapping and corrections for you.

2. A resolution of more than 300 dpi is generally wasted on grayscale and color images, so an image scanned at 600 dpi may be a waste of both time and money. Use a resolution that makes sense for your job instead; consult your service bureau and printer if you're not sure what to use.

3. Be sure to send all necessary files to the service bureau with the actual layout file (electronic mechanical). Supply all images to be used including all scans, illustrations and color separations that will be output. Include any special fonts the service bureau will need.

4. Make templates of any grids or formats you use frequently, such as a three-column grid newsletter or a multi-panel brochure. That way you won't have to set up your crop marks, fold lines and margins every time you do that kind of piece.

5. If you must make text changes or corrections after you have placed your graphics, use the command in your page layout program that will greek or gray out the visuals so only a gray box or silhouette appears on screen. This greatly reduces the amount of time it takes for screen redraw and affects only the screen view. Your visuals will still print out properly.

6. Check that you have selected process colors if that's what you want (PageMaker and QuarkXPress will convert the spot colors of images created in other programs to process for you). Also check that you don't have process colors selected if you want spot colors; otherwise you'll end up with — and have to pay for — more film than you want.

Step Seventeen: Meet with the Client to Approve Mechanicals

Before the meeting you list what you'll need to cover with Taylor when he reviews the mechanical boards:

◆ Explain the placement of each photo
◆ Confirm choice of PMS colors
◆ Review where and how colors are used

You'll use the original comp to point out where the bleeds, color overlays, reverses and screens are on the overlays. You'll have him mark any changes on the photocopied dummy of the brochure.

And just in case any changes affect the fi-

What If the Photos Are Wrong?

What if photos do turn out wrong? It may get caught when you show the contact sheet to the client. Even then, the images on a contact sheet are so small that the missing parts might still have gone unnoticed. That would mean that the mistake could go undetected until the final prints were ready for approval. Then you'd have to do part of the shoot again and wait another few days for proofs and prints. You could lose three or four days and miss your deadline. That's why you build in a false deadline at the final client approval stage when you make up a production schedule. There are just too many things that can go wrong during a project to take a chance.

Just the Fax

Often you must fax clients proofs of brochures or newsletters for review due to distance or time constraints. When you do so, try to talk with the client about the relationship of facing pages. And, if possible, send clients at least one set of physical proofs so they do see the spreads as units. Clients may simply look at one faxed page at a time, not realizing that they should look at how the pages work together as spreads or without knowing which pages go together. Helping clients see pages as spreads will prevent problems such as when clients think part of a picture is missing or don't understand why you've broken copy the way you have.

Client Change Request

YOUR BUSINESS LOGO

Client: _Richard Taylor_   Date: _2/14_
Company Name: _Taylor & Derne Electronics, Inc._
Project Description: _Sales Brochure_   Project Number: _911501_

A. The following changes were requested by the client and considered to be additions or deletions from the original project specifications, time frame and/or price changes: (Use additional sheet if necessary.)

① _New copy to be written for brochure_

② _Copy will be completely retypeset_

I have requested the changes noted above, knowing that these alterations could affect the price quote estimate or time frame originally agreed to for this project.

Client signature: _Richard Taylor_   Date: _Feb. 14_

B. This section is to be filled in by the design company/designer and returned to the client for final approval. This project will remain on hold until the client signs and returns Section C below indicating that he/she understands the changes that will occur in prices and/or scheduling and has accepted full responsibility for these changes.

1. The client change requests listed above will affect the original price estimate as follows: _An additional $375 for copywriting; an additional $315 + 100% markup for 24-hour rush; an additional $315 for typesetting; time-and-a-half for overtime._

2. The client change requests listed above will affect the delivery date as follows: _Delivery will be ONE DAY later than original date agreed to._

3. The client change requests listed above will affect the production schedule as follows: _____

C. I authorize the changes listed in Section A to be made and accept full responsibility for the resulting alterations indicated in Section B.

Client Approval Signature: _Richard Taylor_   Date: _Feb. 19_

---

nal price or schedule, you'll bring a Client Change Request form. (You also bring a copy of the Production Schedule, so you can check the impact of any changes on the schedule.)

When you arrive at Taylor's office at the meeting, he introduces his partner, Bill Derne. Taylor explains that he wants Derne to see and sign off on the brochure. "It's just a formality," he says, "I'm sure everything's fine." You get a sinking feeling in the pit of your stomach because you know Derne isn't going to like something about the project. That always seems to happen when the client brings someone new into the final approval meeting.

Taylor is happy with the mechanicals, but Derne isn't. He hates the copy and the typefaces. Taylor and Derne debate the merits of the copy at length. They finally arrive at a compromise but the copy and the headline will still have to be completely rewritten. You manage to persuade Derne to accept your choice of typefaces by explaining why they're especially appropriate for a piece targeted to a youth market.

Before you leave you fill out the Client Change Request form and have both of them sign it. You point out both verbally and on the form that these changes will substantially af-

fect the final cost of the project. You show them the Production Schedule and explain why these changes may also affect the schedule. Taylor decides that getting the pieces a day or two late is acceptable, so you add that information to the Client Change Request form. At least they're willing to accept responsibility for the costs of the changes. Recently some clients have tried to force those charges back on you, and you were afraid Derne might, too.

Step Eighteen: Make Mechanical Changes

You race back to the studio and call the copywriter. You agree on a fee for the rewrite, which you'll have in two days. You then fax your notes on the final Derne-Taylor compromise to the copywriter. (This is, of course, one of the best reasons for having a fax: the time you save from not having to pick up or deliver written materials to the client, subcontractors or vendors.) You make arrangements with the typesetter and service bureau for rush jobs.

Project Summary

YOUR BUSINESS LOGO

Date: _2/15_
Client: _Richard Taylor_
Company Name: _Taylor & Derne Electronics, Inc._
Address: _57 Industrial Dr._
City/State/Zip: _Center City, NS 99999_
Project Description: _Sales Brochure_

Code	Project Phase	Complete	Incomplete	Hours to Date
02	Research	Yes		2
03	Concept	Yes		5
05	Layout	Yes		9
05	Comp Prep	Yes		Included above
11	Copy		Being rewritten	subbed out
11	Copyediting		Yes	subbed out
01	Client Meetings		Yes	3
07	Art/Illustration	None	—	—
09	Mechanical		Type to be reset	6
08	Typesetting		To be reset	8
—	Photography	Yes	Subbed out	6-art direction
—	Videography	None	—	—
12	Proofing		Yes	1
15	Revisions		Yes	
13	Press Approval		Yes	
—	Outside Typesetting	Yes		

Total Hours to Date: _40_
Aspects of the project that are on hold: _Mechanical prep until copy is approved & type reset_
We are waiting for client approval on: _New copy-must be received by Feb. 17_
Recommended changes: _None_
Problems that could develop: _None, unless further major changes in new copy_

Contact us immediately: Yes _____ Not necessary _x_
Designer Signature: _Ima Designer_   Date: _2/15_

Step Nineteen: Send Another Project Summary, Then Get New Copy Approved

You send Taylor a final Project Summary giving estimates for the additional costs for the rewritten copy and rush typesetting job. You also let him know when you'll bring the new copy for his and Derne's approval.

When you take them the new copy, Taylor and Derne both sign off on it. You have it ready the next morning as promised.

decided not to try creating duotones yourself. The smaller the files the better, when it comes to rush computer charges and time.

If you can modem large files to the service bureaus late at night, you'll avoid having both your own and the service bureau's modem and computer tied up during the prime working time. This may also reduce your service bureau charges; you may have to pay less for the extra computer time than you would during the day.

Proofing Approval Checklist

YOUR BUSINESS LOGO

Project Name: Sales Brochure   Project Number: 911501
Client Name: Richard Taylor   Company: Taylor & Derne Electronics

✓ Place a check mark next to items listed below that were proofed and approved.
NO Use this to indicate items that were missing or incorrect.
N/A Use this for those that don't apply to the mechanical or proof.

Mechanical

✓Page Content	✓Numbers	✓Headlines/Subheads
✓Captions/Quotes	✓Color	□Call Outs N/A
□Graphic Treatments N/A	✓Type Proofed	✓Phone Numbers
✓Logos	✓Layout/Design	✓Crop/Fold/Trim Marks
✓Folds, Perforations	✓Trims, Bleeds	✓Registration Tabs
✓Halftones: Cropped, Sized	□Screens N/A	✓Paper Stock, Weight
✓Postal Indicia/Codes/Permits		□Other: Indicate

Other: Indicate Special Requirements: _____

Blueline/Color Proof

□Trim	□Registration	□Diecut/Perforate/Punch
□Reverses	□Fold	□Placement of Text
□Hickies/Marks	□Proofed	□Placement of Graphics
□Color: Placement	□Clarity of Type	□Clarity of Rules
□Clarity of Graphics	□Halftones/Screens	□Halftones: Position
□Screens: Position	□Halftones: Labeled	□Screens: Labeled
□PMS Labeled	□Other: Indicate	□Other: Indicate

Color Separations

□Color Quality	□Changes	□Clarity
□Quantity	□Size	□Other: Indicate

Other: Special Requirements:
□ _____   □ _____   □ _____
□ _____   □ _____   □ _____

Special Notes or Instruction: _____

This is to verify that I, the above-named client, representing the above-named company, have thoroughly reviewed and approved the project materials described above. I understand that this is my last opportunity to request changes due to mistakes or preferences. I further acknowledge that any mistakes or preference changes that were not discovered or specified at this time are not the responsibility of the designers/design company named above. I accept full responsibility for this final approval and with it hereby authorize the designer to take the approved materials listed above to the printer for the final phase of the project—the printed pieces.

Designer Approval Signature: Ima Designer   Date: 2/14
Client approval Signature: Richard Taylor   Date: 2/15
Bill Derne   2/15

Service Bureau Instructions

YOUR BUSINESS LOGO

Designer Studio: Ima Designer   Date: 2/15
For Questions Call: Ima Designer
Billing Address: 603 Studio Way, #2, Center City, NS 99999
Deliver To: Will pick up; call when ready
PO #: 716   Project Number: 911501
Project Description: Sales Brochure--camera-ready line & FPOs
Service Bureau: Hot Shots
Contact: Kelly Wade   Telephone/Fax: 555-1223
Date Needed: 2/16   Time: by noon   Rush Charges Okay: yes

Submission Format

☒ Floppy   □ Modem   □ Optical   □ Tape   □ Cartridge   □ SCSI Device   □ WORM
Page Layout Program: Quark Xpress   Version: 3.2   XPress Data Files: _____

Font(s) Used In Document

Name: Bodoni   Manufacturer: Adobe
Name: Stone Sans   Manufacturer: Adobe
Name: _____   Manufacturer: _____

Placed Graphics

Graphic Name: Product 1   Format: TIFF
Graphic Name: Product 2   Format: TIFF
Graphic Name: Product 3   Format: TIFF
Graphic Name: Product 4   Format: TIFF

Output Specifications

File Name to Image: TD Sales
Number of Pages: 2   Output Size Excluding Trim Zone: 12-1/2 x 10-1/2
Resolution: 1270 dpi   Screen: 150 lpi
Film: _____   Paper: x   Negative: _____   Positive: _____
Separations: Spot: _____   Screen Color: _____   Illustrations: _____   Process Color: _____
Proof: Matchprint: _____   Cromalin: _____   Color Keys: _____
Mac-driven Color Copier: _____   Other (specify): B&W proof
Special Instructions: Call Dan Sloan re: FPO scans for printing requirements.
Phone: 555-1212

Step Twenty: Final Mechanical Review With Client

You return to the client for final (you hope) approval. You take a Proofing Approval Checklist listing the materials to approve and the changes that were made. You also remember to bring the original photocopied dummy indicating the changes, so the client can proof them against the new one.

Taylor and Derne approved the boards! You have them read and sign the Proofing Approval Checklist—you can't leave without that.

You race to the service bureau with the disk, where they confirm that you can get the job tomorrow. Since the client is already having to pay rush charges, you're glad that you

Step Twenty-one: Deliver Mechanicals to Printer

You call the printer before you leave Taylor's office, to make sure that your contact person, Mr. Sloan, is there. You don't want to leave the boards with just anybody.

Mr. Sloan is waiting for you. You thoroughly review the boards with him, point out all the duotones, the PMS numbers, reverses and bleeds. Then you go over each of the duotones to be sure he understands your directions for cropping and scaling and color percentages.

You verify with Sloan that there is nothing in the finished art that will substantially change the original quote on printing costs. Although you can't think of anything that wasn't

Problem/Solution

What if you go to a press approval and an important piece of type is missing that was originally on the mechanical?

Solution: When the press foreman shows you the blueline that both you and the client approved, the type is missing there. But it *is* on the mechanical, so technically it's the printer's fault. Someone in prepress didn't strip it in. But you and the client are responsible, too, because you signed off on the blueline proof—you more than the client, since most clients don't know what to look for on a blueline.

The printer, however, offers to reshoot the mechanical and make another plate—at no cost to you. You show the client what you've caught. (If you're doing a press approval without the client, call her immediately about the problem.) Be sure to explain that the printer is correcting the mistake at his expense. Although you didn't catch the mistake in the first place, the client will be grateful that you caught it now and corrected it without incurring additional costs.

When you notify a client about a mistake, always point out what could have happened if it wasn't discovered, and how it's being corrected without inconveniencing her. That way when you ask for the additional time the printer needs to complete the job, the client will feel that it's a small price to pay.

UP THE LADDER OF SUCCESS

Printing Instructions

YOUR BUSINESS LOGO

Designer/Studio: Ima Designer Date: 2/16
For Questions Call: Ima Designer 555-6666
Project Description: Sales Brochure Project Number: 911501

Printer: Sloan Printing
Contact: Dan Sloan Telephone/Fax: 555-1212/555-1222

Materials Sent
  (2) Mechanical Boards (RC paper w/FPOs)
  (15) Halftones

Printing Specifications
Paper Stock: L.O.E.-gloss-80# cover Quantity to Print: 30,000
# of Sides: # of Colors: 3 (Blk + 2PMS) PMS Ink #s: 481 & 232
Delivered as Camera-Ready Film:
Delivered as Electronic Disk Files:
Prepress Service/Service Bureau: Hot Shots
Contact: Kelly Wade Telephone: 555-1222
Stripping Required, See Specs Below: Duotones to be created
Bleeds: 2 sides-20% coverage Screens: No Reverses: Yes-2
Halftones: 15 Duotones Film: Yes Separations: No
Proofs/Blueline: Yes Color Key: No Chromalin Proof: No
Print Size: 12-1/2 x 10-1/2 Score: Yes Fold: 1
Finished Size: 10-1/2 x 6-1/4 Bindery: No Emboss: No
Die Cut: No Drills: No Perforations: No
Thermography: No Other:
Mailing: 20,000 bulk mail Pack: Yes
Delivery Instructions 20 to Ima Designer; 20,000 to B&D Mailing Services;
  9,980 to Clare Brooks, Taylor & Derne Electronics.
Date Due: March 8, MORNING PREFERABLE
Shipping Costs: None
Billing: Ima Designer, 603 Studio Way, #2, Center City, NS 99999
Other Instructions:
Printer's Signature: _____ Date: 2/16

---

covered in the original estimate, you know that the most frequent cause of cost overruns is filmwork, such as halftones, mechanical effects and close separations, and that wasn't mentioned in the original estimate. There wasn't a problem, so you won't have to get approval from your client for the increased cost or rework part of the mechanical.

You give Sloan a dummy to attach to the mechanicals to help the prepress and press people understand how the final piece should look. As you look through the mechanicals with him, you refer to the printing instructions attached to the back of one of the mechanicals. These will help him to convey your specifications to his work crew. It will also be there if Sloan isn't around and a problem comes up. Of course, you leave a note on the instructions to call you day or night if there are any questions.

Before you leave, you confirm when the blueline will be ready, and then you're off for a nice long walk. You deserve a break!

Step Twenty-two: You and Client Each Approve Blueline

In two days, the blueline is delivered to your office. You proof it very carefully. Everything appears to be in order, so you initial the proof to show the printer that you approved it. Now, the client has to approve and initial it, too—for your protection, as well as the printer's. So it's back to the client's office for his approval. Then you drop the initialed blueline at the printer's office and confirm press approval and delivery dates.

Step Twenty-three: Press Approval

Three days later, the press approval is at nine in the morning. You meet Mr. Taylor there. You like to have the client attend press approvals whenever possible to take the final responsibility for approving the press sheets. You also think it's a good experience for them to see, firsthand, how the printing process works. The more clients know about graphics and printing, the better they will be as clients.

The pressman puts a sample from the first 100 sheets on a table with special lighting so you can see the color under simulated daylight conditions. This is the only way you can really tell if the color matches the PMS chip. You look over the sheet carefully, first with your naked eye and then more closely with a loupe. Then you explain to the client what you should both be looking for—broken type, hickies, clear photos and solid coverage on the large bleed areas. Everything looks good, so you and Taylor each initial one of the press sheets.

Step Twenty-four: The Brochures Are Delivered

Two days later, the brochures are ready. You have twenty to thirty brochures come to you before the rest are delivered to the client, so you'll catch any problem in binding or trimming. That gives you time to discuss with the printer how the problem can be corrected before you tell the client. Clients can usually take bad news much better if they know you have a solution. (You also want to keep samples for portfolios and presentations.) When the brochures arrive you examine them carefully and don't find any problems. You notify the printer, making sure the delivery man knows how to get to the client's office. And it's over! Or is it?

Project Expenses Tracking Sheet

YOUR BUSINESS LOGO

Project Number: 911501
Project Name: Sales Brochure
Client: Taylor & Derne Electronics

Date Rec'd	Company Name	Inv. #	Inv. Price
2/3	Johnson Copywriting	9921	$450.00
2/15	Johnson Copywriting	9930	312.50
2/15	Stevens Photography	4228	1,200.00
2/24	Hot Shots	74152	30.00
2/24	Typesetters, Inc.	22175	35.00
2/26	ABC Graphics	12024	75.00
3/9	B&D Mailing	5610	750.00
3/9	Sloan Printing	038132	3,000.00

Step Twenty-Five: Billing for the Project

Now that the project is completed, it's time to send the final bill to Taylor. You've already collected two-thirds of the total payment as advances (one on signing and the other at the midpoint of the project) because it's your policy to do no further work on a project until those are paid. You've heard too many horror stories about designers paying for work out of their own pockets and then not getting paid to want to take that kind of gamble with your money. Although you generally collect your final payment on a project before it's delivered, you feel confident that you won't have any problems with Taylor. In fact, you already have an appointment to drop by his office to present your final bill and collect your check.

You had Taylor send the check for the postage directly to the post office. You always

 have the client pay postage costs directly to the post office or the mailing house because nothing gets mailed until it is paid for. This saves you time and headaches, since you aren't racing one check to the bank, waiting for it to clear, then racing off with another.

You take out your billing book, where you've already filed the Price Estimate Work

Sheet and the Project Expenses Tracking Sheet. You check your clipboard to make sure you've got all the Project Time Sheets in the book. No, the last one's still there, so you pull it. After checking that all the invoices are in from your various vendors and subcontractors, you're ready to start on the Project Billing Work Sheet.

You add up your total hours from the time sheets for each phase of the project, enter them on the work sheet, and check that you remembered to include the time you spent preparing the proposal on that first time sheet. You'll include those costs under Concept Development (03). (If you hadn't gotten the job, you'd have filed those costs with your business expenses as marketing expenses.)

You verify that you haven't exceeded your original Price Quote Estimate for your hours. You're just a little bit over from having to paste-up the type twice. (If the overrun was your fault, you'd have charged the estimated amount instead and eaten the difference.) Even though a 10 percent overrun is acceptable, you don't bill the client for extra hours unless there were client changes or extraordinary problems with production. You check the Price Estimate Work Sheet to determine the amount per hour you quoted for your time

Project Billing Work Sheet

YOUR BUSINESS LOGO

Client: Taylor & Derne Electronics, Inc.
Date: 3/2
Project Number: 911501

Work Description	Time	Cost/Hour	Total Time Cost
01 Consultation/Meetings	6	$50	$300
02 Research	2	35	70
03 Concept Development	5	50	250
04 Organization	3	35	105
05 Layout/Design	9	50	450
06 Art Direction	6	50	300
07 Illustration		—	—
08 Typesetting	8	35	280
09 Mechanical Prep	6	35	210
10 Consult Vendors/Subs	5	35	175
11 Copywriting/Editing	Subbed out	—	
12 Proofing	3	35	105
13 Press Approvals	3	40	120
14 Acct. Administration	2	35	70
15 Revisions	—	—	—
16 Client Changes Overtime 1½	6	52.50	315
17 Other—			
18 Other—			
19 Other—			

Subcontractor	Price	Markup	Client's Price
Copywriter/editor	450 + 312.50	90 + 62.50	915
Photographer	1,200	240	1,440
Typesetter	35	7	42

Vendor	Price	Markup	Client's Price
Halftones	75	15	90
Service bureau	30	6	36

Other Project-Related Expenses	Price	Markup	Client's Price
Mailing	750	150	900
Postage	610	—	610

Miscellaneous Expenses	Price	Markup	Client's Price
Printing	3,000	600	3,600
Misc. materials	40	8	48

Total Project Cost: $10,431

Let the Computer Do Your Billings

The Project Billing Work Sheet can also be created in a computer spreadsheet program and used to gather pricing information that can then be transferred to the client's Invoice (which you can also create in your spreadsheet program). You can use the function codes for each Work Description to facilitate fast and accurate transfer of data from one file to another, especially if you're compiling the results of your Project Time Sheets on the computer as well. You can also assign codes to the subcontractors and vendors you use most frequently to make it easier to transfer that information.

There are some specialized software packages available for designers that offer you time-and-billing packages as well as a number of dedicated accounting programs. Or you can use database software plus a spreadsheet program to design your own system. Once you've gotten your data transferred to the computer, you or your secretary can easily update the information on a regular basis. Then you'll have everything ready when it's time to invoice a client.

since you have a variable pricing structure, charging higher fees for concept development and client contact than for mechanical prep or proofing. You enter the cost per hour on the appropriate line, and then calculate the correct charges and enter them.

Next, you transfer all the invoice amounts from the Project Expenses Tracking Sheet and enter the markups for each from your Price Estimate Work Sheet. You've double-checked all the invoices against the quotes as they came in, except for the last bills for rewriting and retypesetting the copy. You pull the Client Change Request and check those additional charges now.

You fill out a blank invoice, entering all the client information and assigning it the next invoice number. Then you copy all the time costs and the entries under Client's Price for all Subcontractor Costs, Vendor Costs and Other Project-Related Expenses, as well as Miscellaneous Expenses from the Project Billing Work Sheet and enter the total. Because you've already been paid two-thirds of your fee, you enter the amount paid for Less Previous Payments, and you subtract the total paid to date from the Total Project Costs to get the Final Project Costs. Then you take all your taxable time costs and project expenses, calculate the sales tax due, and enter that in the appropriate space. (Since sales tax doesn't apply to every phase of a project, you've placed an asterisk next to the cost of any taxable service and can quickly see what you must calculate sales tax on.) You charge all

the sales tax due now, because the previous two payments were advances and as such not taxable. Finally, you add the Sales Tax to the Final Project Costs to get the Total Amount Due. You make copies for your Active Accounts Receivable and Sales Tax Files and are ready to

bring the invoice over for payment. You're finished! Well, almost — only one thing left to do.

When the Project Is Finished, Billing Is *Not* the Last Thing You Do

Before you bill for the project, you write Mr. Taylor a letter briefly explaining that you enjoyed working on the project with him and hope to continue your working relationship. You ask him to feel free to discuss with you or jot down any problems that may have come to his attention during the project or any thoughts he might have that would help make future projects even more successful and productive. This is a standard procedure for you, and clients have praised you for it. Although you do welcome a client's criticism and you know it will make you a better designer, you also know that this really hooks the client into wanting to continue working with you.

YOUR BUSINESS LOGO

Invoice

Number: 567   Date: 3/2   Project #: 911501
Your Address: Ima Designer, 603 Studio Way, #2, Center City, NS 99999
Client: Richard Taylor   Company Name: Taylor & Derne
Address/City/State/Zip: 57 Industrial Dr., Center City, NS 99999

Services Rendered	Time	Amount
01 Client Consultations/Meetings	6	$300
02 Research	2	70
03 Concept	5	250
04 Organization	3	105
05 Layout/Design	9	450
06 Art Direction	6	300
07 Illustration	—	—
08 Typesetting	8	280
09 Mechanical Prep	6	210
10 Consultations with Vendors and Subcontractors	5	175
11 Copywriting/Editing	subbed out	—
12 Proofing	3	105
13 Press Approvals	3	120
14 Acct. Administration	2	70
15 Revisions	—	—
16 Client Changes	6	315
17 Other—	—	—
18 Other—	—	—
19 Other—	—	—

Subcontractor	Costs
Copywriting/Editing	915
Printing	3,600
Typesetting	42
Photography	1,440
Stats, Veloxes, Films	90

Vendor	Costs
Service Bureau	36
Misc. Materials	40

Other Expenses	Costs
Mailing	900
Postage	610

Payments not received within 30 days will be subject to an interest rate of 1½% per month or a fraction thereof from date of invoice. Client subject to reasonable collection fees.

Total Project Costs:	$10,431
Less Previous Payments:	6,466
Final Project Costs:	3,965
Sales Tax:	200
Total Amount Due:	$4,165

CHAPTER
five

Collaborators

and

Competitors

Surviving in this business is definitely a sink or swim situation. You can simply tread water, just getting by, or move past the competition with strong and steady strokes. How well you swim in this crowded pool isn't only a matter of luck or ability; it's a matter of drive and determination. There will always be someone waiting to take your place—someone with more talent, more skills or cheaper prices. And the talent pool is larger than ever before. Fax, airfreight and the modem let designers thousands of miles away compete for work in your hometown. You can't control the competition, but you can control your performance. That's where you have a choice.

People in this business get hungry because they live from job to job never knowing when the next one will come along. As a result, they take any new project offered to them, believing they can squeeze out the extra hours or do something new without allowing time for trial and error. Clients have no tolerance for missed deadlines or sloppy work that resulted from rushing through a job. And they won't call again.

Clients appreciate thoughtful professionals who care about the quality of their work *and* their ability to deliver that work on time. You must ask yourself: Can I do this job, given what I know I can do well? Do I have the time, with my present commitments, to give it my best? If you never take on a project unless you can answer "yes" to both these questions, you'll be way ahead of the competition. Being honest when you have doubts will win a client's respect. They'll not only come back to you again, but also recommend you to others.

Being steady is another trait many designers don't fully appreciate. They foolishly believe steadiness is synonymous with sameness—creative inspiration's killer. There's no doubt about it; creativity is important. But talent and creativity can't stand alone. They've got to be supported by dependability and consistent quality. Your ability to focus your full attention on client needs and deliver a top-notch product on time will keep you swimming at a marathon pace.

Heartfelt desire is the final ingredient in becoming a long-distance swimmer. When you combine what you love to do with slow and steady business practices, the combination is unbelievably powerful. Too many designers think that they can't earn a decent living doing what they love. So they do anything and everything to make money, even if they find it dull and boring. It works for a while, because the sheer joy of starting a new design business and being independent keeps them motivated. But at some point they come to a grinding halt—because they can't keep growing if they don't like, much less love, what they're doing.

If you find out what kinds of assignments make you eager to get started, you'll have taken a major step toward defining the direction of your business. The reason is quite simple: Doing what you love brings out your best. You can't *always* work on just the kinds of projects you love, but actively seeking them out will eventually create an area of specialization for you. A specialist known for always delivering high-quality work—whether it's realistic illustrations, sophisticated logo designs or classy annual reports—gets respect. If that specialist is you, and you love your specialization, you'll see your business grow faster than you could ever have imagined.

Exploring the Design Pool

Designers swimming about in the same freelance pool with you may actually produce quite different types of work. They may work on newspaper and magazine ads, brochures, newsletters, catalogs and annual reports. They may design book, record or videotape jackets, do posters, or prepare charts and graphs. They design business identity packages that include logos, business cards, stationery and signage. Graphic designers can also become involved in three-dimensional design projects such as package design, model-making or point of purchase and other types of store displays. The exact area of someone's specialization varies because of personal preference, ability, experience and opportunities,

or on-the-job demands.

Self-employed designers generally do projects requiring a variety of skills. Unless you have employees or can afford freelance design help, you will take your projects from concept through mechanical yourself. You'll be art director, layout artist and mechanical artist all rolled into one. If you work for ad agencies or larger design studios, however, you may develop a specialization tailored to their needs. For example, you may develop layouts and/or comps from an art director's thumbnails. Or you may work as a mechanical artist under the direction of another designer or a production coordinator.

Let's quickly review some of the opportunities for specialization. Even if you prefer handling projects from start to finish, there may be times when you'll want — or need — to work with an agency or studio. Being able to associate a job title or description with its responsibilities will help you understand what you are being asked to do and, in some cases, to easily identify the role of the person you are working for.

Designers

Designers specialize in translating concepts into the initial sketches for a project. They explore a variety of visual options in the form of thumbnails. In these initial layout sketches, all of the elements that go into the finished piece are loosely laid down. These sketches will indicate where the type will be placed in relation to the photos or illustrations and the copy. When a variety of thumbnails have been completed, a designer will then select several of the best for translation into full-scale layouts. Sometimes clients are shown layouts for approval in the form of sketches or other traditionally produced formats. Often, however, the initial sketches or thumbnails are taken to the computer where a number of variations can be quickly explored and then presented in clean form to the client.

Once the ideas are developed and presented to the client for approval, the designer will either translate, or supervise the translation of, the roughs into a finished presentation comp. Although some comping is still easier to do by traditional methods, comps most often include computer-generated headlines and greeked body copy in the exact typeface and point size to be used. Sample illustrations or photographs may be scanned in or photocopied and placed on laser-printed pages. Many studios and agencies use color laser printers and/or color photocopies to better show clients how a piece will look. These comps are then mounted on presentation boards for client approval.

A designer's primary responsibility is to translate someone else's ideas into tangible form. In an agency or large studio that person will be either a creative director or an art director. In other kinds of businesses, you may take direction from an advertising manager, marketing director or communications director (if there's an in-house design department, the titles are the same as in an agency or studio). How much creative freedom you have in doing this will depend on the person you're working with. At times, you may be given simply the bare concept, "We need to show the product with some kind of holiday theme and there will be a lot of copy." At others, you will be given very precise directions on every aspect of the layout.

Who Me?

Although working on the computer has given designers greater creative control, it has also given them increased responsibility for quality control. When the printer, service bureau or typesetter does work for you on a project, they are responsible for absorbing the costs of fixing problems and mistakes. If you use the computer in your studio to typeset copy or to output film, you are now responsible for any problems or mistakes — and for the cost of correcting them.

Fortunately, there are steps you can take to ward off problems. Know what you can and can't do well, and don't take chances. It's better to pay the printer or the service bureau to do your trapping than to do your own traps and ruin a job. If you're doing a lot of typesetting where appearance and accuracy are critical, find or train someone to be your expert, in-house typesetter.

Proof and reproof everything. Don't depend on the client to catch problems. Clients should certainly be responsible and willing to be accountable for proofing everything carefully to prevent errors. But remember that clients aren't trained proofreaders or copyeditors and can easily miss something that you, too, have overlooked.

Mechanical Artists

Mechanical artists translate the layout or comprehensive into the final format, the mechanical, to be used by the printer. In this era of graphics computers, the mechanical may take the form of traditionally pasted-up boards or it may be a computer-generated printout.

Some designers prefer to leave this final stage of a project to a mechanical artist because it involves specialized technical experience, concentrated attention to detail, and precision craftsmanship.

In the beginning, however, most graphic designers with their own businesses will do all phases of graphic production themselves, from layout to comprehensive to mechanical. Some designers who open their own studios specialize in mechanical production and offer this service to other independent designers as well as advertising agencies or design studios. This type of work, however, is rapidly disappearing except for those with exceptional computer skills and speed. Even clients with no design or graphic arts training are now taking on basic mechanical production.

Designers who work on computers are choosing to do more of their mechanical work themselves. The work just seems to flow naturally from one stage to the next as they move from the roughs (which may not be very rough) to the mechanical. Mechanical artists can become prepress specialists as these tasks continue to move into the design studio. If production-related work is what you do best and what you enjoy most, you can still carve out a niche for yourself. Be prepared to learn and use new techniques, programs and equipment quickly so you can take advantage of new opportunities.

Art Directors

This job description is closest to what you do every day as a self-employed designer. Art directors work closely with copywriters (sometimes under creative directors) to develop the basic concepts for a project or a campaign as well as with other creative professionals — photographers, illustrators, designers or videographers — working on a project. They're responsible for how the project looks, including an effective layout, the images used, and the overall quality and appearance of the finished piece(s) and/or campaign. Art directors may produce — or supervise other designers who produce — layouts and/or comps. If the project involves printed materials, they will oversee the production of all mechanicals and will usually approve the final proofs at the beginning of a press run.

Studio or agency art directors often begin their careers as mechanical artists (computer jockeys) and then move on to become full-fledged graphic designers. A graphic designer will move up to the position of junior and finally senior art director with increased experience in management and supervisory responsibilities.

Unless you're hired by an advertising agency, design studio or design department to handle a project on your own, you'll probably work with an art director. (In small or mid-sized studios or agencies this person may be called the "creative director" instead.) The art director and copywriter will already have set the concept and copy — and possibly even had it approved by the client — by the time you get an assignment. You'll then develop layouts and/or comps or mechanicals, trying to accurately interpret the art director's instructions (which means you have less room for creative flexibility).

Although these jobs are sometimes boring, they can lead to better opportunities. An art director who knows your work and has confidence in your capabilities will often give you greater input on and control over assignments. Use your newfound freedoms wisely; always check with the art director to review your concepts before you proceed to the presentation stage. If you've missed the mark in

what the agency or studio was looking for, that art director's neck is on the line.

Creative Directors

Creative directors supervise and inspire creative teams. (If you run a design studio with one or more employees, you assume the role of creative director even if you don't use that title.) Although they may not actually conceive and produce pieces or campaigns themselves, they are ultimately responsible for how each piece communicates. In medium-sized shops and departments, creative directors may oversee all production from copy to art. In larger shops or design departments, an art director, production coordinator or senior graphic designer works with freelancers and supervises production.

Some creative directors insist on total control over all the final elements in the concept development of a campaign or project. This type doesn't seem to understand that you can't do your best work when you feel like a servant. If you get stuck with one, tough it out and move on. The best kind of creative director is an enthusiastic leader who has that wonderful ability to make everybody feel like their input is valued — even when it can't be used. You can really grow as a designer with someone like that, so learn all you can from him or her. (When you are the creative director, remember the difference in the way you felt about your work when you were the subordinate!)

Creative directors come from a variety of advertising or graphics backgrounds. Most start out as art directors or copywriters, while others may have been account executives. Some creative directors leave to set up their own shops and offer their services to other designers, agencies and studios. Or they may set up their own full-scale ad agencies or studios (becoming your competitor instead of collaborator).

Desktop Publishers

When I wrote the first edition of this book back in 1990, desktop publishing, or DTP as it's frequently called, was in its infancy. Now it is one of the fastest growing areas of graphic design. Desktop publishers have taken over a sizable chunk of the typesetting industry. Although the need will always exist for the superior quality of traditional typesetting, DTP is now a respectable substitute for those publications that do not warrant such high quality and the price that goes with it.

Desktop publishers use computers and laser printers with at least 300 dpi resolution to electronically create just about every kind of printed material, from brochures and flyers to newsletters and catalogs, to signs and identity systems. Desktop publishing is even being used by book and magazine publishers now that the output quality has increased so significantly over the last two years. And when desktop publishers work in conjunction with service bureaus to imageset their materials, the quality is a close runner-up behind traditional typesetting. Many larger companies have purchased computers with DTP capabilities and hired or trained people to produce their printed materials in-house. This has unfortunately had a negative effect on independent designers and ad agencies, who've lost many clients to the DTP explosion. Consequently many designers are now offering DTP services; they will do everything electronically except printing. They can pass on the additional savings to their clients while touting the benefits of using experienced designers rather than just staff people who have learned how to combine word processing with computer graphics.

Unlike some designers who may be highly skilled in graphic design but have little or no expertise in copyediting, many desktop publishers have strong backgrounds in design (often on-the-job publication design) combined with copyediting skills and word processing experience. Some are seasoned copywriters; others got their experience in traditional typesetting. Many desktop publishers also have academic design training.

If you are planning to subcontract work to desktop publishers, check out their background and experience to be sure it's compatible with the kind of jobs you want to give them. One desktop publisher may be much better at following a rough layout and doing

Illustrators

There are many different types of illustrators. Some restrict their work to a specific genre such as marine, landscape or figurative; others work with a variety of thematic subjects. Illustration styles also vary, ranging from photo-realism to impressionism to cartoons and caricatures. Illustrators who work in any of these loosely defined styles are usually thought of as interpretive illustrators. That is, their work expresses their personal interpretation of the subject matter assigned to them.

Technical and scientific illustrators are allowed less freedom for artistic interpretation or choice of subject matter. Technical illustrators are experts in precision rendering. This may include mechanical drafting, engineering drawings, electrical or schematic drawings, architectural drafting, architectural and conceptual rendering. Scientific illustrators also produce precision renderings, but they specialize in one or more scientific disciplines, such as biology, zoology, botany, geology or physics.

an ace copyediting job than she is at conceptualizing a design. While another may be great with the creative parts of a project but not the most reliable to trust with grammar, punctuation and spelling. Others do it all extremely well. Ask to see samples and check with previous clients to get recommendations. If you are a desktop publisher, promote yourself by emphasizing your strengths, but also be honest with potential new clients about your weak areas. They will appreciate your candor and will be more likely to farm out to you jobs that are suited to your personal expertise.

What are the advantages of working with desktop publishers? DTP is far less expensive than traditional typesetting. It offers the client more opportunities to participate in the process of creating the printed piece since the work passes through fewer hands. There are also more opportunities to implement changes and see the results immediately. In addition, DTP offers the designer far more control over all phases of production, from concept to electronically produced mechanicals. The disadvantage of working with DTP is that, when something goes wrong, the buck stops with you, the designer. Because you perform all the production phases, there's no one else to blame. Fortunately, the advantages outweigh the disadvantages.

Your Professional Support Group

While every project is different, each requires collaborating with one or more professionals. Try to think of these people as your support group in the business community. Close ties with a number of fellow professionals you know and trust can help you through times of creative and motivational isolation. These contacts can also keep you in touch with what's happening in both the design and the client market. They can be a godsend when times get lean, and you need all the leads you can get.

Taking the time to carefully select and nurture a good business relationship with each member of your professional support group is

just as important as the quality of work you do. To make the most of your personal and working relationships, you must understand the role each plays when she works with you—and exactly what's expected of you. On the following pages, I will describe in some detail some of the collaborators you are most likely to work with in your business.

Photographers

Photographers who work in advertising and graphics create photographs that depict a client's product, service or audience. These images may also evoke a mood, promote a feeling toward the product or symbolize a concept. (Editorial photography deals with moods, feelings and symbols but is more interpretive, closer to illustration, than most advertising or graphics photography.)

Before you, as the art director or designer on a project, call in a photographer, you must know what kind of photograph you want and have a good idea of what you want it to do for you and your client. A good photographer can, and often will, offer sound advice on getting the best image for the concept you have in mind. But the bottom line is that you have the final responsibility for how the photograph turns out—you're the one who'll hear about it if the client isn't happy!

Copywriters

Copywriters provide the words to work with the images in ads, commercials, brochures, annual reports and business support materials. You may work with staff copywriters at ad agencies, freelance professionals or business or organization staffers who also write copy. There are also copywriters who specialize in certain areas, such as direct mail, technical or medical copy.

You may work directly with the copywriter as the project develops or the client may hand you completed copy. When that happens you'll need to adapt your design to the existing copy. This can be a tough situation, because the material may not fit what you need it to do in the design, or it may be poorly written, uninspiring or downright awful. Sometimes you can persuade the client to rewrite the copy or get new copy written, but you should back off if you sense serious resistance. (Outstanding design can't save a badly written piece, but it can make it look a whole lot better.)

Is there an alternative to constantly wrestling with new or amateur copywriters? Yes. Find a reliable and creative freelance copywriter and agree to work together on a regular basis as a creative *team*. You can then solicit business offering design and copy services as a package. Many clients will welcome the opportunity to leave the writing to you instead of producing their own copy or finding and hiring a copywriter. You're offering the client an additional service — saving them time. And that's a benefit many really want.

Look for good creative chemistry when you hire a copywriter or want to form a long-term association. You don't want to work with a budding novelist who considers every word she has written to be pure gold. You need someone who's willing to try different approaches and adapt copy to fit the layout, but who will tell you when *you* get off target.

Also look for computer savvy. Your life is much easier when a copywriter gives you a disk ready for you to translate or simply pick up and use. When you work with the same copywriter regularly, you can establish systems of coding and disk preparation to make your job easier. (Developing a written list of guidelines that tells copywriters how to prepare a disk for your use can save a lot of time and trouble when you're constantly working with different writers, especially if the client is also the writer.)

Researchers

Researchers are the scouts or detectives of the advertising industry. They provide relevant information to the agency's creative people and the account service team. If you're not part of an agency, you'll seldom be brought into a project before or during the research phase. But if you do happen to find yourself face-to-face with a researcher, please take her recommendations seriously. Don't make the mistake of thinking that your golden creative idea should take precedence over some "stuffy old research." Agency people have little tolerance for anyone who advocates ideas that are based on whimsy instead of factual research.

Production and Traffic Coordinators

Imagine a design studio, design department or advertising agency as a giant intersection with roads coming in from every possible direction, each road being a different project. The traffic coordinator sits in the middle of that intersection, like a traffic cop, and controls the flow of projects into and out of the design area.

Traffic coordinators maintain the master schedule showing what projects are in production and at what stage of completion. Each new project has to be fit into the overall flow of the traffic before the coordinator can set up production plans and projected deadlines. Sometimes the traffic coordinator, not the art director, will contract and supervise freelance designers.

Traffic coordinators are well versed in the procedures and jargon of production. They are detail oriented and will catch the smallest mistake before they notice if your work is exciting or innovative. Since the traffic coordinator's primary responsibility is to keep work flowing smoothly through production, they have little tolerance for missed deadlines.

While small to mid-sized shops will usually have either a traffic or a production coordinator, larger agencies and studios may have both. If a company is big enough to have both, the production coordinator is often less of a deadline watchdog and more of a technical expert. This person can troubleshoot production snags before they occur, becoming a valuable resource for you, especially if you often have to work alone.

UP THE LADDER OF SUCCESS

Typesetters

Due to rapid advances in computerized digital typesetting equipment, typesetters can create dramatic effects with type itself and set very complex charts, graphs and forms. Designers who understand that a good typesetter is far more than a fast and accurate typist who can

Do Unto Others

The computer has added a new temptation to designers' lives: stealing images. It's easy and cheap to pick up an illustration or a photograph from a previous job or other source and then manipulate it into something new and different. But using another's image without getting permission — no matter how you plan to alter it — is not only illegal, it's unethical. It's as wrong as a client taking your design on a disk, making changes, and printing the new piece without getting your consent or compensating you.

The only exceptions are illustrations that you find in clip art collections or books and magazines old enough to be out of copyright. Only photographs on a disk that you have bought the licenses for or have found in out-of-copyright books and magazines can be used without permission. (Combining small pieces of other images into a new one is rather a gray area. When in doubt, don't.) Otherwise you must get permission from the image's creator before using it. If you make a serious effort to find a creator, especially on an older piece, you can often still use it. Keep all records of your search and be ready to compensate a verifiable creator if one turns up later.

use typographic equipment will find a valuable resource and creative collaborator. But most typesetters are reluctant to offer suggestions to a designer unless asked for them. When you explain a project, don't take silence to mean a lack of interest or productive suggestions.

The graphics computers that are turning designers into typographers are putting traditional typesetters out of work. Many typesetters offer large libraries of specialty fonts and faces, including some not available on Macs or PCs, to attract designers seeking a distinctive typeface for one-time use. (Unless you are certain that you will use a face such as "Hobo" or "Baby Teeth" more than once, it makes more sense to have a typesetter set that headline or copy than to waste money or memory on buying a new font.) Other shops have responded to the situation by changing their businesses from manufacturing — converting manuscript into typeset copy — to service — converting disk files from graphics computers to reproduction quality type. They may also supply composite color film from their clients' disk files. Most typesetters who've made the switch now call themselves service bureaus.

Service Bureaus

It is rare to find a service bureau that can meet all of your graphic needs. Each one usually specializes in the imagesetting equipment it offers. You'll need to shop around for several service bureaus that can provide the form of output you need for specific jobs. Most designers find that they work with an average of three different service bureaus on a regular basis. The following information will help you evaluate service bureaus and decide which ones would be best for the kind of work you do.

Why work with a service bureau if you could (theoretically, anyway) do it yourself? Service bureaus will produce better quality pieces than you can create yourself. You would have to invest large sums of money in high-end scanners, imagesetters and color output devices to achieve the same results. For example, the average laser printer has a

resolution of only 300 dpi (dots per inch); the average imagesetter gives you 1270 to 2450 dpi. Obviously that makes a big difference in the appearance of the type on the page. A good service bureau can also help you troubleshoot problems and offer guidance on getting the most from the available technology.

Equipment and Software

A service bureau is only as good as the equipment it has and the people who run it. Before you select a service bureau, the most important things to look for are compatibility between their equipment and software and yours and operators who understand your needs and can produce the quality of work your project requires. The following information will help you know what to look for when you begin your service bureau search.

◆ Scanners: A service bureau will have either a grayscale scanner (which will pick up the tonality of photos, illustrations and graphics) or a color scanner or both.
◆ Laser Printer: You'll want to find a shop that outputs at least 600 to 1,200 dpi.
◆ Color Laser Printer: This proofing printer may be all you'll need for color comps.
◆ RIP: A raster image processor takes your images and translates or "rasterizes" the PostScript code into a high-resolution image. If a service bureau operator tells you your files are "getting ripped," that means they are being transferred into a readable image. All service bureaus must have RIP equipment — the higher the quality, the better.
◆ Imagesetter: A PostScript imagesetter reproduces RIP images in high resolution — from 1,200 to 4,000 dpi — onto paper or film.
◆ High-Resolution Color Imaging System: This is definitely not standard because of its high price tag. This machine not only outputs high-end color from your files, it can correct flaws or totally change photographs or illustrations.
◆ Film Recorder: This allows you to translate computer images into high-resolution, (4,000 dpi) 35mm color transparencies.
◆ Software: Ask the service bureau what software programs and which versions it uses. The software *must* be compatible with yours. Even if they tell you they can convert your older version of the software

to their newer version, be careful. Your document will automatically be upgraded when the service bureau opens it. When you get your document back, you will not be able to open it without the newer version of software.

Warning: Never give a copy of your software to a service bureau.

Also, computer viruses are a real nasty problem when you are sharing disks with service bureaus. You will need to get a good virus detector and a virus vaccine program. Use them faithfully.

When it comes to choosing a service bureau, ask questions and listen carefully. How do you feel about the way you are being treated as you ask your questions? This is a good indication of what you can expect from their service.

Unless you plan to do one-color work exclusively, look for a color scanner and a high-resolution imagesetter. The bureau should also be able to produce color proofs. Ideally, someone on their staff should have hands-on experience producing color work on the Macintosh and knows the nuts and bolts of the printing process. This person should be familiar with a wide variety of programs and file formats. Look for a person who will be able to answer your questions and make recommendations about how best to approach a job to achieve the results you want. And you also want someone who will be there when problems develop mid-project. Ask if they have someone who will check your finished prints or films to see if any problems occurred during the imaging process.

How to work with your service bureau: A service bureau should give you the information you'll need to prepare your files for submission. To help the bureau understand exactly what you want, take them a copy of the page layout(s). Double-check to make sure you've used the correct software version. When you take your files in, make a copy of the Service Bureau Instructions sheet provided for your use on page 67. This will help you ensure that you have passed along all the information the bureau needs to properly process your files. In addition, always be sure to include your name, company name and phone number on each disk in case it gets separated from your instruction sheet.

From service bureau to printer preparing your files: If you are submitting films to a printer, it is not the printer's job to check over your films and search for errors such as misregistrations, incorrect color separations or bad traps. Do that yourself before you deliver your films.

To get the results you want in print, use the following checklist to prepare your files for the service bureau:

1. Check all of your traps and knockouts.

2. Clearly indicate all color separations and identify process colors and spot colors to avoid misinterpretation by service bureau staff when they make the negatives for the printer.

3. Check all color separations on your laser printer before you have them imageset, so that you can catch problems before they go out.

4. If you show imported art in a file, always include on a separate disk the original file it was created in (i.e., the TIFF, EPS, PICT or PICT 2 file), just in case the imagesetter needs the original file.

5. Use standard fonts and indicate the font library. If you do use an unusual font, include the font in your file.

6. Either use a printer with in-house imagesetting capabilities or be sure your printer is familiar with the imagesetting process. And always ask your printer exactly what he or she needs from you before you go to the service bureau.

Doing It Right

Service bureau regularly encounter a number of problems with the disks submitted to them. The following information identifies the most typical problems and gives you tips on how to avoid them.

Unreadable graphic files: This happens when your software and the service bureau's are incompatible. Check with the bureau before you work with a particular program to be

Your Friend, the Printer

I can't even remember the number of times a printer has saved my skin or a client's during a project. But it has happened often enough that I have come to rely on printers' expertise. We once did a project that involved a direct-mail brochure. The client had his heart set on using a very expensive, special order silver paper. During the quote stage, one printer asked some questions that not only got him the job, but saved our client money and eventual embarrassment. He asked, "How will this piece be mailed? It is going in an envelope or will it be a self-mailer?" I told him it would be a self-mailer. He then wanted to know if it would be bulk mailed or sent through regular mail. It was to be bulk mailed. He then advised us to rethink using the silver paper because it would scratch terribly when it went through the sorting and bundling bulk-mail machines. If he hadn't thought to ask those questions, our client would have been outraged to find that the brochures went out with scratches all over them. And we would have been held responsible.

Always be sure to explain to your printer exactly how your printed pieces will be distributed and handled. Ask what you can do to prevent possible problems or improve the look or quality of the printed piece without adding to the expense. Your printer can be your best friend during the course of a project. She can help you do it right from the beginning and troubleshoot problems as they occur from prepress through delivery.

sure they have that program and that you are working with the correct program version number.

Incorrect type spacing: Your files print out, but the spacing is irregular. That means you have used a font that is incompatible with your service bureau's software equipment. Or you have chosen a style option, such as bolding or italicizing, that causes the file to be misread when transferred to other types of printing equipment. To correct the problem, the service bureau will either have to load substitute fonts, or you will have to go back into your files and choose a compatible font. Always get a font library catalog from your bureau before you begin a project; that way you can be certain about the fonts they offer.

Missing graphics: If you created your graphics with an image file such as TIFF, EPS, PICT or PICT2, and you didn't include the original file with your page layout file, there will not be enough graphic information to print your images. Sometimes the graphics won't be missing, but they'll be distorted or rearranged. This, of course, is just as frustrating. So always include your original graphics files, and inform the service bureau what program(s) your graphics were created in.

Incorrect color key match: This usually means you are using an RGB color model instead of the CMYK model that is used in the four-color printing process. The color in RGB is too brilliant and doesn't behave like CMYK, which simulates the four-color process. So you will need to switch your on-screen color to CMYK. Using Pantone for spot-color jobs will work, but don't use it for four-color work. You may also need to check the print specifications of the inks in your color menu. You may have specified certain inks to overprint that cause problems in later jobs. You will also need to calibrate your colors on a regular basis using a gamma correction program. And check to see that your service bureau does the same.

Unprinted color separations: The source of this problem could be as simple as not having all your colors on in the print options menu, so check for that first.

Spot-colors print out as four-color separations: If this happens, it means you didn't shut off the CMYK colors in your print options menu and specify spot-color.

Registration problems: If images are out of register, it's because you didn't specify traps and chokes when you created them. Some designers don't do this as they go along. Instead, they try to do it after the images have been created. That's risky. It's too easy to miss something on screen.

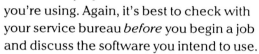 PostScript errors: Sometimes a PostScript problem occurs, and elements will be missing from your layout or will show up someplace else. This is typically a problem with the software you're using. Again, it's best to check with your service bureau *before* you begin a job and discuss the software you intend to use.

Printers

Print shops come in many types and sizes, ranging from the quick print outfits to large companies that can handle large-run four-color jobs. Between these two extremes are many small- to mid-sized companies that do two- or three-color jobs, short-run four-color jobs and so on.

As you work with different printers, you'll learn which ones are the most effective for different kinds of jobs. You'll discover which ones produce top-quality work for a reasonable price and which do only fairly good work for rock-bottom prices. While you'll use the better quality printers more often, sometimes a client's budget just won't stretch any further than rock bottom. Other clients are happy with only a fairly good print job and *prefer* to save the money.

It pays to scout out your printers carefully. When approaching a new printer, ask the owner or sales representative to show you samples of their work. If you are satisfied with the quality of the printer's work and they agree to meet your deadlines, ask for a written price quote. Be sure to find out if they regularly handle the kind of project you're presently working on. If the answer is no, but they agree to do it anyway, chances are their price will be higher than the price from a printer who does these jobs regularly.

Ask if and how they handle electronic files (some printers even have in-house service bureaus). Do they have experience printing from electronically generated film? If so, ask to see samples. Finally, arrange to tour the printing plant if it's close enough for you to do so. Printers who are reluctant to let you see their plants may have something to hide; think twice before giving them work, no matter how good their prices are. While on the tour, carefully study the facilities, the employees and how the work is being done.

It's a good idea to get quotes from three print shops of similar size and capabilities and compare prices. Let the printers know up front that it's your practice to always get three bids before making a decision. When reviewing bids, consider the level of quality your client expects and how much they are willing to

The Right Person for the Job

I once interviewed a photographer who specialized in shooting full-color architectural interiors. His portfolio was absolutely stunning and the chemistry between us was great. But he grew increasingly uncomfortable as I explained the project. I needed a black-and-white shot of a manufacturing company for a trade journal ad. It was a fairly low-budget, no-nonsense photograph that I assumed would be a piece of cake for a photographer of his caliber.

I was about to ask if there was a problem when he volunteered an explanation of his discomfort. He said apologetically, "Don't get me wrong. Things are slow right now and I could really use the work, but I don't think I'm the right photographer for this job. I work best with color and form and the freedom to transform interiors into photographic still life environments. Although it may appear easy to just go out and shoot a building exterior, I'm really not at my best with straightforward, centered shots. I think I may disappoint you."

I was shocked. A photographer turning down a project for fear of disappointing me? Once I might have dismissed him and his honest appraisal of the job as being too egotistical. I would have wanted someone who'd jump when I said, "Jump." But that kind of attitude isn't in your—or your client's—best interest. We need to try to match a project with the person who can do the best possible job.

I really respected that fellow who was in touch with his strengths and weaknesses and had the courage to admit to them. I definitely remembered him when the right project came along, and he didn't disappoint me then.

pay for it, then base your final decision on that. The cheapest bidder may not be the right printer for a particular job.

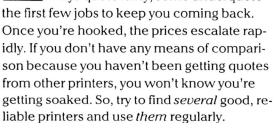

If you've asked the same printer for a price quote on several different jobs, try to give him at least one of them. If you always have to pass on a printer because the prices are out of line, tell her why. Printers like to know what their customers are thinking—or if their needs aren't being met. They may even be willing to adjust prices or practices for you in order to get your business.

Try not to give too much of your business exclusively to one printer—no matter how good the initial work or the quotes are. While most printers always quote fairly, some underquote the first few jobs to keep you coming back. Once you're hooked, the prices escalate rapidly. If you don't have any means of comparison because you haven't been getting quotes from other printers, you won't know you're getting soaked. So, try to find *several* good, reliable printers and use *them* regularly.

Contracting for Freelance Services From Other Professionals

Word of mouth or client recommendations are usually the best place to start if you don't personally know someone who does the kind of work you need. If you strike out there, try the listings in your local advertising trade magazines or the yellow pages.

When you interview individuals you're thinking of working with, review their portfolios, books or samples carefully. Keep the following criteria in mind:

☐ Do they have quality examples of the kind of work you need for your project?

☐ As you describe the project and what you expect from them, do they appear comfortable with your requirements?

☐ Do they contribute useful and sensible suggestions as you review the upcoming project?

☐ If your project calls for special expertise (medical copywriting or technical illustration skills, for example), do they have it? If they don't, they may not be able to compensate for it.

☐ If your project calls for special equipment (such as unusual lights or backdrops), do they have it? If not, can they borrow or rent it? (In this case, get a firm agreement that securing the equipment is their responsibility and that they will have a backup source if needed.)

☐ Do they understand the project's time frame and deadlines? Can they work comfortably within them?

☐ What kind of references can they give you? (Ask one or two of their former clients if the job was completed to their satisfaction, on time, and within the approved budget. Would they use this person or studio again?)

After you've narrowed the field down to the two or three people who seem most likely to deliver what you need, you've got to think about costs. Ask each for a written price quote with an itemized listing of all expenses. You will often have to pay extra for special expertise or to cover the cost of expensive props or equipment. Keep in mind the trade-offs between quality and cost as well; sometimes you do get only what you pay for.

Decide if the estimates look reasonable to you (try to find out what other designers have paid for similar work) and are within your client's budget. If the price quote is too high, but you'd still like to work with a particular person or business, explain your price restrictions. If the job sounds interesting or important, he or she will often try to accommodate a given budget—providing it's not unrealistic. Review the prices with your client before making a final commitment.

Before the job begins, have any outside professional sign a work order that you've prepared. The work order should clearly outline the job description, the agreed-upon price (exclusive of client changes—specify amounts for those separately) and the various deadline requirements for each phase of the project.

How to Develop Good Working Relationships With Collaborators

Working with collaborators involves not only selecting the right people for the job, but also developing and nurturing good working relationships with them throughout the project and beyond. A good working relationship begins with clear communication about the project's requirements, what the client expects, what you expect, deadlines and budget restrictions.

As a project gets underway, part of your job will be to supervise your collaborators' work, not necessarily by telling them what to do, but by presenting your concepts and then soliciting their expert advice and creative ideas. From there, you will need to gently guide them so they can stay on track and give you what you're looking for.

The relationship doesn't end when the project is complete. Paying your collaborators on time is essential if you want to continue the association and guarantee that they will be available when you need them again. Also, let them know how much you enjoyed working with them; this will strengthen the bond between you. A few added touches—like making sure that they get copies of the completed project for their portfolio and passing on any compliments you hear—can go a long way toward solidifying a good relationship.

In your working relationships with your collaborators, try to be open and nonjudgmental. The results will be an increased creative fervor that can actually push the project's concepts and execution to new and unexpected heights. To achieve this level of involvement, it's essential to honor and value your collaborators' suggestions while being careful not to let the seeds of competitiveness take root.

Competitiveness can occur when either the collaborator or the designer feels threatened in any way; then ego steps in. At that point, the work no longer comes from the heart. If you sense this happening, on either your part or your collaborator's, squelch it quickly by refocusing on what is truly important—the integrity of the project. When ego steps in, integrity takes a hike. Creating from the heart means creating from a sense of love for the medium and the message. When creating from the ego, mind indulges a need to feel superior by diminishing the input of others. Ego always destroys a relationship, while the heart enhances and deepens it.

Working with collaborators is one of the more rewarding aspects of design work because it exposes you to and lets you learn from people whose experiences may be vastly different from your own. This cannot help but expand your creative viewpoint and improve the quality of your work.

What to Do When Someone Lets You Down

Sooner or later you're bound to hire someone who fails to meet your job requirements. Your printer promises you that you can pick up your direct mail sales brochure at three. When you arrive, the job is still on press. The printer blames a broken whatzit. He promises to have the job ready first thing in the morning. The next morning it's still not ready. Then the client blames you because the direct mail campaign won't go out on time.

Similar problems affect every designer at least once — and probably many times — during his or her career. It isn't easy to handle these situations tactfully and successfully, but it is possible. Who's to blame in each of the previous scenarios? It may be *you*. Did you give the printer a written schedule clearly outlining deadlines? Did you build in a false deadline a day or two earlier than the absolute deadline to protect yourself?

It's trite but true that an ounce of prevention is worth a pound of cure. Give outside services written production schedules with false deadlines, and make follow-up phone calls. Don't assume that other people will make it their responsibility to check back with you. To prevent problems, routinely touch base several times during the course of a project with every person working on any phase of it. Always put deadlines, job specs, prices, equipment, locations, etc. in writing and get it signed.

Even when you've done everything possi-

ble to prevent problems from happening, they can erupt anyway. The first thing to do is also the hardest — stay calm. Blowing up at an illustrator who drew an antique car when you needed an old truck won't get your truck to magically appear. Your illustrator, now embarrassed and equally angry, may throw the unwanted drawing in your face and walk out. Can you locate another illustrator who will turn somersaults to meet your expired deadline? Probably not.

Getting angry virtually guarantees that the person on the receiving end will retaliate with a similar, and often more powerful, display. Instead, keep a cool head and *explain* your problem. Get whoever has let you down, for whatever reason, on your side. A calm, patient explanation, coupled with an expression of your fear that you will lose this account and a great source of future business for *both* of you could get someone to turn those somersaults you so desperately need right now. If that doesn't work, try suggesting that the client may act against both of you if you can't come through. However you have to do it, make *your* problem *their* problem as well.

Although it's hard when you're scared, angry, and upset about a problem on a job, make sure you're not overreacting or looking for someone to blame for your screwup. If you are, you probably won't recognize what you're doing until days or months later, and by then the damage will be done. Apologize all the same when you've treated someone unfairly — sometimes damage control is still possible. Word travels fast in the graphics and advertising community. And people don't forget when they've been badly treated — especially if they've been somebody's scapegoat. A reputation for being difficult to work with can mean a nonexistent network of people to depend on for backup work, referrals and leads on new clients.

Nearly every businessperson values his or her good reputation and wants to get your business again. Keep that in mind as you grit your teeth and *negotiate* a reasonable settlement (no matter how wrong you "know" they are).

CHAPTER

six

Your
Clients

Making Contacts

Contacts are everywhere. Cultivate your suppliers. They work with a lot of potential clients and have many opportunities to recommend designers. Make friends with your colleagues in ad agencies, public relations firms and design studios. Even if you don't do any work for them, they can often send some your way. Present *satisfied* clients can provide you with plenty of referrals. For example, a realtor recommends you to his accountant, who recommends you to another of her clients. Or work for a chemical company leads to work for a pharmaceutical company leads to work for a hospital. Don't overlook your family, friends and business acquaintances. They, too, can be excellent sources of leads.

 lients are the heart and soul, as well as the bottom line, of your design business. They need you to translate their ideas into reality, their mental images (no matter how fuzzy) into something that can be seen or held. This means that clients are interested first in your skills as a communicator and problem-solver, then in your talent as a designer. Clients want something that looks good to them, but it's got to meet their needs also.

Think about it for a minute. The first step in any design project is figuring out what the client wants — and why. (Sometimes it's hard enough just figuring out what they want: "I think I need a sign, or something, anyway, to tell people about this sale.") Brentom Research Associates wants a logo, so people will not only know who they are but be impressed by what they are. Harvey's Hardware wants a sign that will bring twice as many customers as usual into the store for the big sale. The World's Greatest Advertising Agency wants an ad that will not only produce sales but maybe win an award or two. Good communication is essential to this discovery process.

Getting the client's message across to the target market is based on good communication and problem-solving. You've got to take the client's message and turn it into something the customer will notice, understand and act on. What does the client want the potential customer to know or do? Why might the potential customer want to know or do that? Then you go into the problem-solving phase as you try to translate the client's message. What should a piece look like and what should it say to best reach the desired audience?

So, who are these clients? They come in as many varieties as ice cream: advertising agencies, other graphic design studios, big corporations, small companies, publishers, nonprofit organizations or the guy or gal next door. Their projects can be as exotic as Raspberry Praline Fudge or as plain as Vanilla. They all have one thing in common, though — they all want quality design services from a professional designer that are completed on time and at a reasonable price.

The Two Basic Client Groups

Whoever pays your fee is your client. This is a very straightforward setup when the person buying your services is the one who wants the design project. If a business owner hires you to design her new direct mail package, she tells you what she wants and you go directly to her with your questions.

It's a little more complicated when your client is an ad agency or design studio. In this case, they're acting as middlemen between you (who are working for them) and their clients. When you deal directly with a company or nonprofit organization, you're like the farmer who owns a fruit stand — you sell directly to the buyer who uses it, with no middleman. With an agency, you're like the farmer who sells his produce to a grocery store. The grocery store is the client, although the shopper in the grocery store is the one who really uses the food.

This means that you focus on pleasing the agency rather than the person who's actually going to use the poster, ad or sign. You've got to please that distant, unseen client as well, but your primary goal is meeting your own client's needs. Agency and studio people generally want creative control of a project because they're the ones that have to answer to their clients. So, you'll probably do production work, not creative, unless you've built up a good, long-standing relationship with the agency or studio.

Although the money from working for an agency or studio is good, many designers prefer to deal directly with a client who will ultimately use the finished piece(s). Designers feel this allows them more hands-on involvement from the creative, concept development stage through production. There's also often the opportunity to direct all phases of the project, such as printing and typesetting, for more creative control.

Your personal working style will probably determine whether you choose agencies and studios or individual businesses and organizations as your clients. You can, of course, work with both types of clients, depending on your current interests and the state of your cash flow. Having a diverse list of clients is critical today. There is no longer any such thing as a stable industry or a sure-to-be-in-business-for-ever company. Mergers, acquisitions and business failures change the economic landscape constantly.

If you want hands-on involvement in all phases of a project, you'll probably choose to deal directly with a client who's actually buying a project from you. If you want to be involved only with parts of a project, you'll probably build primarily an agency/studio clientele. If you're just starting out as a designer, working with an agency or studio will let you polish your technical skills, build a portfolio, gain experience making design decisions — under the guidance of experienced professionals — and get paid for it.

Advertising Agencies and Design Studios

There's a lot of overlap these days between the work done by advertising agencies and that done by design studios. Either may produce promotional materials, such as direct mail pieces, print ads, brochures, posters and catalogs. Although some design studios do handle extensive advertising campaigns — coordinated print, audio, video and collateral efforts — ad agencies do much more work in that area. While some agencies get involved in package design, corporate identity programs or annual reports, clients often choose to work with design studios instead. These are projects that require design and graphic production services but not the media or marketing campaigns that agencies specialize in.

You'll have your best chance of getting steady work from smaller agencies or studios. In fact, two or three small agencies and/or studios can keep a freelance designer pretty busy. You'll also have a better chance of doing creative (rather than production) work with a small shop. Smaller studios like to use freelance designers because they often have a different approach or design style that adds variety to the studio's work. Occasionally a large advertising agency will bring in an extremely creative freelance designer to act as a special project art director. This is, however, the exception and not the rule.

You can pick up leads on local ad agencies and design studios in your yellow pages (or the business-to-business yellow pages). This gives you names but will tell you little about the agency or studio. Specialty firms that do direct mail or outdoor advertising will often have separate listings, though. You can also check local business papers or the business section of the local newspaper.

Often your best source of leads is the local grapevine. Other designers, photographers, copywriters, printers, service bureaus and typesetters can tell you who has work for outside designers, what kind of work it is, and what the shop is like to work for. Make contacts through your local chapter of AIGA, AAAA or Art Director's Club, where you can pick up some helpful insider information and meet some potential employers.

To learn more about a particular shop, call them (keep it very brief) and ask which clients they service and whether they use outside design help. If the shop does use outside designers, ask for a contact. (This will usually be a production/traffic coordinator, art director or creative director.) Don't forget to thank anyone you've talked with — even the receptionist — for his time.

On a larger scale, *Adweek* and *Ad Age*, the major advertising journals, will not only give you profiles of many agencies but industry gossip about who has what accounts and what accounts may be changing agencies. *Artist's Market* (Writer's Digest Books), *Adweek Agency Directory* (Adweek Books), and the *Standard Directory of Advertising Agencies* (National Register Publishing Co.) are all updated annually and good sources of leads. *Graphis*, *Communication Arts*, *Print* (*Casebooks* and the *Regional Design Annual*) and *HOW* magazines produce annuals that give agency and studio information with the client's name, as well as featuring shops in their regular issues.

Public relations firms use many of the same services that design studios and ad agencies do. PR firms may pay a little better than some agencies and offer more creative

No Easy Choices

Sometimes agencies and studios will contract with a freelancer for steady part-time or full-time temporary work. This may sound like a nice compromise between security and freedom, especially if times are lean. But (seems like there's always a "but," doesn't it?) you may find that a part-time or temporary full-time position can hurt your design business in the long run. If you take on a full-time stint for a few months, you're going to be out of circulation for that time. So be careful. Regular part-time work is easier to juggle around your own work, but always remember that you can't drop everything to beat a deadline if you start falling behind.

Charging Agencies and Studios for Your Services

Both agencies and studios charge their clients hourly fees or per project package prices for the services they perform. They also mark up prices (anywhere from 15 percent to 100 percent depending on what the market will bear) for all outside services that are charged to the client.

Smaller ad agencies and design studios can't charge their clients as much as larger ones do.

You may need to adjust your rates to work with a smaller shop. (You won't get much work from an agency that's charging less per hour than you'd charge them!) Explain what you're presently getting an hour, then ask the person interviewing you, who will appreciate your being up front about it, if that rate is acceptable. If your going rate is too high, you'll need to know the lowest amount you can comfortably drop to. But before you suggest a lower figure, let the person interviewing you throw out the first offer. It might be more than you expect.

Most agencies and studios aren't going to rip you off; they just need to be able to tack a decent markup onto your fees while keeping them within their own hourly rates. There are, however, some sharks out there, so check out your prospective client first.

opportunities but work may be irregular. You can find listings of these in many of the same periodicals that cover advertising. There's also a directory devoted just to this industry, *O'Dwyer's Directory of Public Relations Firms* (J.R. O'Dwyer Company, Inc.).

Probably the best initial approach to more distant clients is direct mail self-promotion. (See chapter seven, "Pounding the Pavement," for more on self-promotion.) Obviously it's most cost-effective to batch your visits to agencies or studios in more distant cities. If you get called for a portfolio review out of town, try to set up some other appointments in the same area. (It's not always possible but worth a try.)

Agency and Studio Priorities

Working with agencies and studios is easier when you understand why they make the decisions they do. I discovered the freelance designers that I've brought in to work at my agency assumed they knew what was most important to me and my business. A lot of the time they were dead wrong. I hope the following description of agency and studio priorities — in order of importance — *won't* surprise you. If it does, you may need to rethink your working relationships with these clients.

Client Needs: Clients are the foundation of an agency or studio — in fact, *they are the business*. To stay in business, every studio or agency must make client needs top priority.

Profits: Businesses that don't make a profit don't grow. If they're breaking even — making just enough to cover expenses — they may survive for a while but won't be very healthy. Profits pay for new employees to generate more work, buy new equipment, and expand services and facilities. Of course, there are no profits without clients and no growth without finding new clients and increasing revenues from existing ones. Which takes us back to Priority Number One: Client Needs.

Quality Work: Every agency or studio strives to produce quality work. However, there are times when quality work won't meet a client's needs. Discount retailers, for example, know that brash, cluttered pieces appeal more to their target market than attrac-

tive, elegant ones. And at times, clients just want something that any right-minded designer wouldn't use to paper a doghouse. Because client needs are job number one, an agency or studio will lower its standards and produce what the client requests. Only very successful agencies or studios can afford to turn away clients who request low caliber advertising or design. (Some agencies moving up may do this, even if they can't afford it, to attract a certain clientele.)

How Jobs Flow Through Agencies and Studios

If you've never worked with an agency or studio before, you may not know how work flows through their system. Knowing who works with a project, how and why will help you better understand where you fit in and what's expected of you.

Stage One: A new project is introduced by an account executive to management.

Stage Two: When they feel a project has one of the two "Ps" — Profit or Potential — management gives it a go-ahead. Then specific members of the account team, including researchers, art directors, copywriters and production people, are assigned to it.

Stage Three: The traffic/production coordinator slots the project into the flow and puts together a tentative production schedule.

Stage Four: All members of the account team agree when and how to proceed; a final production schedule is drawn up. The account executive then asks the client to approve this schedule.

Stage Five: The research team makes their recommendations, based on study and evaluation of the project's targeted audience, the competition and current trends. The creative team will use this information to build a creative concept or idea.

Stage Six: The creative team informally presents their ideas to management and the account executive. If the concepts are approved, the production team prepares comps for the client.

Stage Seven: The art director puts together cost estimates for creative development and production. Management and the account executive must then approve these costs.

Stage Eight: When the project and its costs are approved by the client, the creative and production team begin actual production. Each phase of production must be approved by the account executive and the client.

Stage Nine: When all production work is complete and the client has approved and signed off on the finished project, the agency bills the client.

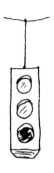

Fresh, Creative Approaches: These are the lifeblood of advertising and design. Clients spend big money on advertising and design because people are attracted by the new and different and can more easily screen out the familiar. However (and this is a very big however), creativity and innovation alone won't guarantee that the audience will respond the way the client wants. The client's comfort level with innovation is also important. No matter how fresh and creative it may be, work the client doesn't feel comfortable using won't get used. So, agencies and studios want to do creative work but that comes second to meeting the client's needs (Priority Number One, again).

What Does All This Mean for You?

You need to show agencies and studios that you understand their priorities and concerns. If you can combine creative flair with a willingness to work within the necessary limitations, you'll get very steady work—and income—from agencies and studios.

A common mistake freelancers, especially beginners, make is concentrating their efforts on impressing the ad agency or studio who hired them with their creativity and talent. Instead, focus on understanding what the agency or studio wants to give the client. Always ask about the boundaries of your role on a project. If you blithely assume you know, you may be very disappointed when you bring in designs for approval.

Printers

Many printing companies offer design services to their customers who don't need or can't afford a regular ad agency or design studio. While some printers do have in-house designers, most bring in a designer only when they need one. If you're just starting out, work-ing with a printer is a good way to build up your portfolio and bring in a small, but fairly steady income. If you're fresh out of design school, doing these basic projects for a printer will help build up not only your portfolio but also your production and design skills. Working for a

printer might also be a good way to justify your computer, since you can do most of your production work right on the computer.

Projects from printers will generally be low budget and often one-shot deals such as flyers, posters, stationery or simple brochures and pamphlets. Most of the design and mechanical work needed will be simple and straightforward. Doing good design work on a limited budget can be an enjoyable challenge. On the other hand, you don't want to invest more time than you can afford in one of these projects. Printers charge their customers fairly low rates for design, so you won't be able to charge the printer very much either. (Printers often prefer to work with designers who offer only basic, competent design and production skills but whose prices are lower.) While it's always important to do your best work on each project, keep a careful eye on how much unbillable time you may rack up on a printer's project (see page 89 for more on when and why you should work for little or no money).

Publishing Companies

Most of the design and production work for publishers is done by their staffs. Tight deadlines and frequent last-minute changes make it difficult to use outside designers. For the same reason, most of the work available from publishing companies will be production rather than design related, and freelancers with some knowledge or experience with publication layout and design will have an edge.

Opportunities for doing creative work for a publishing company are more rare, but they do exist. Newspapers experiment with different formats and mastheads. Publishers have magazines redesigned to keep pace with changing tastes and design styles. Book publishers will occasionally work with outside designers on interior and cover designs. If you're also an illustrator or have a strong background in type design, you'll have a better chance of getting publication work. Depending on the type of project, a publisher may want someone with a very distinctive design

What's a Marketing Director?

Marketing involves the principles and procedures of positioning a company's product or service in the marketplace. In order to develop advertising and promotional strategies to achieve marketing goals, companies need to know what will motivate people to buy their products or use their services. The marketing director either does or supervises the research to identify those specific motivating factors. This information (market research) will help a designer zero in on just the right creative concepts to captivate the targeted customers.

If you are working with a marketing director, heed his or her advice. He or she understands both the company—what it does, how and why—and the potential customer very well. If you haven't previously been exposed to the importance of market research in designing advertising graphics, you can learn much about how it works from a good marketing director.

style and a lot of flair or someone whose work fits into the house design style.

You'll have a better chance of doing creative work with a small publisher, who may not be able to afford the salary for a full-time designer. (You may even have to explain to some "Mom and Pop" type publishers just what you can do for their publications.) To learn what publishers, if any, are in your area check *Literary Market Place* at your local library. Other good sources are *Writer's Market*, *Artist's Market*, *Novel and Short Story Writer's Market* (includes many small presses), and *The International Directory of Little Magazines and Small Presses*. Rates vary a great deal in publication work but are often low compared with other kinds of work. Be up front about your rates but be prepared to reduce them, especially when working with smaller publishers.

Small Businesses

Small businesses are everywhere: restaurants, drugstores, bowling alleys, real estate offices, beauty parlors, law firms, contractors and large and small retail stores. Your average small business won't have enough work to hire a regular ad agency or good-sized design firm but will occasionally need the services of a designer. Many small business owners want signs and posters, use stationery and forms preprinted with their business name and address, or go to printers and typesetters if they need a brochure, flyers or logo. Although there are certain risks involved, start-ups are heavy users of design services. So are young, rapidly growing businesses. An independent designer can build a nice pool of clients by searching out and pitching to local businesses.

To get leads on small businesses who could use your design services:

◆ See who's already advertising in newspapers or mailers
◆ Ask local printers and typesetters for referrals
◆ Join the Chamber of Commerce
◆ Check out malls and shopping centers

◆ Join organizations such as church, sports or social clubs
◆ Work with nonprofit volunteer groups
◆ Walk through your town's business district
◆ Read the yellow pages
◆ Check out businesses around local attractions
◆ Do promotion for local special events.

Obviously this is only a small sampling of ways to get names of potential clients. But a list of names by itself won't do you much good. You need to get to know your local small businesses and their owners.

Most local businesspeople are fairly informal and will respond well to a casual call to introduce yourself and your business. You won't need a fancy presentation or portfolio, just your business card and some printed samples. Be prepared to talk about what you can do for them and why money spent on a designer will be a good investment.

Most will want attractive, relatively inexpensive materials that call favorable attention to their businesses. They'll be interested in problem-solving and results. Will new letterhead improve their business's image? How? Will a "fancy" poster increase sales? How much? Beyond these basics, each small business's needs will be different, a reflection of the products and services provided. A grocery store owner would want simple, bold posters to promote sales, while an antique shop would need attractive business cards and stationery. Try to get a handle on a business's needs before you call. Study the advertising and promotional materials they're already using, if any. Stop by a store to see what kinds of merchandise they carry, check out the menu and atmosphere at a restaurant, or see who visits a local beauty parlor.

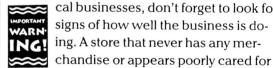 While you're checking out the needs of local businesses, don't forget to look for signs of how well the business is doing. A store that never has any merchandise or appears poorly cared for or a restaurant that never has any customers may be having financial problems. (Of course, some businesses appear to be thriving until the day they suddenly fold, but this is generally the exception and not the rule.)

When in doubt about working with someone, don't. You not only want to get a job, but you want to get paid for it.

Corporations and Large and Mid-Sized Companies

Business has discovered design. In addition to their traditional relationships with advertising agencies, companies and corporations are expanding in-house design staffs and also turning to independent designers. There are as many kinds of corporate projects as there are corporations. Designers may be called in to work on everything from a single simple brochure to a corporate identity system. In addition to the traditional projects such as logos, advertising, brochures, annual reports, in-house newsletters, promotional publications, posters, promotional packages and stationery, designers are now getting calls to work on training materials, signage, sets for sales meetings and conferences, party invitations and environmental design.

Competition for the bigger businesses is intense. Top design studios such as Pentagram Design, the Duffy Design Group, and Chermayeff & Geismar Associates hustle for those accounts. Knowing that there's tough competition isn't an excuse for not trying to get your own piece of the action, though. The next major account you go after might be *your* big break.

When approaching a mid-sized or larger company cold, make sure you target your efforts to the right person. An information services director might do soft-sell promotional or strictly informational materials but not annual reports. A corporate communications director might handle annual reports and public relations materials but not marketing or advertising. A manager of marketing communications or sales manager may handle all sales-related literature and nothing else. (Firms that sell products to other businesses use a lot of sales literature, so it can pay to seek out the right person in sales.) If you get the opportunity to show or send samples of your work, make sure they're appropriate.

Also take the time to get familiar with what-ever the company does. You don't need to know the details of all its operations, but you should have a general idea of the products or services it supplies. If you can get a feeling for its corporate culture, too, it can put you way ahead. You won't get a very warm reception if you send an avant garde piece to a dyed-in-the-wool conservative outfit.

Trade shows are an excellent way to investigate an industry. You'll find leads, learn about the types of support materials used industry-wide, and get good background on individual manufacturers and their problems. Most industries also have their own trade publications (check your local library for their names and addresses) that will supply you with names, events and developments. Directories are also good sources of names and addresses of prospects; for example, there are *Thomas's Register of Manufacturers*; *Standard and Poor's Register of Corporations, Directors and Executives*; and *The Directory of Corporations*. Follow the business press carefully; *The Wall Street Journal*, *Forbes*, *Fortune* and *Business Week* can provide many leads.

Watch closely segments of business that are undergoing rapid change. Small, fast-growing companies can often give plenty of work — identity, promotional and informational materials — to a designer. Because they're growing and changing so rapidly, they're an excellent source of repeat business as well. A lot of takeovers or other changes in a volatile industry can signal opportunity. Many former executives respond to losing their positions by starting up their own businesses. Since all start-ups must register with the State Bureau of Taxation, you can pick up leads to many new businesses there.

How can you improve your chances of landing a corporate or big business account? One way is to become a specialist in a particular area of design. Focus on designing logos, brochures, trade advertising or whatever else you're especially good at and really enjoy designing. Another way is to specialize in an industry or segment of an industry — high-tech industries, restaurants or china makers, for example. To go this route, you'll need to have an in-depth understanding of the needs and

Video: The New Frontier

Video is gradually becoming the new frontier of graphic design. While television commercials are a staple of mass-market advertising, video has other applications as well. It's gaining wider acceptance as an alternate marketing and image-making tool for business-to-business sales in highly specialized markets. Salespeople find videos a more convenient, effective way to show prospective customers exactly what their company has to offer. And personnel and training departments use instructional tapes to assist with on-the-job training and motivation programs.

In addition to creating graphics for and often even producing videotapes for corporate and industrial clients, designers are often involved in producing coordinated support materials. For example, a training film could be supplemented by manuals or handbooks. You might be asked to design a set of graphs and charts that will work both as part of a video and in print.

Work closely with the video production house and/or service bureau if you're working on a graphics computer to make sure the materials you create will reproduce well. Reproducing graphics on film is quite different from print reproduction.

What's an Advertising Manager?

Many companies and nonprofit groups will have an in-house advertising manager or director. These people handle much of the organization's needs on their own or with a small internal staff. Advertising managers hire a freelance designer to reduce overload or to bring special expertise to a particular project.

Never forget that the advertising manager – not the organization! – is your client. Your goal is to give that manager what he or she wants, not what you think the organization wants. You'll score points for understanding that person's individual work needs and doing your best to make his or her job easier.

Many advertising managers come from backgrounds unrelated to design or advertising. Some may know a lot about promotion and marketing but not much about design or production. Others have come up through the organization's ranks and may be experienced in design, copy, production, etc. Don't get me wrong: Many of these people are extremely good at their jobs! But you don't have any way of knowing that at first, especially with a new client. Try to determine right away what an advertising manager's strengths and weaknesses are so you can communicate well with him and both do your best work.

trends of that industry or business. This means becoming an expert not only on the product or service itself but also on its market(s) and how it's promoted and sold. *Pro bono* work (also know as freebies for a good cause) can be a way of calling attention to your design talents — while contributing to your community or a cause you believe in.

Entering award competitions is another good way to call yourself to the attention of corporate clients. It's excellent advertising and corporate clients may feel a little more secure about going with a designer whose talent has been recognized by the industry. Advertising in one or more of the major showcases (*American Showcase, The Creative Blackbook, The Workbook* or *a.r. The Annual Report,* for example) will put your name in front of a lot of corporate marketing people. A showcase ad is very expensive, but if you're trying to get more high-end clients, it may be a worthwhile investment in the long term.

Nonprofit Organizations

Any organization that relies on endowments and contributions rather than generating extra return on income ("profit") is considered a nonprofit organization. Most of us are familiar with the traditional charities and service organizations that fall under this umbrella: the United Way, the Red Cross and all the groups dedicated to combatting various health problems. Zoos, performing arts groups, and many museums and historic sites or organizations are also nonprofits.

Because they're dependent on fund-raising efforts, nonprofits must produce a lot of informational and promotional material, such as annual reports, newsletters, direct mail packages, posters, T-shirts and press kits. Working with nonprofits can help you build up a specialization or do different types of projects from those of your regular business clients. Some nonprofits are more conservative in attitude and style and will prefer a designer with a traditional approach. Other nonprofit organizations are more innovative and will give you a chance to do more experimental pieces.

It's easier to get your foot in the door with

nonprofits than with many businesses. Like businesses, nonprofits need quality materials that get results, but they don't usually need the level of market and sales expertise that ad agencies and larger design studios offer. The structure and organizational policies of a nonprofit will also be different from those of a for-profit business. Taking the time to learn a nonprofit's particular idiosyncrasies will make it easier to work with that organization and will help build repeat business.

Although many of the larger nonprofits can and do hire advertising agencies to manage their efforts, there's still plenty of work available for freelancers and small design studios. Budgets will vary, depending on the size of the organization and type of project they want to produce. If you can be flexible with your prices, you'll get not only repeat business but also many referrals to other nonprofits needing reliable designers. There are real opportunities for a designer to carve out a nice consistent business by working with nonprofits. In addition to earning a decent living, you may get a feeling of personal satisfaction from producing work for groups that are dedicated to helping people without personal benefit.

Institutions

An institution is any organization that has a social, religious or educational purpose; it may be for profit or not for profit. Institutions include hospitals and nonprofit health care facilities; trade associations; colleges, universities, trade and technical schools and some museums; and historic sites or foundations such as Colonial Williamsburg. Although even many for-profit institutions operate on tight budgets, they can be a good, steady source of work.

Institutions are generally dependent on fund-raising and government grants, so both nonprofit and for-profit organizations produce promotional and informational material. Educational institutions and trade associations also need a lot of recruitment materials to maintain and increase their student populations or membership.

Because their budgets are often limited, many institutions are willing to take a chance

The In-House Writer as Client

Many areas of corporate communications that were once seen as the exclusive domain of high-priced PR firms and ad agencies have now gone in-house because of tighter budgets. While the result has been more opportunities for small, independent designers to work with these corporations, it has also created a new client relations issue for small shops – the in-house writer/corporate communications manager who has little, if any, practical design experience or experience working with designers. Be prepared to alter your working role when accepting a project with this type of client. You may become designer, guide *and* project coordinator. Make sure that project goals and schedules are defined. Throughout the process, respect your client's expertise – this project may not be the only thing on her plate. She may want to give you added responsibility. A team approach is essential.

the largest organization, however, may occasionally offer opportunities for work with one of its departments.

Satisfaction

The list and descriptions of potential design clients in this chapter is by no means the last word. I'm sure you've thought of a lot of opportunities that I've overlooked, and that's great. To the extent that you're also thinking of clients in terms of their wants and needs, that's even better. Understanding those wants and needs is the key to keeping your clients satisfied. And keeping your clients satisfied is the key to a successful design business.

Marketing yourself and your work is a long-term proposition. It begins with an initial introduction, "Here's who I am and what I can do for you." And it continues through each project, "Here's a design that will solve your problem in a way that fits your values and expectations." Make your clients feel they're important to you, that you'll make them look good, and they'll return the compliment by giving you repeat business and referrals to colleagues.

on less-experienced designers and generally offer more creative freedom. Larger or more conservative organizations provide fewer opportunities to break into this market or do highly creative work. Large hospitals and educational institutions especially may need a level of expertise and service that larger design studios and ad agencies can supply. Even

CHAPTER
seven

**Pounding
the
Pavement**

You Are What You Are

One of my staff designers was very good at turning concepts into beautiful, dynamic designs. Once he understood what the concept was and what you wanted him to do with it, he was off and running. He wasn't very good at coming up with ideas or getting from idea to concept, but it didn't matter for the kind of work he did. Unfortunately, he decided he was such a hotshot designer that he could make a lot more money working for himself. He got a lot of work at first, because people knew he did great designs. But it didn't take long for word to get around about what he *couldn't* do—come up with ideas to design from. Within a year, he was back to staff work, because people weren't comfortable working with someone who'd oversold his abilities. He later told me that he was actually happier doing staff work; overestimating his design skills was one of the biggest mistakes he'd ever made!

elling is an art. I'm serious; this is not a gimmick to get you to read a chapter on the subject. There are as many opportunities for you to be creative or inventive when promoting your work as you'll find at the drawing board. That doesn't mean it's easy or fun. On the other hand, how much fun is design when it's 3:00 A.M. and you've got nothing down for that 8:00 A.M. presentation?

Selling has gotten a bad reputation over the years because most people think selling is sleazy. The word reminds us of high-pressure telephone sales pitches and used car lots full of great buys. But you don't have to think of it that way. Selling design is simply persuading the client that you can provide a valuable service for his money. If you really believe that's true—and you'd better or you shouldn't be in his office in the first place—then what's so bad about that?

Personally, I think the fear factor is the biggest obstacle to selling. We're afraid of *rejection*. What if I do a promotion piece and nobody responds? What if I call on twenty prospective clients and they all say no? What if they don't like my work? What if they don't like me? Before long, we've convinced ourselves that it's useless to try, so we avoid or ignore selling our design.

The reality: Any of those awful things can happen—and probably will—at some point in everyone's career. Not everyone will like your work or want to hire you as a designer. You're going to have to deal with rejection, which hurts. The good news: Rejection is not fatal; it just feels that way. Seriously, though, your track record will improve if you work as hard to sell your design as you do to create it. And it will get easier to live with the rejections when you've built up some confidence in yourself and your work—they go down much easier when you've coated them with some successful sales.

Begin your marketing plan by deciding to treat yourself as well as you do your clients. Put the same time, effort and thought into developing your own identity package and promotional materials as you would a client's. If you've already done some corporate identity or advertising work, you're already familiar with parts of this process. If you haven't, don't worry. This is your chance to get some experience with researching markets and developing identity and promotional materials.

Then you take your show on the road. Although you may be very uncomfortable with cold calling or showing your portfolio, it's an important part of your education both as a businessperson and as a designer. The feedback you get gives you the opportunity to fine-tune your work as well as your skills in working with clients. Later you may be able to turn the actual selling over to someone else, but you'll work better with that person if you understand how to do it yourself.

Where Is Your Design Business Now?

If you were creating an identity package for a client, you'd begin by gathering information about the company—its product or service and its image—then work with the client to establish objectives for the identity program. You need to know what the market for the product or service is, what people think about it, who the competition is, and what people think about them. When you evaluate your own business, you must be as objective as possible about both your design and business skills. It's terribly tempting to build your image around the business you want or hope to have—but doing so can be disastrous. You'll only end up wasting valuable time and money if you aren't brutally honest about what you can and can't do. It won't take long for reality to catch you.

Information Gathering and Analysis

The first step toward developing your identity package and eventually a marketing plan is to determine what your strengths and weaknesses as a designer and businessperson are. To get you started on your evaluation, here's a little self-test you may find helpful. This test isn't the final analysis of your design business, but it will show you the kinds of questions you need to ask to determine where and what your design business is.

1. Why did I go into business? What did I hope to achieve?

2. What services do I presently offer my clients?

3. Do I have a specialty or special skills?

4. Do I have experience working in or with clients from any particular business areas, such as health care, high tech, industrial, retail?

5. How would I describe the quality of my work in the following areas on a scale from 1 to 5, with 5 being excellent?

___ Developing design concepts
___ Translating ideas into designs
___ Creating dynamic, effective layouts
___ Typography
___ Desktop typesetting/publishing
___ Making mechanicals (including computer-based layout)
___ Doing illustrations
___ Copywriting
___ Editing
___ Production management (buying services, preparing for reproduction)

6. Do I have a particular design style? Or do I have a slightly different style for each project depending on that project's purpose and special needs? How would I describe my work in general: whimsical, humorous, direct, sophisticated, etc.?

7. What elements of my design are most eye-catching? And why?

8. How consistent is the level of quality of my work? If it varies, when does it do so and why?

9. Have I employed the same design solutions on a range of different design problems?

10. Are there any elements that will make my work look dated in a year? Does any of my work look dated already?

11. Do I change my styles or work often, doing what's trendy at the moment? How does that affect the way my work looks?

12. What projects have I enjoyed most? Disliked most? Why?

13. Which of the following describe my attitude toward the work I'm doing? (Place a check mark next to any that apply.)

___ I prefer to stick with what I know and do well.
___ I'm a go-anywhere, do-anything person.
___ I like to do a variety of activities each day.
___ I prefer to stick with one job until it's done.
___ I'd love to work with four-color all the time.
___ I really enjoy the challenge of doing quality work on a limited budget.
___ I prefer collaborating with, rather than working for, my clients.
___ I do my best work when I'm left alone to develop my ideas.
___ I prefer working with clients who know what they want.
___ I'd rather have the freedom to develop my own ideas on a project.
___ Producing mechanicals is boring.
___ I like to watch my projects come together when I do the mechanicals.
___ I'd rather have a number of clearly defined, short-term projects I can finish quickly.
___ I'd rather work on long-term projects, getting in at the beginning and developing them gradually over time.

14. How would I rate my performance in these areas (ranking from 1 to 5, with 5 being excellent)?

___ Knowing how to position clients in their markets
___ Analyzing a client's market and competition
___ Staying within a budget
___ Meeting deadlines
___ Turnaround time
___ Keeping clients informed about projects
___ Giving clients the best possible prices
___ Helping clients decide what's best for their project

15. Who are my present clients? (If moving out of an agency or studio: What clients will still give me work? If just starting out, what clients do I think I'll have?) Where are they located? What kinds of businesses are they?

16. What kinds of projects do my clients give me?

17. How difficult do I find them to work with? Why?

18. How profitable are they?

19. How much money do I make from my business?

If you also provide illustrations, copywriting, editing, photography or other services to your clients, evaluate what you do, how you feel about the work, and how profitable it is for your business.

Once you've completed your self-evaluation, look through it for patterns. Are your strengths also what you enjoy doing? Are you better at coming up with ideas and working them out? Or are you better at the production aspects? Are you better at creative work or at working with clients — or are these about even? Do you lean toward preferring total involvement and control on a project or toward doing bits and pieces of a lot of things? Compare your strengths, weaknesses, likes and dislikes with the projects you're getting. Is there a good fit?

Then write out a profile of your design business, including your design skills and the services you offer. For example, if you're doing a lot of production-related work or short-term projects, you have a primarily service-oriented business. If you're doing a lot of one- and two-color work on a small budget, you have low-end clients. If all your clients are in the same industry — retail, service, health care — or you're doing the same kind of project for a variety of clients, you're specializing (whether or not it's intentional). What do you have to offer as a designer beyond basic design and production skills?

Include what your strengths and weaknesses are. Are you very budget-conscious or careless? Are you stronger at working with type or layout or handling illustrations? Can you do beautiful, low-cost designs — but miss deadlines in order to get the pieces as perfect as possible? Do you spend so much time on design that you sometimes slop through the

mechanicals to stay on schedule?

What Do I Want to Do?

Once you've defined where your business is now, it's time to decide where you want it to go. That direction depends on how you feel about what you're already doing. Do you want:

♦ To do more of what you're doing now? Why?
♦ To get a broader range of projects? Why?
♦ To explore a whole new field? Why?
♦ To develop a specialization or change yours? Why?
♦ To make more money or win more awards? Why?
♦ To get better work? Why?
♦ To _____ (fill in your own)? Why?

If you answered more of the same, congratulations! If not, how well do your current projects fit your strengths? If there's not a good match, what do you need to change? Perhaps you've drifted into taking any job as long as it pays well — or at all. Perhaps you're not making clients aware of all your abilities. If you want to change fields or specializations, are you actively seeking new clients or depending on referrals? Referrals are a great way to get new clients, *unless* you want to break into a new industry, develop a new specialization, or want more varied projects.

Once you've determined why and how your present situation differs from where you want to be, think about what it will take to get there. If you're not getting the kinds of proj-

Reality Check!

Take out your portfolio and any good recent work that's not already in there. If most of your good recent work isn't in your portfolio, this is a good time to edit and update it. How do you feel about the work in your portfolio? Does it reflect your strengths and a broad range of your capabilities? Think about whether it reflects the direction you want your business to take. If you can't immediately see possibilities, de- cide whether you can actually do what you want — or if you're indulging in wishful thinking. If your four-color work is never as good as your newsletter designs, can you really develop the skills to move into four-color ads or brochures?

ects you want from present clients, can they give you different opportunities? Or will you need to go after different clients? Do you need to improve some of your design skills or develop new ones? If you're satisfied with where you are, think about how you'll find more clients that will give you the same opportunities. If you've done all your work in a single industry, consider expanding into others where you can find similar work. Make a list of as many different ideas as possible, no matter how crazy they sound.

Now, define your objectives and set some goals for yourself. Let's say you want a broader range of projects than you get now. You might set yourself an objective of seeking out clients who will need a variety of services. You could also target a certain type of project you want to start doing—annual reports, four-color ads, posters—and pursue clients who need those services. Once you've chosen that objective, you need to set goals that will help you achieve it. Be positive and specific. Set such goals as "get five new clients by the end of June" or "target clients in the health services industry." This gives you the first pieces of a marketing plan for your design business. The next step is identifying potential clients and letting them know you're out there and want their business.

The Right Clients

If you're not getting the kind of work you want, you don't have the right clients. And even if you do, you still need to expand your contacts. That means finding clients who want the kind of work you want to do. In the last chapter, "Your Clients," we looked at the different types of clients and the services they're most likely to buy. Once you've defined the broad audience for your marketing efforts, refer to that chapter for more detailed information on different kinds of clients and where to find them. For now, it's enough to determine what large groups of clients represent your best prospects. For example, every business needs identity materials, but a local insurance company might want only black-and-white letterhead and business cards. A

mid-sized manufacturing company is more likely to want a complete identity system and be willing to pay for two- or three-color work.

Look for examples of the kinds of projects you want to get. Flip through annuals, creative directories, newspapers and magazines and note the designer or ad agency and client responsible for pieces you wish you had produced. Check out posters and promotional material for public events or performing arts groups. Then brainstorm a little: Who else might need work like the samples you've seen? Public relations firms use many of the same materials as ad agencies. Service organizations, such as hospitals, buy annual reports just as Fortune 500 companies do.

Next break your lists into categories, looking for patterns. You may have advertising

Reality Check #2

Take out your portfolio and other recent work. Is it of the same caliber and quality as the samples you admire from other designers? You may not have done exactly the same kind of work, but you may have been practicing those basic skills. If some of your work matches your wants but some doesn't, you may need to eliminate that kind of work and clients from your list at least for now. If you feel that little of your work fits the kind you most want to do, give yourself some self-assignments and find out if you *can* do that kind of work or must adjust your ambitions. If your reach currently exceeds your grasp, don't give up. Try to get the kinds of projects that will help you improve your skills and develop others you need. Then when you're ready, go for it!

agencies, design firms, colleges, foundations, doctors, computer companies or health service organizations. Then choose three groups for your initial investigation. Start out with only three groups to investigate. This will keep your research project to more manageable levels. You'll need to learn something about each industry and the wants and needs of potential clients in it to make your marketing efforts most productive. You also need to get your list down to the level of specific names not just of companies but of the individuals there who will actually buy your services. If you don't know the names, phone the agencies or companies and ask. Most receptionists will gladly help, es-

What's in a Name?

Many designers simply use their own names for their business names, Sibley Peteet Design, for example. Others include a tag line or specifier that explains what they do or describes their specializations, such as Shelby Designs and Illustrates. Because they tell exactly what you do, tag lines and specifiers are a good way to stand out from the crowd, especially if you're just starting out.

Some designers operate under business names only, Pinkhaus Design, for example. If you go this route, try to choose a name that is not only memorable but also tells something about your business. Some names that really made an impression on me are: Ink, Inc., Graphic Design at the Top, After 5 Graphics, Art Direction Unlimited, Ads to Go and Overnight Graphics.

Choose a name that you can live with. You'll confuse your clients if you change it often. Some good reasons to change — and do some interesting self-promotion — are a merger with another firm, expansion by taking on partners or associates, or a major change in your services.

pecially if you don't want to talk to the person in question. Just say you're putting something in the mail and want to get the name right.

Highlight any local businesses or organizations that may appear on your list. If there aren't any local businesses, try your local yellow pages or business yellow pages. It's most cost effective to thoroughly explore the local market and refine your goals and methods first, and then go after more distant clients. You can sometimes move out of that local market pretty fast, but it's still a good place to start.

Hey, World, Here I Am!

"Hi! Remember me? We met at that party at the beach last week." You met at least a hundred people at that party and almost all of their faces are now a blur. You definitely don't remember this particular face at all. Like most of those other people, nothing about this one stands out in your mind. Unless this person does something special *now*, you'll walk away and not look back.

It's even harder to make a lasting, favorable impression in business than at a party. You must communicate who you are, what you do, and how you're different from the competition in an interesting way in about thirty seconds. And every other designer is doing the same thing at the same time. That means you have to cut through a lot of visual noise to make sure clients will remember *you* when assignments come up.

The first step toward standing out in the crowd is to decide what message you want to communicate. Demonstrate the value of working with you to the clients you want. All your promotional materials — your firm's name, your stationery, portfolio and self-promotion pieces — must work together to get

UP THE LADDER OF SUCCESS that message across. If you're marketing your services to a wide variety of clients, your basic identity package must work for all of them while you tailor your portfolio and self-promotion pieces to specific client groups.

Never attempt to develop an identity package without a clear idea of what you want it to

Reality Check #3

Test your theories about what clients need which services with a quick informal telephone survey. Pick ten local businesses that fall into the three groups you've targeted for promotion. Call each, introduce yourself, and explain that you're a designer scouting for new business. Try to speak to the owner of smaller businesses. For a larger business, ask who is responsible for design or advertising. Don't use design jar-gon when you call. Operators and secretaries understand functional descriptions and titles but probably won't know insider design terminology.

Ask if the company uses graphic design services. If you find out they don't need design services, thank the person for his or her time, and go on to the next one. If they do use designers, ask what kinds of services they use and their major concern in selecting a designer. Always ask the name of the person you're speaking to and to whom you should send promotional materials. If it's the same person, you've made a contact; if not, you know whom to approach for a follow-up.

Once you know the needs of the clients you've targeted, you can address those needs specifically in all your marketing and promotional materials. For example, you've learned that hospitals do produce annual reports but on very tight turnaround. You can then stress your fast turnaround times when you bid for those jobs. If you interview several potential clients in a particular industry and none want the kinds of services you plan to provide, you should put investigating that group on hold for a while. You at least know what their needs are if you decide to approach them in the future.

accomplish. You want to be remembered as a designer with definite, valuable skills who can communicate a message clearly. Although you can develop your promotional materials in any order, I recommend that you start with your identity package. Not only because you'll need these items first and won't change them often, but also because developing these will help you decide how you want to be perceived and the best way to promote that perception. Then, arranging your portfolio and developing self-promotion materials will come easily.

Your Identity Package

Designing stationery, business cards and business forms is an exciting challenge because it's an opportunity to display your skills as a visual communicator with some style and flair.

You could be sober and steady, elegant and sophisticated, or whimsical and humorous. But it's not enough just to show your personality or an image of your business, you also need to reflect the personalities of your present or prospective clients. Conservative businesses and professionals such as doctors and lawyers may shy away from using a designer they perceive to be too off-the-wall. At the same time, you don't want to come off as stodgy or boring if you have clients who are more artsy.

After you decide the image you want to project, choose the message you want to communicate. Do you want to stress your ability to come up with creative solutions? Do you need to show people you do both design and illustrations? Will you emphasize your communication skills or speedy turnaround time?

The final consideration is how your competition present themselves. What services do similar-sized design firms offer? What clients are they targeting? While you do compete with local advertising agencies and the larger design studios, your major competitors, at least initially, are other individual designers and small design firms. Start by checking the listings for designers in your local yellow pages, even though not all designers can afford such ads. See if you recognize any of the names and can remember their specialties. If you can't pinpoint many of your competitors' services that way, check with your local Art Director's Club or AIGA chapter and any industry trade magazines that cover activities in your area.

If none of these methods produce the information you want, conduct a telephone survey of local designers. Call each designer or studio whose services you haven't identified. When you reach the designer or a secretary, tell them that you're conducting a survey of design services in the area. If they are willing to talk with you, ask only two questions. "What kind of design work does your studio do?" and "How would you categorize the majority of your clients — corporate, nonprofit, retail?"

If you get guarded or minimal answers, don't try to get more information. You don't want to appear pushy or to be prying into their businesses. You simply want to learn what they offer so you can decide to offer similar services or to tap into a less crowded market by offering different ones.

Try to track down examples of your competitors' work and promotional materials. Study the types of work they're doing and their design styles. See what design or graphic elements and copy they're using. If you can't review their promotional materials, you can probably still make an educated guess from looking at their work. If the graphic elements that you thought reflected your business image and personality seem very similar to other designers' styles or materials, consider how you can convey the same ideas about your business in a different way. You don't need to include a lot of splashes of color or dozens of graphic elements to say "creative."

Now you're ready to position yourself to your targeted clients. Set a budget for your 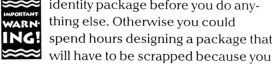 identity package before you do anything else. Otherwise you could spend hours designing a package that will have to be scrapped because you can't afford to produce it. Even worse, you might fall in love with a design you can't afford and decide to do it anyway — a recipe for financial disaster.

It's probably easiest to develop your logo ideas first and build the rest of your identity package around it. If your budget is small, de-sign your letterhead so you can photocopy business forms onto it or print them onto it with a laser printer. (Depending on your letterhead design, that would work with the forms included in chapter two of this book.) You can always design custom forms later.

My emphasis on considering your business forms to be an integral part of your identity package may come as a surprise to some of you. After all, *prospective* clients never see them. Wrong! Every present client is also a future client, so never take them for granted. Any communication between you and your clients, even an invoice for your services, is a chance to make a memorable impression. Well-designed business forms enhance your

Effective, Not Expensive

You can demonstrate your creative flair without spending a lot of money by investing time and creativity instead. Printing in one-color doesn't mean always using black ink. Work with your printer to find a colored ink and colored stock that will give you the look you want and still be legible. Add a swash of extra color with a metallic-ink marker, colored pencils or watercolors over or around your studio name or logo. Rubber stamps and different colored ink pads are another inexpensive way to add extra color(s). Have your firm name, address, phone number or logo cut into a stamp and use that on your stationery or business cards. Since stamps come in a variety of shapes, you should be able to find one that will fit your design needs.

Explore other options such as photocopying a texture onto the paper as an edging. If you're a designer and an illustrator, incorporate some of your artwork into your design. Can you translate your name or your business name into some kind of graphic, maybe a rebus? Calligraphy or an outstanding type design can add a touch of elegance to the simplest printed piece.

This survey was developed solely to provide research-based information for Rhode Island School of Design Division of Continuing Education students. RISD/CE does not intend the results of this survey to represent a comprehensive, national profile of portfolio requirements. Used by permission of Rhode Island School of Design.

Rhode Island School of Design Portfolio Survey

Rhode Island School of Design's Division of Continuing Education offers three certificate programs — Advertising Design, Interior Design, and Scientific and Technical Illustration. Each program offers a scope and sequence of courses encompassing both conceptual and practical aspects of work in the field. To receive a certificate, a student must successfully complete a specified number of required and elective courses and also pass a final portfolio review.

In December of 1988, the Continuing Education Programs Office developed a "Survey of Portfolio Evaluation Criteria." One hundred and fourteen businesses in Rhode Island and Massachusetts received the questionnaire. The businesses were identified as being potential employers of RISD certificate candidates and were comprised of advertising agencies, interior design firms, and organizations which employ technical or scientific illustrators (such as publishing companies).

There were two objectives in conducting this survey. The primary objective was to evaluate portfolio requirements established by Continuing Education for its certificate programs to ensure that they reflect current standards by which practicing design professionals judge job applicants. The secondary goal was to compile a body of relevant, research-based information in order to furnish it to students participating in RISD/CE's 1989 Winter session seminar, "Portfolio Preparation and Presentation for Certificate Candidates." This seminar is designed to assist students with all areas of portfolio development.

Of the 114 businesses surveyed, a total of 37 (or 33%) responded by the deadline. A copy of the survey appears on the following page. The numbers listed next to each survey item represent the percentage of respondents who chose that answer.

The last part of this report lists specific individual responses to our request for additional comments. Many respondents chose to use this part of the questionnaire as an opportunity to reinforce the importance of various portfolio evaluation criteria used by their companies to screen potential employees.

Below are additional comments made by survey respondents regarding the specific portfolio requirements of their companies.

"As always, creativity is the most important consideration. Next would be the application of creativity to real-world design problems. Finally, the portfolio should include backup to all creative efforts. 'Think roughs,' so the candidate's preliminary creative efforts can be evaluated."

"A résumé format and design is a great way to show talent and imagination on an actual project."

"We look for people who have good design ability, show adaptability working on many things at a time, speak well, and whose portfolios show an understanding of professional-quality work."

"I value the interview as the most important factor in hiring a candidate. An attitude of willingness to work hard and learn on the job is critical to being hired at this agency."

"Applicant should have a sense of humor — verbal communication skills, eagerness, aggressiveness and salesmanship."

"In both advertising and design I look for an applicant's ability to define a problem and solve it creatively. This must be evident in the portfolio. Thought before action."

Rhode Island School of Design's Division of Continuing Education
Survey of Portfolio Evaluation Criteria
Advertising Design Results

When reviewing a job applicant's portfolio, each firm has different criteria for judgment, depending on the job and the company's priorities and goals. With the results of this questionnaire we hope to establish broad guidelines for RISD's certificate candidates which will aid them in composing and constructing their own portfolios.

Please circle the number which best describes the degree of importance you place upon each area of portfolio presentation when considering an applicant for an entry-level position with your firm.

	Always Required	Often Required	Occasionally Required	Not Required	Not Applicable
1. The work is neat, with no smudges, erasures, etc.	75%	25%			
2. The sequence of work is logical.	33%	40%	27%		
3. Photographed works are of professional quality.	37%	31%	25%		
4. Work exhibits a broad range of abilities.	47%	29%	18%	6%	
5. Work shows proficiency in a specialized area.	29%	18%	41%	12%	
6. Labelling is neat and descriptive.	24%	18%	24%	24%	10%
7. Work is self-explanatory and needs no verbal clarification.	18%	41%	24%	17%	
8. Work includes a developmental piece which shows a project from conception to completion.	6%	24%	41%	18%	11%
9. Work is assembled and mounted in a professional manner.	65%	24%		6%	5%
10. Work shows competency in a variety of media.	29%	53%	18%		
11. Work shows imaginative concept development.	82%	12%	6%		
12. Work shows consideration for reproducibility (blue lines, reductions, etc.).	47%	29%	18%	6%	

Please choose the three statements above which are the most important factors in your review of an applicant's portfolio and indicate the numbers here: 11, 4, 1

Is the applicant usually present when you review the portfolio?   Yes — 94%   No — 6%

Do you review slides included in a portfolio?   Yes — 89%   No — 11%

The size of the portfolio which you find easiest to review is (please circle or describe):
8½" × 11" — 7%   11" × 14" — 36%   16" × 20" — 43%   18" × 24" — 14%

What format do you prefer for the presentation of three-dimensional work (please circle)?
slides — 30%   prints — 35%   original work — 35%

The optimum number of pieces in a portfolio is: 5-10 — 6%   10-15 — 78%   15-20 — 16%

The format you prefer for a résumé is: traditional — 24%   creative — 41%   doesn't matter — 35%

In hiring an applicant, what percentage of importance do you place on each of these areas of the hiring process?
portfolio review — 54%   interview — 33%   résumé — 13%

Please describe any other standard you have for portfolio evaluation that is not included above and/or is specific to your company: (See comments on page 164.)

Portfolio Review Do's and Don'ts

- ☐ **Do come prepared with information about the company.**
- ☐ **Don't show off your knowledge about the company.**
- ☐ **Do find a conversational icebreaker to open the meeting.**
- ☐ **Don't wait for the client to lead the discussion.**
- ☐ **Do dress professionally.**
- ☐ **Don't overdress.**
- ☐ **Do keep your presentation brief and to the point.**
- ☐ **Don't show every piece you've ever done.**
- ☐ **Do stay focused on the client's needs.**
- ☐ **Don't just think about what you'll get out of this job.**
- ☐ **Be polite and friendly.**
- ☐ **Don't act buddy-buddy even if you have mutual friends.**

No Smoking

If you smoke, don't do it during the meeting, even if the client is a smoker and offers you one. A cigarette in hand is restricting and it tends to lessen your professional demeanor. Also, since so many people are adamant against smoking these days, try to avoid smoking just before a client meeting. It can leave you smelling of smoke and that can be a real turnoff to a nonsmoker.

image as a talented designer who can make *anything* look good.

Your Portfolio

The maxim "What you see is who I am" is especially true of your portfolio. It's an excellent opportunity to show prospective clients what you have done and by extension what you can do for them. Your portfolio must work to reinforce every other aspect of your promotion and marketing efforts. You won't get much work if your identity package sends a message that your portfolio contradicts or if that portfolio says you can't deliver on the promises made in your self-promotion materials.

You should review your portfolio at least once a year, but every six months is better. You're more likely to keep your portfolio updated with your most recent, best work and make sure the pieces you show are appropriate for the kinds of clients you want. You should also review it every time you launch a new self-promotion campaign, need to reorder stationery, or if your needs, interests or clients change. If you notice that the work in your portfolio doesn't reflect the image you're projecting in your other promotional materials, you need to do something about it immediately. Maybe you just need to do a better job of editing your portfolio in order to more accurately reflect your capabilities. On the other hand, you might not be letting present and prospective clients know about all the services you can offer. Or you might be promising results you aren't delivering—especially if you're *not* getting the amount of repeat business you think you should.

How to Prepare a Portfolio

A portfolio, also called a book, is a sample of your best recent work. It should include ten to fifteen examples that demonstrate the full range of your graphic skills and creativity.

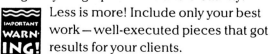 Less is more! Include only your best work—well-executed pieces that got results for your clients.

Each work you include in your portfolio must be yours. If an agency or company produced a piece while you were there but

you weren't directly involved in it, don't use it. You can, however, include something you did as part of a group project. Explain what part of the work is yours and give credit to other team members.

Design your portfolio carefully. The first and last pieces should always be your best work. For a general portfolio review show pieces that reflect experience with the client's industry or a range of your work. When you're showing your portfolio for a specific project, include primarily samples of that type of project or work for similar clients. Clients like to see how you handle the various stages of a project, so you might show a few concept layouts, a comp and the finished piece from one project.

Include only those pieces that are in good condition. Torn, smudged, tattered, yellowed, crinkled, blurred or stained pieces are not acceptable. Each piece should be neatly mounted on the same neutral colored but sturdy backing with an even border of approximately two to three inches all around. If you have a number of small pieces to display on a single page, mount them together in an uncrowded and visually interesting arrangement. In a ring binder portfolio with acetate sleeves, mount your work on both sides of a heavy, matte-finished paper trimmed to the sleeve size. (Many of these binder portfolios come with the right kind of paper inserts so you won't have to cut your own.) Mount each piece securely with tape or glue to guarantee that nothing falls out during a meeting. Include an unmounted copy of any fold-outs, brochures or booklets you have mounted, so the client can examine each.

Always use the best portfolio case you can afford. You'll find a range of cases in art and office supply stores. Decide what you want to include in your portfolio before you buy, so you don't get stuck with one that is too small for your work.

Portfolio Review

Even if a prospective client calls you because you were highly recommended by one of your clients, it's very unlikely that you'll get the project without showing your portfolio. On the other hand, you can't depend on your portfolio alone. There are many designers with dazzling portfolios who lose jobs because they don't know how to handle that first client meeting.

What could go wrong when all you have to do is show your portfolio? Plenty. Let's look at one disastrous portfolio review from the client's point of view. Just as you begin to tell the designer why you've called him, he says, "Let me tell you about myself." For the next forty-five minutes you yawn through a play-by-play account of his entire career—including how his dog died while he was working on that two-page magazine spread, but he completed it in spite of his grief (and it won a national design award). He proudly describes how meticulous he is with mechanicals and his years of experience with color separations. When he finally leaves an hour and a half later, you decide that you never want to see another graphic designer as long as you live!

The quickest way to turn a client off is to focus a portfolio review on yourself. I know that sounds contradictory, because you're showing your work. But a portfolio review is really about the client. As every good salesperson will tell you, "The more you ask your clients about themselves, the more wonderful they will think you are." That means you should know something about the company when you bring your portfolio—what type of business it is and a little about its market. You should, however, mention what you know about the company only if it relates to the conversation at the time. Demonstrate an understanding of and interest in the client's product or service; don't show off. If this isn't a cold call, try to get some background on the project you may be offered. Then you can tailor your portfolio to show that you've handled similar projects successfully.

Start the meeting off on the right foot. When you walk into the client's office, look around. Is there anything about the decor, the artwork, family photographs or collectibles that would get the client talking about herself? If so, a short conversation about it can set

a friendly, relaxed tone for the rest of the meeting. This will help you get over feeling self-conscious and will put the focus where it belongs—on the potential client.

After a few minutes of casual conversation, turn the discussion to the project under consideration by asking about the client's position or involvement with the company. Go into that meeting prepared with a list of open-ended questions that will encourage the client to speak freely. In fact, this first meeting is an excellent time to fill out a Client Information Sheet (see pages 40-41 and 117-118) but first get the client's permission to ask a few questions and take some notes. You want to learn as much as you can about the client's goals and what she is looking for in a designer. Once you understand the client's needs, you can better decide what you have to offer to help fill them. Then move on to the specifics of the project. If the client doesn't have a project in mind and this is just a general information interview, then ask about the type of graphic work the company has produced in the past, and what they are looking for in a designer.

When the client asks about you or your work, always try to make your answers relevant to what you perceive the client needs or wants. When you show the client your portfolio, explain only those pieces that would interest the client or that specifically relate to this project. For a general portfolio review, you would show work you did for similar companies and pieces that demonstrate a variety of design decisions. Don't think about yourself and what you can get out of this client. Keep your attention focused on her, and what you can do to help the client achieve her goals.

Keep your meeting within a reasonable time frame. Limit the portfolio presentation itself to five or ten minutes. There's nothing more deadly than a long-winded designer talking about every project she's ever done. If you notice that the client is looking at his watch or standing up, take that as your signal to gracefully exit. *Always* leave behind a sample of your work and your résumé to help remind the prospective client which designer you were.

Appearances Count

It's not enough to have a portfolio full of outstanding work beautifully displayed. Even if you're the world's greatest designer, a client will be completely turned off if you show up in her office looking as if you just climbed out of bed. You don't have to wear a Brooks Brothers suit or a designer original to make a good impression, but clean and neatly pressed clothing is a must.

Clients learn as much from how you behave as how you dress. You should stand, move and speak as if you feel poised and confident even if you're shaking inside. Learn what you can about a client's business, needs and history with design projects. If you've planned your approach and are prepared with an appropriate portfolio and thoughtful questions, you'll feel more confident. Be excited and upbeat about getting the job, but don't pursue it too aggressively. Rehearse the client meeting from your first step through the door to your exit. Be polite and friendly, whether or not you're offered a job. And *always* leave your card, résumé and some type of promotional material behind. Today's "Sorry, we don't have work for you" may be tomorrow's "This just came up and we thought of you."

Before You Do Another...

If you already have developed one or more self-promotion pieces, evaluate what you've done before doing another. If your current effort is working, keep it or do more of the same. But if it didn't get results, you need to decide why and make some changes. Some criteria to consider are:

- ☐ Are you addressing the client's needs?

- ☐ Is it appropriate to your target market?

- ☐ Does it communicate your message clearly?

- ☐ Is the piece well-designed?

- ☐ Is the printing and paper quality first-rate?

- ☐ Does anything about it look cheap?

- ☐ Are there any typos or other mistakes?

- ☐ Are your address and phone number easy to find and read?

Self-Promotion Packages

If you aren't working on a self-promotion project, you're already behind. Even if you've got plenty of work right now, in six months you'll have done a lot of great work and have nothing more to do. Successful self-promotion requires the same kind of discipline that you give to work for your other clients. That means setting a budget and schedule and determining what you want the project to do and the form it should take. No matter how busy you are, schedule your promotion projects *right now*! Treat them like regular paying jobs and stick to your schedule.

When you get a project from a client, he sets the goals and the parameters for it. You have to create that framework for yourself before you begin any self-promotion project. Doing a piece that looks good isn't enough. Decide what you want the promotion to accomplish before you begin, and then determine how best to achieve it. What you do depends on who you are or what you want to be, your experience, and what you're doing now.

You need to think about what form a promotion will take: a brochure, a poster, an ad, a postcard, a calendar or a party. Creating a

piece that matches the type of work you want to get can be very effective. Develop an annual report for your business or an imaginary one to show what you can do. Design a brochure as a series of advertising spreads or send postcards that resemble ads to appeal to that market.

But the bottom line is that you must do *something*. You must promote yourself to prospective and present clients regularly. Get started now by pulling out your marketing plan, that target list of clients, and your calendar and production schedules. Once you've gotten the ball rolling by putting a plan in writing, it's a lot easier to keep it going.

That last item (above left) might sound too obvious to miss, but I've seen many attractive promotions that I tossed out because I couldn't figure out who sent it! After you've studied it, show your piece to friends, relatives and business associates and ask for their honest opinions. Ask these questions to test their responses to important points:

- ☐ What does this piece tell you about the designer?

- ☐ If you didn't know me, would you look at it if you received it?

- ☐ If you needed a designer, would you hire me based on this piece? Why or why not?

- ☐ What, if anything, would make this a stronger piece?

If several people make the same comments, that will give you a good starting point for rethinking your promotional pieces.

Occasions to Promote

Although it's best to plan some regularly scheduled self-promotions, you may find it easier to stick to a deadline if you tie a project to a special event. You'd feel pretty silly sending a Christmas greeting to clients in February (unless you want to send a message about beating deadlines), so you can force yourself to sit down and get it done. Although Christmas is prime time for holiday promotions, don't overlook the possibilities presented by other holidays. Dunlavey Studio in California has developed all their promotional materials around the Irish roots of the studio's founders and often sends gifts to clients at St. Patrick's Day.

Real or manufactured special events offer great opportunities for letting clients know who you are and what you do. In addition to opening your studio, you can tie promotions to relocating, taking on a partner, your studio's anniversary, winning an award, entering a new market, offering new services, local special events, or a studio party. One very successful design firm throws an annual "Going Out of Business" Party in memory of the original event that actually helped keep them in

business. Wedding and birth announcements are fun to do, but ask yourself who will *want* to know that you're a new parent or just got married. Colleagues, fellow designers and long-time clients are more likely to appreciate such announcements than prospective clients who don't know you.

Who Gets It?

Choose the mailing list for each promotion carefully. Sending out a scattershot mailing to every name you have is not the most cost-effective way to promote yourself. Which present, past or prospective clients are most likely to help you achieve your goals? You won't get much work designing annual reports if you mail to small businesses, for example. Decide exactly how many people you want to mail to. Do you need to reach everyone in an industry or only certain members of it? If you're offering a new service to present clients, not all of them may need it.

Unless you're just starting out, you should already have lists of present and prospective client names and addresses from which to pull the right names. You should verify that all the information is correct before you mail. People often change jobs, and misaddressed mail will just end up in the trash. If you don't have a suitable list, compile one before you design.

Doing It

A self-promotion piece can be anything—brochure, flyer, mailer, poster, introductory letter, invitation/announcement, even an object such as a T-shirt or a box of cookies. Each option has its pros and cons, so choose the medium for your message as carefully as you would a client's. Flexibility is another concern here. If you are going to use a promotional piece as a leave-behind, then it must work effectively in *both* contexts. Don't try to make one piece do too much, however. A capabilities brochure might not be the best direct mail piece because of its size and weight, even if it's highly effective during presentations or as a leave-behind.

The vehicle you choose should be appropriate to your target market. Art directors might appreciate a T-shirt more than a buttoned-down businessperson would. You should also consider what your competitors are doing for self-promotion. For example, if everyone else is doing posters, yours might

get lost in the shuffle; do something else so you will stand out.

Ideas for outstanding promotions are everywhere: annuals, showcases, competitions, etc. Seek out springboards for your creativity, but then put your imagination to work. The best promotions are those that not only have a strong concept but which reflect the individual designer's or studio's personality. Think about it: The pieces that catch your attention are those that look special and unique, because they're as individual as the designers who created them.

If you come up with the perfect idea but can't afford or can't execute it yourself, set up a promotional partnership. The finished project should benefit all participants, not just you. Be sure to sell the benefit up front. "I want to do a promotional piece, how about a joint effort?" is a real turnoff because it's too focused on your needs. "I have a great idea for a piece that could really sell *your* services" makes it clear this is a two-way street. Sometimes giving credit and samples to a collaborator will be enough benefit or you can swap services. At others, you may have to modify your dream idea in return for the help you need. A copywriter might want the piece modified so he can use it for his self-promotion, too. A printer might contribute her services if you agree to showcase a technique or service she wants to promote. *Everybody* wants to collab-

orate with printers because that's the biggest part of the cost, so you must present an absolutely sensational idea that clearly benefits them, and then treat them as a collaborator. Don't ask for special treatment on deadlines and try to tailor the project to their equipment as much as possible.

Whatever you do and however you do it, sending out a promotional piece is *not* the last thing you do. You should follow up. Call about eight days after you think a recipient should have received a piece. Ask if the prospect received your piece and what she thought about it. If she says she didn't get or doesn't remember it, offer to confirm the address and send it again. Do it if she agrees, but don't push if she doesn't.

Alternative Promotions

You can also promote your business by joining organizations where you can make useful contacts, giving talks on design to groups, or doing volunteer work. Every time you show your portfolio, attend an industry trade show, or enter a competition you're promoting your business.

Although many designers hate to do it, they've discovered that making cold calls is an excellent way to get new clients. It takes a lot of patience and persistence to make this approach work, because you have to deal with a barrage of rejections. But if you have reasonable expectations and can always remember it's nothing personal, sooner or later the law of averages will swing around on your side. That's a fact. All you want to achieve from a cold call is to set up a meeting at which you may make a presentation to convince the prospective client to give you a project. Try to get the prospective client to at least agree to look at your literature (send it right then) and then follow up.

Presentation Folders and Labels

Most printers carry or can special order a wide variety of presentation folders. You can create your own cover design and have personalized folders printed, but usually a minimum order of 500 is required. Unless you are going to make frequent presentations, specially printed folders are really unnecessary. Order blank folders from the printer as there may be no minimum order required. Most printers also carry rolls of self-adhesive blank labels in different styles and sizes that come in quantities of 500 or 1,000. Then you design your own labels. A one color, printed and embossed roll of 1,000 labels can cost less than $100. Gold or silver embossed labels are particularly attractive but more expensive. Ask your printer about the options and costs for folders and labels. You'll find inexpensive but less attractive presentation folders and blank labels at office supply stores.

Presentations

Presentations let company officials have input on the choice of a designer and design direction and concepts for a project. A company will ask you to make an initial presentation to help them decide which of several competing designers will be offered a project. You may also be asked to do a presentation when the client needs other company personnel to approve your concepts for an extremely important or expensive project—an identity package, annual report or a series of advertisements.

Some presentations are relatively informal, and you'll show only a few rough sketches or layouts and explain the creative ideas. Presentations to a committee are usually more formal, and you'll need a written proposal that describes the project and a proposed budget, a production schedule, sample copy, and several comprehensive layouts to show what the finished piece will look like.

Always learn exactly what the client ex-pects to see in a presentation before you agree to do it. Don't present unless you feel you have a solid handle on the project's requirements and what the client needs, that your work is equal to or better than your competition's, and that the project is worth the time and money you'll invest. If the purpose is choosing a designer for a project, decide to participate based on the amount of time and effort it will take. You must take the project almost to the mechanical stage, which means hefty out-of-pocket expenses—stats, Pantone paper, press type, color laser prints, etc. Then there are the time costs; depending on how many hours it takes to prepare, you could have from several hundred to several thousand dollars worth of potentially unbillable time. Can you recover that investment if you get the job? How much will you lose if you don't get it?

The Proposal

Your written proposal must be neatly typed, without typos, misspelled words or erasures. Begin with the reason for the presentation. Next, list or outline the goals and objectives of the project and explain how your proposed concepts will achieve those goals. Do your homework: Research the client's product or service, know who the competition is, and work with the client to identify her goals for the project.

If the project will have an impact on the company's public image or be used to sell the company's products or services, include a market research report. If you've had experience doing research, you can develop this report yourself. Otherwise, you can bring in a market research consultant to prepare that part. You may be able to persuade the consultant to deliver that report for you as part of the presentation. Always explain to any consultants or freelancers you work with that this is only a presentation and that they will be working on speculation just as you are.

Fully describe the creative strategy—what you'll do, how you'll do it and why. Include photocopies of the presentation design work and any copy that will be used with the proj-ect. Some designers show samples of their work for other clients to show how they've successfully handled similar projects. The proposal concludes with a fully itemized budget for the project and a production schedule.

Provide copies of the proposal for all presentation committee members. Call the client's secretary before the meeting to verify how many people will be there and bring a few extra copies as well to be certain you'll have enough. Your proposal should be more than just several pieces of paper stapled together. Insert each copy of the proposal into a cover or binder with typed labels personalized for each member of the presentation committee. Include on the labels the company's name, the subject of the presentation, and either your name or your business's.

You can distribute copies of the proposal at the beginning of the presentation, but ask the committee members to put them aside until afterward. That way you can be sure that they'll be listening to you instead of reading through the proposal. Some designers are uncomfortable with all those eyes staring at them during the presentation and prefer to have the committee read the proposal throughout the presentation. While you'll develop your own personal style, hiding behind the written proposal can hurt your presentations. I strongly recommend you take a course in public speaking (most colleges with continuing education programs offer them) to improve your presentation skills and increase your self-confidence.

Preparing Your Presentation

Never go into a presentation with only one idea. If the committee doesn't like it, you're sunk. Three to five different creative concepts developed into finished designs is best, especially if you're not sure what styles or ideas the committee will prefer. Don't overdo it by presenting more than five designs because too many choices can totally confuse the committee. Members may focus on different designs, develop widely varying opinions of your work, then split when it comes down to making a final decision. Or they may think that you didn't have a clearly defined design strategy and just created pieces that are all over the place.

You can draw layouts for a single-sided, flat piece entirely by hand, but take great care to make the type styles and graphic treatments closely resemble what the printed piece will look like. It's more expensive but more effective to use press type, press-on textures or colored papers, and photocopies of sample photographs or illustrations pasted in place. If you have a computer or access to one, you can save a lot of time by creating type or scanning in textures or illustrations for output on a laser printer. Each design should then be mounted on neutral mat board with a matching or complementary colored cover paper.

You don't need to present a comp of every page in an annual report, catalog or long brochure, but you should present several different page layouts. You may need to produce a dummy to show the effects of printing on different paper stocks or to demonstrate a piece that will be an unusual size or shape. You will have to produce full-size or to-scale models

for three-dimensional pieces such as packaging design. Computers are invaluable for packaging presentations since you can generate and have printed a number of variations quickly.

Rehearse, Rehearse, Rehearse

Always rehearse several times for a presentation. Don't try to learn every word in your written proposal — if you forget a word or phrase you could completely blank out — memorize only the major points. Just know what you want to say and roughly how you want to say it. Concentrate on making smooth transitions from one segment into the next.

Try to rehearse somewhere similar in space and furniture placement to the room where the actual presentation will take place. If it's an unknown, ask the client if you can see the room ahead of time to decide where to put your designs or easel or any other equipment. Rehearse not only what you plan to say, but how and where you'll move. Try out different gestures, too, until you feel comfortable with the flow of the presentation and your body movements become second nature. Check your timing. Make sure you have planned out what you want to say so that you know you will stay within a reasonable time frame. And budget time at the end for questions.

Delivering the Presentation

Presentations are often called "dog and pony shows" because they're performances which should dazzle your audience — the committee. Just like any good performance, a presentation should be timed, fast-moving, informative and entertaining. You have only twenty to thirty minutes to sell yourself and your ideas, so make the most of it. Dress appropriately and conservatively so the committee won't spend more time staring at your clothes than your designs. Plan your presentation and budget time for each segment of it. A typical format is:

1. Introduce yourself and try to put everyone at ease

2. Describe the project — its goals, market, etc.

Don't Oversell

Never promise more than you can deliver. Present yourself in the best possible light, but be honest about what you can and can't do. Give some specific examples of your achievements, but no matter how much you need the job, don't invent experience and don't take all the credit for joint efforts.

Don't get carried away by your own sales pitch and oversell yourself or your services. You can be so anxious to get a job that you commit yourself to an unrealistic deadline, an unrealistic price, or an untried technique. It's tempting to decide that you can worry about that later, but there are worse things than losing one job now. It takes very few slip-ups to get a reputation for being unreliable – and that could cost you a lot of work down the road.

Keep the Presentation Moving

If it's at all possible, stand and move around during the presentation to keep your listeners from getting bored or sleepy watching a talking head. Don't pace back and forth like a caged tiger, but use gestures and move a bit as you uncover each design to make your presentation more dynamic.

Never uncover your designs until you are ready to talk about them. Unveiling them should be the climax of your presentation. Build up to showing them, then let each be the star of the show in turn. This will give momentum to your presentation and add drama and flair.

Don't bore the committee by standing there just reading your note cards for twenty minutes. Use your notes only for reference, to cite figures correctly, or find your place.

3. Present your conceptual ideas by showing your comps

4. Tell them how these designs will achieve the project's goals

5. Review the budget and production schedule

6. Answer questions

Keep your presentation moving along at a steady but not rapid-fire pace. If someone asks a question, don't be afraid to pause for even several seconds to think about an answer. A few moments of silence before you speak can add great dramatic power to what you have to say. If you can't think of an appropriate answer, calmly state that you want to give that question further thought or offer to get back to the questioner with an answer after the meeting. Make a note of the question and then move on.

Conquering Presentation Anxiety

The most difficult part of a presentation is those first minutes when you have to take control and begin speaking. That's when presentation anxiety hits full force. How do you know if you're suffering from presentation anxiety? When that initial excitement at the prospect of the creative challenge ahead and the opportunity to get a project turns into a gnawing fear in the pit of your stomach. That fear of failure steadily builds to a fever pitch, reaching its height as you walk into the presentation.

The best way to get rid of presentation anxiety is to distract yourself for as little as thirty seconds and then, poof, it's gone. I remember the first time it worked for me. I had to make a presentation for a hospital annual report to a three-person committee. I knew two members, the public relations director and the hospital vice president. And finally, there was the president of the hospital. I didn't know him, but I had seen him a few times talking with doctors and administrative people. Whenever his name was mentioned at the hospital, I saw people cringe. I was terrified of him, too.

I prepared for the presentation for almost a month. I knew what the annual report had to accomplish for the hospital in terms of its public and private image. Based on my research into the hospital's past, present and future direction, I had come up with a brilliant concept that directly linked the hospital's future to the philosophy of its founders. But the night before the presentation, I could barely sleep. When I did drift off, I dreamed that I was in the hospital hiding under tables and inside laundry carts so that no could find me and force me to give the presentation. But they finally did find and dragged me into the boardroom to present my ideas to that ogre of a hospital president!

As I took the elevator to the third floor for the presentation, my heart started playing leapfrog. I kept taking deep breaths but nothing happened. I wanted to turn and run, but managed to reach the boardroom anyway. The vice president and public relations director greeted me warmly. Then I was looking right at my nemesis. He returned my handshake while staring at his shoes. They were nice shoes, but not worthy of all that attention. Then it hit me: He was uncomfortable. He had trouble making eye contact with me. The more he contemplated his shoes, the more I wondered why he was so uncomfortable. Maybe he was *shy*? Who knows? But I did realize that he was a real person with his own set of anxieties.

Then I noticed that my anxiety attack was gone. My heart had stopped pounding, and my hands weren't trembling. I had walked into that room less than a minute earlier with every fiber of my brain focused on me, me, me! But when I got interested in something else, I forgot about me. And that's the trick. You have to forget about yourself and focus on something else. It doesn't matter what it is, as long as it can distract you long enough for you to catch your breath and get comfortable.

It doesn't take much distraction to scare off presentation anxiety. If you're giving the presentation in your studio, have light refreshments set up. Then you can talk casually with people as they help themselves to coffee or food. By the time everyone settles down and you're ready to start, you'll feel relaxed and in control. If the presentation is at the client's office, you can ask questions (that you plan ahead of time) which have answers that serve as an introduction to the presentation—questions about the project's audience or the company's history. Just be sure that a committee member will know the answers. Using charts, graphs or audiovisual aids to introduce yourself or the presentation is an excellent way to ease into the presentation. Begin handing out the proposals while you give a brief introduction. Remember, if you know your material and you've rehearsed well, you just need to focus on something other than yourself to relax.

Turn a Rejection to an Advantage

You left there knowing you did your best. You were on target, your ideas were good or maybe they were even great. Then you get that letter or phone call that goes, "Sorry, but we decided to go with another designer. Thank you for your time, anyway." You want to curl up and die, and you vow *never* to make another presentation as long as you live. Well, that's one way of looking at rejection. But it's not the best way.

So how should you look at rejection? Start by reminding yourself that it was purely business and had nothing to do with you as a person. When you've accepted that, decide that it's an opportunity to learn. Although you didn't get the job, what did you learn about the client, the company and their industry?

What did you learn about the market for the client's product or service? File what you've learned to use in future self-promotion and marketing efforts for that client. You can use this information and even the creative ideas with another client.

How would you rate your performance? What could you have done differently? Think about the questions the committee members asked. Although you felt you'd done well, perhaps some points were unclear. Did they follow your presentation easily? Did they seem to understand how you arrived at the concepts you chose? Looking back, did it seem they felt comfortable with those concepts?

When you get a rejection letter or phone call, try to learn why you didn't get the job. Tell the client you appreciate being invited to do the presentation. But you'd like to know why you didn't get the job, so you can improve your design and presentation skills. Were the designs, schedule or budget off target? Was there something you didn't see or do? The client will admire your openness to criticism and your desire to learn and grow from it. And you can bet that the next time they have a project in the offing, you will be remembered. Plus you will find out, firsthand, how you could have improved your presentation or why someone else's ideas were better for the company than yours. This valuable information will be yours to use when you prepare your next presentation. Without it, you'll repeat the same mistakes.

Visualize Success

Sports psychologists have discovered that athletes can improve their performances by repeatedly visualizing themselves competing successfully. The same technique works for presentations. Visualize yourself giving a successful presentation. Imagine yourself walking into the room and greeting the members of the presentation committee. See yourself chatting casually with people and then comfortably slipping into the substance of your presentation. Watch yourself move around the conference table and the chairs, picking up your designs, pointing out the details you want the committee to notice, making your points about the relationship between the visuals and your creative strategy. Imagine their questions and your answers. Then see yourself looking at smiling faces as you say in a pleasant and upbeat voice, "Well, folks, that's about it, unless there are more questions. Thank you for your time and attention." Feel the confidence that comes from knowing you've done your best. If you repeat this visualization exercise several times before each presentation, you'll feel more confident and move more smoothly through them.

CHAPTER

eight

Growing

Your

Business

rowing your business is much like planning a party—the keys to success are planning and preparation. When you give a party you must estimate how many guests will come so you can have enough food. You plan the entertainment and arrange the room so everyone will be comfortable. And you prepare for the unexpected—more people come than planned or your stereo conks out. You can't control exactly how the party will turn out, but by working out the details and anticipating problems, you can improve your chances of success.

You can't know exactly how many clients you'll have at any one time. That makes running a design business like planning a party for which no one RSVP's—you take your best guess and prepare for the unexpected. Unlike a party, though, you don't overestimate your needs but try to manage with slightly less than you think you'll need until you can't stretch your resources any farther. You study patterns from previous years and make tentative plans based on those. You attempt to predict the results of any marketing efforts and factor those in. Finally, you work out contingency plans so you're ready if things change.

You must manage your business's growth carefully in order to build on past successes and avoid failures. If your client base is expanding, you've got to invest time in learning about their businesses while keeping your present clients happy. Keeping the customer satisfied—yes, your clients *are* customers—is vital to your business's success. That takes more than doing good work at a reasonable price. It takes anticipating and meeting client needs and making your clients feel that they are important and valued.

At its best, the designer-client relationship is a collaboration. The client provides you information and insights into the product or service and the intended market. You provide the client your communication skills and creative talents. Designer and client understand they're working toward the same goal as a team, and each concentrates on bringing his special expertise to the party. At its worst, the designer-client relationship resembles a wres-

tling match or tug-of-war. This happens when clients aren't sure what they want to say or do but are hoping they—or the designer—will sort of stumble onto it. It can also happen when the designer doesn't feel confident about his work. And of course, there's the client who thinks she knows more about design and communication than the designer and insists on running the whole show. Not to mention the designer more concerned with his idea/image/self-expression than what the client really needs. Usually, the experience falls somewhere in-between—not as good as we hoped but not as bad as we feared.

There are no magic secrets for building good client relationships; good customer service requires courtesy, consideration, communication and common sense. In this chapter we'll see how those qualities can be applied to building strong relationships and solving problems.

Getting Bigger and Better

Most of your business's growth will come from broadening and expanding your client base. If your clients represent several different kinds of industries, you gain experience working with businesses that involve diverse markets. You'll also have protection if a particular industry experiences a slump, because you'll have clients in other industries. Having more clients will bring in the revenues to expand your business in other ways, such as adding employees, enlarging facilities, buying or updating equipment, and increasing your salary or benefits.

In the previous chapter, "Pounding the Pavement," we discussed ways to expand your client base through marketing and self-promotion. There are, however, two other ways to expand your client base. You can form a partnership with another designer or merge with or acquire another design firm or a related business. Both methods have advantages and disadvantages, but they can accelerate the growth of your client base considerably.

Forming a Partnership

The right partner can bring the financial backing, personal expertise or business contacts to

Too Many Clients

When times are tough, you feel you can't have too many clients. But it can happen—you start getting hot and pick up a lot of new clients. If you begin to get in over your head, you can give business away—ask another designer or design firm to take an account in return for a percentage of the profits. This lets you hand off accounts for whom you no longer wish to work while doing a favor for another designer. If you especially want to take a project but temporarily can't handle the extra work, you can hire a freelance creative team to actually do the work under your supervision.

UP THE LADDER OF SUCCESS

expand your business and help shoulder the emotional burdens of running it. Try to find a designer whose abilities complement yours but whose design style and personality are compatible. You may want someone to focus on the financial and operating aspects or the marketing of your business while you run the creative side. Decide what you want to get from and can bring to a partnership before you go shopping for one. Don't team up with someone just because you like him or her; that's not an indication of how well you'll work together as a business team. Don't get a **IMPORTANT WARNING!** partner you can't stand in order to get his or her skills, money or clients, either.

It seems that when partnerships are good, they're very, very good — Carbone Smolan and Pentagram leap to mind — but when they're bad they're horrid — we've all heard those horror stories. Jane and Sue break up their design firm because Jane spent *their* money as if it were her own. Tom left the firm because his partners Dick and Harry were dictating what he should and shouldn't do. Partnerships usually run aground because of personal problems, but many of them have their roots in the legal structure of partnerships (see page 10).

Mergers and Acquisitions

When you merge with or acquire another design company or related business such as a photographer, video production house or ad agency, you can expand your company's capabilities and offerings as well as your client base and billings. If you choose a business that expands your present services and provides different areas of expertise, you personally have an opportunity to grow in new directions.

Choose your merger or acquisition partner carefully. You won't do your business any good if you hook up with a business that's in financial trouble, has a poor reputation, or is about to lose an important client. Check them out carefully and don't get involved unless you're sure this is a good deal for you. Protect yourself legally by having a lawyer who's an expert in this area draw up the merger or ac-

quisition agreement. And consider the impact this new work setup will have on your job description and that of your employees. A certain amount of confusion and discomfort always accompanies a reorganization. Try to work out systems and any new or revised job descriptions in advance to reduce office tension and stress.

Managing Growth

Growth, even under the best of circumstances, can create periods of instability. For each new client you have to devote numerous hours of unbillable time just to become familiar with that client's business and needs. If your workload increases suddenly from one large or several small new accounts, you may find yourself scrambling around to find em-

Don't Put All Your Eggs in One Basket

Taking on too large an account can be hazardous to your financial health. If a new account represents more than 50 percent of your present total billings, you could wind up overextended by hiring additional employees and buying the equipment, materials and services you need to do the work. If you subsequently lose that account, you will have lost more than half your business and will have to deal with the consequences.

You face the same risks when an existing account grows to be more than 50 percent of your billings. Letting one account become too large a part of your business is very easy to do, especially if it's a large company with several divisions. Work for one division leads to work for another, and so on. This is fine unless you let your work for other clients slide in favor of this growth opportunity. What do you do if you then lose that account? Or find yourself turning away work for one division to do a project for another? Your dream client can turn into a nightmare right before your eyes, so never get in too deep with any one client.

While you can't always dictate when growth will happen, you can control it. It's a matter of setting your priorities and sticking to them. As long as you can keep the bottom line in sight — you're in business to get and keep clients by doing good work for a reasonable price while making a profit — you can make sound, effective business decisions. Run your business; don't let it run you. Failing to do so can trap you in a swiftly descending spiral, and you might end up worse than when you began your expansion. You may even end up bankrupt.

Prepare Your Business for Lean Times

Even when business is booming, you should be prepared for possible rough waters ahead. Before you begin your next round of business expansion, cut your existing debt. This will improve your bottom line and increase your profit margin on future growth. Clean up your accounts receivable and replace slow payers with better clients. Make a contingency plan telling what and how you'll cut expenses if hard times come. Establish a business line of credit before you need one in order to get the best terms. And above all, concentrate on good client relations — satisfied clients are more likely to help out by sending you any work they have.

The Telephone — an Image Maker or Breaker

How you answer the phone tells clients more than you might realize. Often your first opportunity to make an impression on a new or prospective client is over the phone. What do you want people to think about you and your business? Do you sound articulate, self-confident and assertive? Do you sound friendly, professional and courteous? These are certainly the kind of qualities that would enhance the image of any professional designer. If not, what kind of image are you projecting? And would you want to work with that kind of business?

The best way to find out what you do sound like is to tape-record all your calls for a while. At first, you may feel uncomfortable knowing the tape is running, but after the first few calls you won't notice it anymore. Review the results at the end of day and decide what image you're projecting. Play the tape for a friend or a trusted colleague if you can't be completely objective. Then make a conscious effort to correct or change any problems with your telephone voice or manners. Listen to what you say and how you say it, trying to catch and correct your problem areas. Rehearse phone calls with a friend to build good telephone habits and manners.

ployees or extra freelancers. Not to mention all the additional expenses that come with any growth. That's why planning and managing growth carefully are so important. In the midst of all of the changes, daily business must go on with a minimum of stress and confusion and so must you.

Customer Service

Your clients will expect, even demand, good service from you, the designer. That means not only consistently good work at a reasonable price but making your clients feel valued and important. It's easy to do when clients know what they want and are willing to let you decide how to get it. But dealing with clients who are extremely demanding or who simply can't make up their minds leaves us feeling we'd rather dig ditches than be designers.

A mental trick I find helpful is trying to view a client's restrictions as a challenge, not an obstacle. Anyone can do a wonderful design on an unlimited budget with no creative restrictions. It's the truly talented designer who can make a low-budget, two-color mailer attractive and effective.

You improve your chances of avoiding problems if you try to anticipate client needs from the beginning. As the owner of an advertising agency, I've both bought and sold design services. I'm going to use that dual perspective to help you put yourself in the client's shoes. I'll go over what I've found clients expect from a designer, and ways you can handle the types of problems that pop up most frequently.

What Do Clients Expect From You Once You're Hired?

You made it through the interview without a hitch. You can feel it. Sure enough, you have an assignment. Now, you've got it made. Right? Wrong! You have to think of every project, whether it's your first or fortieth for this client, as a trial project. A client may like you personally and even value your work but he never stops judging you.

The following are questions clients continually ask themselves about designers. Keep

them in mind every time you walk into a client's office or talk with one on the phone. If you work to make the answers to each a yes every time, you may turn out to be the busiest designer in town.

☐ Has this designer lived up to my expectations?

☐ Is her work living up to the pieces I saw in the portfolio?

☐ Is the quality of her work consistent? Is it fresh-looking each time or am I seeing the same old ideas in a new form?

☐ Is she handling this project responsibly and competently? Are my calls returned promptly? Does he respect my needs and input on the project?

☐ Has she met budget and every deadline?

☐ If things go wrong, does she accept responsibility for the problems or mistakes and get them corrected?

An Ounce of Anticipation . . .

Working with clients is similar to playing a game of chess: It's easier to win if you stay five moves ahead. To keep the odds on your side, assume you're going to run into problems or obstacles on each project. Then actively plan new and exciting ways around potential roadblocks. Knowing the solutions ahead of time will also help keep your energy focused exactly where it should be — on the quality of your work.

Challenge #1, The Unrealistic Deadline. Clients can unintentionally turn an easy job into a nightmare by setting unrealistic deadlines — asking the designer to do a three-week project in three days. It often seems that clients do this just to make your life difficult. But more often than not, they simply don't have any idea how long each stage of producing a piece can take.

Before you accept a project, decide whether or not the client's deadline is workable. If it's not, give your client specific reasons why that time frame isn't possible and propose an alternative. It helps to explain, or to demonstrate whenever possible, exactly how a particular job is done. For example, if your client is only allowing two days to print a four-color, eight-page catalog, then try to arrange a tour of the printing plant. Actually seeing the many steps involved in taking a mechanical from stripping to press proofs will help your client understand how long it takes the printer to prepare and print a job. If you can't arrange or the client can't take time for a tour, try showing samples of the stages with a flow chart marked with the time each takes.

Occasionally a client refuses to change a deadline because it's tied into a special promotion or sale. When this happens, suggest changes in the project to ease the deadline crunch. Suppose your client wants a two-

When All Else Fails

No matter how good your intentions or how strong your negotiating skills, eventually you will run into a brick wall with a client. No matter what alternatives or incentives you offer, the client believes that there's a right way, a wrong way, and my way – which is what we're going to do. At that point you have two choices: fight or walk.

Both fighting and walking offer certain rewards but also pose definite risks. If you fight and win, you may end up with a great piece and a client who's impressed by your talent and your tenacity. Or you may get your way on this piece and lose your client. If you walk, you may save yourself from producing a piece that won't please the client but wind up losing the client anyway. But there are times when you'll just have to take a chance. I can't give you any guidelines for picking your fights or knowing when to fold. You only learn that from experience.

Although I generally vote for caution and diplomacy when dealing with clients, I remember vividly one time I had my back against the wall and came out "swinging." I was offered a hospital annual report, which would take a minimum of five months to complete – and was given only two months to put it together. I had already done the annual report for this hospital the year before, and I knew that there was no way this could be rushed through in two months. But I didn't want to lose a $50,000 project either.

I spent the weekend reworking my production schedule a million times. I reviewed every possible option and some that were, frankly, a little crazy. The logistics were overwhelming. Where would I find enough freelance help – both to help on this and cover the workload at the agency if I pulled my staff off current projects? Could I get enough photographers to shoot all the images I'd need in an incredibly short time – and how would the hospital react to the bill? Could I use several printers and typesetters to save time, or would that cause more problems than it would solve? No matter what I did or how I did it, I always came to the same conclusion. Unless a miracle occurred and *absolutely nothing* went wrong on the project, it was virtually impossible to deliver that annual report in only two months.

After a sleepless Saturday night, I decided that I could see only one way out. I called the hospital's public relations director at home Sunday morning with a prepared speech in front of me. "Since I met with you on Friday, I've gone over the schedule a million times trying to figure out how we can do this project in two months. I'm sorry to have to say this, but my professional reputation is on the line. Because I feel this is virtually impossible to do within your time frame, I will only go ahead with this project if the president of the hospital will sign a waiver releasing me and my agency from any legal responsibility if we try but don't make it."

The public relations director said he understood my position and accepted my condition. "First thing Monday morning, we'll go into the president's office together and tell him." My heart sank into the pit of my stomach. I had hoped the public relations director would get the waiver himself, if he agreed to the idea at all. No such luck.

Monday morning, the public relations director presented my stipulation of a waiver to the president. He obviously didn't understand my position or appreciate the request for a waiver. "If you don't complete this annual report by the annual meeting, this hospital will never do business with Ganim Advertising again!" he bellowed.

"Sir, if we complete the annual on time but do a rushed-through, half-baked job, you'll still never do business with Ganim again," I said quietly but firmly. "So either way, I have nothing to lose. But I do stand to lose a reputation I've worked long and hard to earn, if the annual report is poorly done. And if I don't ask for a written agreement protecting my company, we could be liable for a legal suit if the deadline is missed or something major goes wrong. At the very least, you could refuse to pay for a $50,000 project. And believe me, when a project is rushed through – especially when we have to cut a lot of corners as we will on this one – something will definitely go wrong. I can't afford to take a $50,000 risk. And if you were in my position, I don't think you would either."

There was a long silence during which I held my breath and prayed. The president finally looked at me, smiled and said, "You're right; I wouldn't take that kind of risk with my business. I'll sign that waiver for you. Just do your best."

Socializing With Clients

Socializing with your clients at business luncheons, cocktail parties and dinner meetings is part of this business. But if you're tempted to become friends with rather than just be friendly with a client, you may be asking for trouble. Personal disagreements can sour even the best working relationships and lead to your losing a client. If a friendship does develop, try to separate your friendship from your business relationship. When a client becomes a friend or a friend becomes a client, treat him in exactly the same manner that you would any client. Only discuss business during a scheduled business meeting, not during a social engagement. Make no exceptions to your standard business policies, such as contracts, payment arrangements and professional courtesy. Never assume that a client who is your friend will always be satisfied with your work.

color brochure with full-color photographs, and there isn't enough time to shoot the photographs and have color separations made. Suggest you cut production time by using black-and-white photographs instead. If the client complains that the brochure will be too dull without the color photos, suggest dressing up the brochure with a third color. To help sell the idea, show your client some samples of effective and attractive brochures done that way to help them feel more comfortable with your suggestions. As an added incentive, explain how much money they can save if color photographs are eliminated from the production cost. There are few clients who can resist the savings pitch.

Challenge #2, Unworkable Budgets. Clients unfamiliar with design and production costs may set an inadequate budget. At this point, you have four choices. You can flatly refuse the job, but risk getting a reputation for being hard to work with. You can accept their limits, but have to eat a loss. You can agree to their limits now, but try to sneak in the necessary increases later. Or you can avoid bad feelings and even turn the situation around by showing them why the budget doesn't work.

Put together a detailed cost estimate beginning with a description of the project and the available budget. Follow that with a list of project specifications and the estimated cost for each item on the list. This shows them exactly what their budget will cover and how much more money it will take to complete the job according to their specifications. As you review the cost estimate, explain how prices are determined and what the going rates are for design and production services in your area. Try to get competitive bids for at least one or two outside production services, such as printing, and include these (with your markup) as well.

If your client still maintains that you have to find a way to work within an unrealistic budget, suggest some money-saving alternatives and show effective samples. If they *still* won't budge, explain that you can't stay in business by losing money. Remind them that they are in business, too, and surely they can understand the problem you're facing. Always try to

find a way to turn the situation around to their point of view.

You can also suggest that they call another designer for a second opinion, even provide them with a name or two. If their budget really was unworkable, it won't take them long to discover they were the ones out of line, not you. They just may be back with a new appreciation for you and more money to spend.

Challenge #3, Multiple Cost Estimates. Clients often have no budget in mind and expect you to tell them how much a particular project will cost. That can be fairly simple if the project is clearly defined in terms of direction and the final form it will take. When it isn't, you are faced with the time-consuming and unbillable task of putting together multiple cost estimates. These are monsters because you first have to work up a variety of options and prepare separate estimates for each.

Here's a typical scenario: You have a client who wants a brochure, but he doesn't know how much he wants to spend. He's also not sure whether he should have 2,000, 5,000, 10,000 or 30,000 copies printed. He would like to know how much it would cost to print each of those quantities as well as the price differences for two, three or four colors. That comes to twelve different estimates right there. To complicate matters even more, let's suppose he doesn't know whether or not to include photographs in the brochure. To make that decision, he wants to know what it would cost without any photos, how much for black and whites, and how much for color pictures. Of course, he doesn't have a clue how many photographs he'd use, so you have to give him a ballpark price based on an average number of photographs.

Before you resign yourself to wasting days rounding up all this information, try to get your client to focus on the goals for this project. Then help eliminate options that won't meet those goals. Explain why it's more economical to print 10,000 copies than 2,000 and why 30,000 may be overkill. Show the client other brochures in two, three and four colors and then point

Straight Talk

We all learn from the time we're young never to say what we really think if we might hurt someone's feelings. But we carry this attitude too far and, by the time we're adults, we've become experts at saying nothing or disguising our potentially unpleasant thoughts as harmless throwaway phrases or roundabout questions. "The garbage needs to go out" or "Would you like to take out the garbage?" are classic examples. Our listener can't give us the information we need, answers the wrong question, or ignores the issue as unimportant. "No, I don't want to take out the garbage" or "Well, if you really wanted me to take out the garbage, why didn't you say so?" We then get frustrated because the person we're talking to isn't a mind reader and doesn't respond appropriately. Asking a listener to understand what we're actually saying when we appear to be saying something else is called indirect communication. Direct communication, on the other hand, is stating what you mean or asking for exactly what you want. "Please take out the garbage."

Another cause of indirect communication is our fear of the word no. "No, I won't take out the garbage." But what if the answer would have been yes? "Sure, I'll take out the garbage." We're too often the victims of negative thinking, finding out too late that the other person would gladly have gone along with our request – if we had just asked straightforwardly. Even if the answer *is* no, there's still the option to negotiate: "If you take out the garbage tonight, I'll take it tomorrow." And a negative answer is better than no answer at all. The garbage will go out one way or the other and you can deal with the real issues directly, too. "You don't do your fair share of the chores!"

Indirect communication can also involve talking to one person about another person. I made this mistake several years ago with an employee, a junior designer, whose performance had deteriorated to intolerable levels. Before I spoke with him about my concerns, I unwittingly mentioned my grievances to a client whose office was in my building. Several days later, the whole thing came back to bite me when one of my female employees was in a ladies' room stall and overheard this client telling one of her employees that I was ready to give the axe to our junior designer. My employee was furious and took this information back to my designer. I was out of the office at the time that all this came about. When I returned, the designer had packed up his things and stormed out, leaving a presentation that was due at a client's office the following morning unfinished. I not only had to deal with my other employees, who were now upset with me for not being honest with this designer, but I also had to stay in the office until one in the morning to finish the next morning's presentation. I learned from this bitter experience never to talk behind someone's back. Now if something bothers me, I go directly to the person involved and get it out in the open where it can be dealt with openly and productively.

out why four colors are a wasted expense if there aren't color photographs. And don't forget to mention that photographs in general should be used only if there's something or someone that absolutely must be shown. Otherwise graphics and color are a far better and less expensive choice.

Even after understanding the price differences from printing different quantities, the client is still not sure how many brochures to print. It's not a question of costs; he doesn't know how many he'll use. Does this mean doing all those cost estimates and hoping he makes a decision based on cost? Not yet. Ask who will receive this brochure and why. How will it be distributed — mail, salespeople, telephone requests, general handouts? Then based on the method of distribution, what's the total number of people who could possibly receive this brochure? Questions such as these should help your client to get a better focus not only on how many pieces will be needed, but how many can realistically be used. If these questions don't get answered, you may need to steer the client toward hiring a market research firm to consult on this aspect of the project.

If your clients have no strong opinions about the colors, photographs, paper and other design or production matters, ask them if they would like you to recommend what you consider to be the best choices for them. You'll find that most clients will trust your professional advice and judgment. In fact, they'll even welcome it. It's surprising how many clients really don't want the responsibility for making these decisions.

Now that you've discarded some options as impractical or inappropriate, try to get rid of some more by looking at costs in more detail. Clients may not know how much they want to spend, but you can bet they know how much they *don't* want to spend. Use that as a preliminary cutoff point for your cost estimate. Unless they say, "I don't care, the sky's the limit," and they almost never say that, then a price ceiling will immediately eliminate a number of variables.

At times, you'll still have to work up multiple cost estimates. Although the client asked

How the Business Community Views Designers

Many small, independent designers and freelancers complain that they are not treated with respect by their clients and the business community in general. Bankers, for instance, often view them as operating unstable businesses with a low track record of longevity and financial success, thus making it more difficult to secure loans and lines of credit. That impression is frequently shared by prospective landlords reluctant to rent to designers who are just starting out, accountants who have never worked with creatives and thus have difficulty understanding the nature of their businesses, and other businesspeople with whom designers need to establish a credit base. The only exceptions are printers, service bureaus and other vendors who deal with designers on a regular basis.

As designers, we know that this perception is inaccurate. But we also know that, as with any group, there are certain members of our profession who relish being seen as eccentric, flighty, aloof and undependable. They attribute these qualities to their refusal to give in to convention – it would destroy their creative spirit, they claim. And they are the ones who, unfortunately, have contributed to the stereotype of the so-called "oddball" creative personality type. These few have left a legacy that the rest of us have had to work doubly hard to overcome.

How can we change the public's perception of the "oddball" creative? By continuing to do exactly what most of us have been doing all along: Taking ourselves, our work and our contribution to the national economy seriously. The majority of us are doing our best to dispel the images people have of nonconformist creatives who are unable to function in traditional corporate or institutional environments. We are doing this by dressing professionally (which means appropriate to the clientele we are serving), operating our businesses thoughtfully and responsibly, and observing the ethical standards set by such professional organizations as the Grapic Artists Guild and the American Institute of Graphic Arts. However, there is another component to changing public opinion that involves our responsibility to serve as role models for the newcomers entering this field. And it applies most to those of us who have an opportunity to serve as teachers in academic or vocational programs preparing people to enter our profession. Given this opportunity, we need to make it a standard part of our curriculum to introduce professional standards to our students and impress upon them the negative consequences that can result when they fail to observe these standards.

Winning respect from other people always begins with respecting ourselves. If we take ourselves seriously and project that attitude into all that we do, others will see us in the same light.

---

for them, he or she may wind up confused by all those choices. This makes it difficult to reach a final decision. Avoid this by ruling out as many as possible in advance on the basis of cost or practicality. Then explain each remaining option when the time comes to present your estimates. Use examples whenever possible to illustrate what the different options will look like in the finished piece.

Attempt, without being pushy, to help your client make a decision before you leave. Otherwise you may hear, "There's so much to consider. Let me think about it, and I'll get back to you." Unfortunately, many of them never do. When that happens, let a reasonable amount of time pass and then contact them. If they hedge, be polite but direct. Ask what their problems or concerns are. Tell them you want to help them produce a product they can be happy with at a price that's comfortable. That will usually get them talking. Find out what their objections are and do your best to solve them. If you can't, you'll just have to chalk it up to experience.

Challenge #4, Clients Choose the Lowest Cost Estimate, Not the Best. Some clients will be adamant about cutting costs. To them, the lowest cost estimate may appear to be their best choice, and it may be. But lower prices usually mean a reduction in some aspect of the project's quality. Explain to your clients what trade-offs their choices involve and what impact they'll have on the piece. For example, a cheaper paper may not take ink as well and ruin the effect of the type. Eliminating a third color may make a piece look cheap. I've always found it difficult to get clients to understand that shaving costs on the printing side will often cause the design itself to suffer and look second-rate. To avoid Client Shock Syndrome when you deliver the completed project, bring samples to the meeting when budget cuts are being decided. Those samples are the only way to actually show your clients what they'll get if they opt for lower printing prices. Make absolutely certain they understand that the trade-offs are their choice, not your mistakes.

Freedom to Say No—Nicely

Most people dread the thought of saying no because they never learned how to do it diplomatically. Obviously, you won't be number one on someone's list of favorite designers if you make a habit of gruffly snapping out a "NO!" when you can't do something. But when the no is softened with a tactful evasion or the offer of a solution, it can be effective. "I'm completely booked up" sounds better to a client than "I'd rather die than do another product catalog." When you have to say no, explain briefly your *business* reasons for doing so, and make every effort to assist your client in finding a solution or replacement.

 The *big* mistake many newly self-employed designers make is telling their clients everything. The client doesn't need to know all the gory details of your problems with other clients, other projects or even your suppliers. Saying that you're swamped with work is enough. If you're offered a project by a client you don't want to work for again, just say you're tied up; don't go into details about your previous unhappy experience. If you don't want a particular project or kind of project, explain you're unable to take it right now and refer the client to other designers who might be available. When it comes to explanations, less is often more.

How do you say no? Let's say a client calls you with a tight deadline project when you've already got several going. Instead of a flat refusal or a pointed remark about people who call you at the last minute, try "I'd really like to handle your project, but I'm swamped with work now. Let me recommend someone that I know would do a great job for you. I'll give you a call as soon as my schedule is a bit lighter; maybe we can talk about future projects you're considering. If I know something is coming up, I can hold an opening for it." You've given a polite, business-related reason that also implies consideration for all your clients. You plan your work so you can give each project your best, and you don't want to do anything to compromise that. You've offered a solution by recommending a reliable replacement. And you also let that client know that you are interested in working with them and want to be available to do so in the future.

Never, never, NEVER offer personal reasons for not doing something. Your clients will respect and accept—even if they don't like—a decision based on business reasons. They won't understand, even if they say they do, if you are unavailable for a meeting because you have to pick up something for your dinner.

It's not that I advocate lying—I don't. But if your reasons for not doing something a client wants you to do are personal, don't talk about it. You aren't obliged to explain the details of your life; in fact, most people don't want to know about them. If a child's, spouse's or parent's illness will affect several days' work or a deadline, it may need to be mentioned; but not otherwise.

It's Not Always Smooth Sailing

You've had a good working relationship with one of your clients for the last two years. When the client called you last week for another project, you felt a coolness. At first, you brushed it off, but it continued throughout the project. Although there was nothing you could put your finger on, you sensed something was wrong.

When trouble starts with a client, you probably won't have to ask yourself more than twice if something is wrong. But if you don't trust that funny little feeling inside that tells you when trouble is brewing, here are some of the warning signals.

- [ ] A client who was once friendly and outgoing, suddenly seems distant and cool for no reason.

- [ ] The client suddenly begins to criticize or question everything you do.

- [ ] Longer and longer periods of time lapse between projects for a client, which may mean the client is trying out other designers.

- [ ] A client takes an unusually long time paying a bill.

Clients can demonstrate displeasure or dissatisfaction through a wide variety of behaviors. You need to be sensitive to any change in the way the client relates to you, but balance your sensitivity to another person's behavior with common sense. You can get paranoid if you let yourself overreact to a client's every little mood shift that may have nothing to do with you. That's why I say that you won't have to ask yourself *more* than twice if something about you is troubling a client. The first time you notice a change toward you, chalk it up to circumstances. But if it happens twice, sit up and take notice.

Once you've spotted a problem in a client relationship, you can ignore it and hope it dissipates in time or you can attempt to discuss it. In this case the best defense is a good offense. No matter what has happened in your relationship with a client, it's always much better to meet it head on. Something left unresolved can fester, doing serious damage to not only this relationship but to your reputation.

Be direct and unemotional. Don't take it as a personal affront. This is business and the situation usually has a business reason behind it, not a personal one. But do be concerned, and express a genuine desire to understand what happened. If the problem is something you did or didn't do, try not to be defensive. We all make mistakes, so admit it, apologize, and then go on.

When the client denies there's a problem, let the matter drop—even when you still feel something is amiss. There's always the chance that the client's attitude really doesn't have anything to do with you but is due to work pressures or personal problems. But sometimes a relationship turns sour and you'll never know why. Maybe something you said or did has been forgotten while the negative feelings remain. If this is the case you'll probably never know for sure, and there isn't a lot you can do about it. The only thing you can do is to think back to the last time you were with this client, when everything *seemed* to be fine. Can you remember anything you may have said or done to which the client reacted in an unusual way? Was there anything that left you feeling uncomfortable? If nothing strikes you, stop trying. Worrying about it won't help. In fact, it may make things even worse. Just hang in there if the client lets you, and be on your best behavior. Time is a wonderful healer.

When a client just can't bring himself to confront you personally, an end-of-project client satisfaction letter (see page 130 for how this works) may help clients tell you what they liked or disliked about you or your work. It can reopen lines of communication that might otherwise be closed permanently because it gives the client an opportunity to explain what he or she thinks without the discomfort of a face-to-face encounter. It also lets you react to the client's opinions in private. You can then choose to act or not act on the comments.

Making It Right

When you discover that a problem does exist between you and a client, what can you do to correct it? Sometimes an apology is enough, but when more is needed you have to find out what the client wants. Think over what you know about your client, what hints she has given you about what she values. If you need only smooth ruffled feathers, then token presents—wine, flowers or tickets to a ball game or a concert—may be appropriate and appreciated. But if the trouble concerns an error you made that caused the client to lose money or time or angered her superiors, then you may need to return what was lost in order to rectify the situation. Give the client a percentage reduction (equal to her previous loss in time or money) on the next project's bill. Let her know what you intend to do to compensate for the slip-up that occurred. If you are uncertain how the client would prefer you to make amends, then ask what you can do. The client will usually tell you. It might be a discount or it might be an action to set the record straight. For example, if your client's boss is upset as the result of what happened, she might truly appreciate it if you called her supervisor or sent a letter explaining that the mistake in the last brochure was entirely your fault. This action could satisfy your client far

more than any material gift or discount you could offer.

If in return for a mistake the client wants something you consider unreasonable or impossible, negotiation can result in a compromise that satisfies you both. Negotiation means give and take as you work toward a win/win situation in which both parties get something they want, and each person involved feels he or she comes out a winner. Letting the client have his way every time is not the answer. If you give everything away without getting something back from the client, you'll feel resentful toward that client. And the client may feel that you can be easily manipulated. Always offer less than you're actually willing to give, so that you have room to move if the client counters your offer. The opposite is also true: Ask for more than you really want, then let the other person talk you down, and let him feel as though he has gained something. This is win/win negotiation. If you can master this art, you're well on your way to business success.

You and the World

Always strive to make a good impression on everyone you meet. Maintaining good relationships with your vendors and subcontractors is just as important as having good client relationships. Vendors who like working with you can become your greatest source of referrals for new business. If they dislike you, they can discourage clients from considering you.

In the short term, it can often seem smarter to focus on getting the best deal or the cheapest price. But that can be shortsighted. A business that views you as a regular, loyal customer is more likely to help you out when you need work done on a very tight deadline or a price break to stay within a project's budget. Make an effort to develop long-term, mutually beneficial relationships with several vendors and subcontractors who consistently do quality work at a reasonable price.

Show vendors and subcontractors the same respect you want from your clients. Don't ask for extensive work on spec. Always try to give specific budgets and time frames for projects when asking for quotes or commitments to do work. And *always* pay your bills promptly! While it is standard practice to take a full thirty days to pay a bill, delaying payment beyond that point is unfair to your creditors and hazardous to your credit rating. No one wants to do business with someone who's unreliable or untrustworthy. Don't give yourself unnecessary handicaps by being a designer no one wants to work with.

The image you create and project affects all those who come into contact with you. They, in turn, carry that image of you to countless others. It's a ripple effect that you should never underestimate—especially since it takes only a minute to ruin a reputation that you've spent years building. Showing professional courtesy and consideration to everyone is the foundation of a good business reputation. It's true that there seem to be plenty of successful rude, surly people out there. But you can bet your bottom dollar that most of them didn't act like that on their way up.

Little things mean a lot. Thanking everyone who helps you and complimenting anyone who does a good job for you sends a strong, positive message. Making a contribution to your community—donating your services for a good cause—can leave a lasting favorable impression.

But the real test of your image is your behavior under fire. It's easy to be nice and polite when things are going well, but it's critical to do so when it seems everything is going wrong. How do you react when a problem arises? Do you panic? Do you blow up at the culprit or bearer of the bad news? What would you do if the 2,000 annual reports scheduled to be delivered to a local hospital that morning still hadn't shown up by 5:00 P.M., and the hospital's desperate public relations director is calling you every five minutes? And the printer calls you back to say that the reports were delivered to the wrong hospital? Would you scream, cry or chew out the printer? These are all natural responses, but they won't solve the problem and could hurt your reputation.

When You Have to Fire Someone

Sometimes you have to fire an employee. This is a traumatic moment for you, too, but being prepared will help you get through it. Thoroughly document the causes for dismissal in advance in a file that includes all the employee's evaluations and other written directions for improvement. It's not enough to know you've made every effort to resolve the problem, you must be able to prove it. When the time comes, be understanding and tell the employee in private. Be kind but direct – make it clear he is fired – and always tell the truth. If someone was

 incompetent, say so or you could leave yourself open to lawsuits. If you blame the firing on downsizing or reorganization, and don't subsequently fire others, the fired employee would qualify for a discrimination suit. As harsh as it may sound, *never* give notice; dismiss him immediately. Having someone who's been fired still in the studio is bad for your other employees' morale. Provide good severance pay, offer to pay for the trip if you've hired someone from out of town, and get them out of there. Then explain the situation to the other employees before the rumor mill gets going.

Put the printer on hold for a minute if you need to vent your emotions, then scream, cry, swear or throw things. Take a couple of deep breaths, get back on the phone with the printer, and ask what she can do to solve the problem. You, of course, want the printer to go get those annual reports and personally deliver them to the right hospital (or at least send someone to take care of it). But let the printer propose that or another solution before you insist on yours. This will probably get your reports there on time (and that is the bottom line) and leave both of you feeling good about it. Only when no solution is forthcoming should you bring out your big guns and demand one.

Someone always owns the responsibility for a problem and its solution. If that person in a given situation is you, take the responsibility and solve it. If the responsibility belongs to someone else — partner, employee, printer, photographer or client — give the person responsible the chance to solve it. Let the person know you've been placed in a bad spot — as a last resort a controlled display of anger can be effective with someone who can't or won't recognize a problem — then wait to see what solution, if any, is offered. Don't start off trying to push a solution down someone's throat and don't jump in and fix the situation unless you absolutely must. That may solve the immediate problem but will leave you feeling angry and resentful and make it harder for you to control your anger the next time.

Managing the Side Effects of Growth

The two major side effects of your business's growth are an increase in the number of employees you have and in the amount of space you need to house your business. Don't increase staff or space first then hope to find enough work to pay for them. I've seen a lot of design firms collapse under the weight of employees hired in expectation of bringing in more work. On the other hand, don't wait till you're drowning in work before you hire someone. The same is true of adding studio space, because a new office won't bring in new clients while badly cramped work space can hamper your efforts to work at all.

Decide what you want, determine the most effective way to do it, and only then go ahead. What kind of help do you need? How many hours a week? How much space do you really need? What will it cost? Plan ahead with *what if* and *when* strategies. When I'm billing X dollars each month consistently, I'll hire a part-time secretary to handle record keeping, prepare invoices, and answer the phone. I can afford that even if my billings drop a little.

Employees

When you take on new business, increase your hours and those of your present employees or bring in freelancers before you hire more full-time staff. Always add staff gradually to spread out the impact of the necessary rearrangement, reorganization and training. Adding only the people you absolutely must have will reduce the financial burdens of additional payroll, increased insurance costs and the extra overhead.

If you hire more people than you really need you can find yourself having to take in more business to support the additional employees, then taking in even more employees to keep up with the escalating business in a vicious growth cycle with a business that only feeds on itself. You can end up working to support your employees' salaries, benefits and yearly raises and unable to afford to give yourself a raise.

When do you need additional help? When you've got as much work as you can carry and can't take on anything else. When you're doing work that someone else could do for you — pasteup, bookkeeping, clerical or basic design work. Remember, you must both manage the business and design. In order to do both without managing all day and designing all night, you've got to delegate work effectively. Establish design direction for a project, then turn it over to an employee who will work on it under your supervision. Hire a secretary to answer your phone and manage paperwork.

You must be a good manager to have good employees. If you can't tell someone what to do and how you want it done, don't be surprised if it doesn't get done. Only when you've set guidelines, clarified goals and objectives, and provided your employees with the necessary tools and authority to do a job well can you expect their best in return.

Establish good systems and procedures (see chapters two and three for more on how to do this) before you hire a single employee. Give everyone adequate training and make it clear that this is how work is to be done. Monitor each employee's work carefully. Don't ever assume something is being done right—make sure it is.

Look for employees who have worked in areas with which you have no experience or who complement your abilities and personality to add both depth and breadth to your business. Never hire a clone of yourself. Don't even consider hiring someone who doesn't have good references. You may think that this person will work better for you, because this is a wonderful opportunity or a better job. But nine times out of ten that won't happen.

You need a secretary when answering the telephone and record keeping take up more than one or two hours a day. Delegating these routine tasks will free you and your partners or design employees to spend more time on billable activities. A secretary can do more than answer the phone and handle clerical duties. Depending on his communication skills and ability to handle detail, the person you hire may be able to relay information to and receive estimates and schedules from subcontractors and vendors and order all your office supplies and equipment. If you can find a gal or guy Friday who also has training as a bookkeeper, you can combine the two roles.

Don't expect a secretary to take over the moment she walks into your office. You'll have to work with her and familiarize her with your systems and procedures and your preferences. Don't expect her to be a mind reader. If you want or need something, ask her. If you don't like something she is doing or want it done differently, tell her what the problem is and what you'd like changed the first time she does it.

You need a sales representative or account executive if you have a highly marketable talent or skill but have trouble selling your services. Another alternative is taking in a partner to handle all the marketing, and perhaps financial matters, for you.

An independent sales representative usually gets individual projects, not clients, for a number of designers and other creatives. He receives a commission, usually 10 to 15 percent, on each project you accept. Be sure that you have everything the rep will do on your behalf spelled out in a contract. Have your lawyer review it thoroughly.

An account executive is your in-house salesperson who brings in new clients, not just individual projects, and will also handle most of the client contact for you. Clients tend to prefer meeting the designer who'll work on their project, so plan on continuing to attend some sales calls and presentations. An account executive should have prior experience in sales, client and account management with a design, advertising or public relations background.

Expanding Your Studio Space

Sooner or later you'll need room to add new people and more equipment. You'll need to give your employees more space to work and nicer spaces to work in. Larger, nicer studio space also projects a positive, successful image to clients and fellow designers.

Choose your new office space on the basis of present and projected needs over at least the next year. Even if you find a space that appears to more than meet those needs, try to get only a short-term lease with an option to renew at the same price. If you outgrow the space (or business slows and you want less) during the term of the lease, you're free to move. If you're still comfortable where you are, you can renew.

Calculate the costs of moving carefully. If you're banking on the income from only one or two large accounts to finance your move, you could end up in hot water. It's better to work up your numbers based on your *average* income for the last several years, which should include some slow periods. Also remember that a

Don't Rent: Own

Buying a building is an excellent investment if you can afford the down payment and have a solid client base to support the mortgage and taxes. Although the market may have its ups and downs, real estate is generally a good long-term investment. And the tax write-offs are great.

Like any other investment, make sure this is a viable one. Mortgage payments and taxes come due in lean times, too, so don't commit to a larger ongoing expense than you can safely handle. One or two new large accounts won't provide an adequate guarantee that you can carry a heavier cash outlay. What if you've bought the building and then lose one of the accounts?

If you have additional office space, you can cover at least part of your mortgage and taxes from rentals. But consider the costs of doing so carefully. If you can't rent out the extra space, your building can quickly turn into a financial liability instead of an asset. You may also need to hire the services of a business manager to manage rentals, repairs and other tenant issues.

larger rent payment won't be the only additional expense of moving. Besides the moving expenses themselves, you'll need to buy or lease more furniture. You'll need to get all your stationery, business cards and forms reprinted with the new address and phone number. And you'll probably see an increase in your utility bills.

Allow for several days of downtime to pack, unpack and get resettled in the new space. Decide *before* you move how you will handle projects that need to be completed and rush jobs that will arrive during the time period you will be moving and getting settled.

Recession-Fighting Strategies

Economists say that recessions come and go in four-year cycles. And since no business is recession proof, if you are planning to be in business for at least the next ten years, you may have to weather two recessions. Some businesses never survive a recession, while many others do. What's the secret? First and foremost is knowing that you can survive and even thrive during a slump in the economy. Aside from assuming a positive attitude, what else can you do to ensure your survival? You can adapt your business methods and procedures to the economic changes.

Adapting your business methods and procedures begins with recognition. If what worked for you during peak times no longer works because the economic climate is different, then it follows that you will have to try new things. I've outlined some ways to bring in clients, trim the fat from your expenses, and put more money in your pocket when the economic outlook turns bleak. But before you begin, consider this one fact: When the economy is in a recession, businesses must advertise more than ever. That, of course, means they still need all kinds of graphics materials, but now they must spend less money than before. The business is out there during a recession—it may even increase—but the budgets are much lower. Your new focus has to be on how you can still make a profit while working for lower returns.

Hire Freelancers

Freelancers' fees are substantially lower than yours (30 to 50 percent), and they can do design and production under your supervision. You can then take in more work without tying up your own higher rate time. You can charge less on a project, take in more work, and still make a healthy profit.

Barter

You can substantially lower your expenses by using the good old-fashioned barter system. You can trade your graphic services for the things you need, such as rent, equipment, materials, printing and even subcontractors' services. You can trade your design time with a photographer or a copywriter for his or her work on one of your projects. I've traded my time for massages, dental work, painting and remodeling in my home and office. I've heard of people who have bartered for high-priced items like cars or copiers. Any company or service business that uses advertising or promotion in any way needs design services. When you barter, you are doing work at your standard retail price, but it is only costing you your wholesale or discounted rate. So if you do a job that is worth $1,500, it may only cost you $1,000, yet you receive in-kind items or services worth $1,500. If you do get into the barter system, check with your accountant, or contact the IRS and ask for publication 334, "Tax Guide for Small Businesses," because you still have to report and pay taxes on any income you derive from trade in tangible property or services. And that income must be reported at its fair market value, not the discounted rate.

Also, make up an agreement that spells out the conditions and details of what you are trading and what you will get in return along with dates of delivery or performance. It's also helpful to make up redeemable certificates in different dollar denominations, or a computer-generated certificate on which you can just plug in the dollar value, and give these out to your barter buddies.

Bartering can expand your visibility and your market base. Once you get into this method of trading, there's no limit to the companies and businesses you can approach who will be glad to get to know you and use your services. Once you've received what you wanted in trade (after all, how many copiers can you use?), many businesses will want to continue using your services on a cash basis.

You can even go national with this concept. There are trade exchange organizations that set up barter deals between businesses. You have to become a member, which usually involves paying a membership fee and being listed in a members' directory where other businesses can see you and use your services. Some exchanges offer inexpensive advertising services, such as brochure distribution of their members' flyers to other members. The interesting thing about trade exchanges is that many of them deal in barter credits. For example, if you do a graphics job for $3,000 for one company, you may not receive your goods or services back from that particular company. Instead, if that company has nothing you need, your $3,000 is credited with the trade exchange, and you get what you need from some other member company. There are other advantages to this system. You can purchase something on credit by offering a dollar amount against future services. If the trade exchange doesn't have a company who needs your services at the moment, you don't have to wait. You get what you want, and your services are credited against a future taker. If that future taker never materializes, you will in essence, be getting your goods or services for free.

For more information on trade exchanges, contact National Commerce Exchange in Tampa, Florida, (813) 539-8719, or send a stamped, self-addressed envelope to the International Reciprocal Trade Association, 9513 Beach Mill Rd., Great Falls VA 22066. Also check your local phone book under trade exchanges or barter brokers.

Lower Your Expenses

Begin by moving into lower-priced offices, which doesn't have to mean moving to a less attractive or smaller space. You can often find nicer space for less money in the "burbs." Or you can team up with other designers, photog-raphers, copywriters, etc. and share space, thus cutting your expenses. You can also offer each other more work by collaborating on projects, which will increase your exposure while bringing in more income. If you have staff members who are not absolutely necessary or equipment you don't need, let them or it go. Learn how to run a tight ship and you'll never have to worry about sinking.

Shop Competitively for Vendor Services

Really shop around for the best prices from printers and suppliers, and pass the savings on to your clients. I know this contradicts my previous advice to avoid clients who try to nickel and dime you or choose to work with you based on price alone, but during a recession the old notions have to go. You must be more cost-effective to attract clients. One of the best ways is to ask for more competitive prices from your vendors and subcontractors. It may be more difficult to get reduced rates from subcontractors because, like you, they would have to discount their hourly rates and that could be a hardship. Put yourself in their shoes: How can you say that yesterday your services were worth $60 an hour and today they are worth only $40 without compromising your reputation and losing your self-esteem? But vendors such as printers, typesetters and service bureaus are operating on volume, and they often employ semiskilled workers. Therefore they have more room to discount than does an independent creative person.

Expand Your Expertise

Complete courses and workshops — for example, in computer software or illustration — that will give you new skills and thus a broader skill base to sell from.

Network

During a recession, networking becomes more important than ever, because companies don't want to take chances on unknowns. When they have to fire their high-priced ad agency and find a lower-priced

design studio, they are going to ask printers, photographers, art supply stores and service bureaus for recommendations. Always keep your suppliers and subcontractors informed that you are expanding your market, bringing in new clients or promoting a new specialty.

Many designers offer a discount rebate to present clients who make a referral that results in a new project or account. This could be a 10 to 15 percent cash rebate on their last bill or a percentage off the next project.

Be Positive

Don't complain about the business climate. Behavior follows attitude, and negativism will make you look like a loser. Instead, always tell people things are great, and you've got more work than ever. Is it lying? It may be. But it's the kind of lie that I believe is absolutely necessary — for your sake as well as others. It's not about misrepresenting yourself; it's about keeping your attitude positive and optimistic.

CHAPTER

nine

Planning

Your

Future

wning a business is similar to owning a car. What you want from it determines the kind you have. Owning and operating a Rolls Royce is quite different from riding around in a pickup truck. The same is true of any design business. The kind of work you want to do, the amount of money you want to make, and what you're willing to invest, all affect the kind of business you'll have.

Keeping a business healthy requires the same care you'd put into keeping your car running well. You need clients to bill and a billing system to tell you what they owe. You need equipment and supplies to get the work done. You need to bring in new clients and do good work to keep the ones you have. You need policies and procedures to tell you where you're going and how well you're doing.

It takes time and effort to learn how to do all these tasks well. But gradually you get better at taking care of business, and it takes less time to do so. You're still busy, but you have the time to start thinking ahead. It's similar to getting a car fixed: Now that you've got dependable transportation, you want to go somewhere.

That's great! But where do you want to go? I've talked a little about planning throughout this book, beginning with the business plan in chapter one, "You're in Business!" And I've discussed the different ways you can make your business a success. Defining success, though, is up to you — not your family, friends, colleagues or competitors (not even me). You have to consider what *you* want for *your*self and *your* business.

If I'm So Successful, Why Am I Unhappy?

When I began my freelance business, surviving was all I cared about. Once I got beyond that point and could plan what I wanted from my business, my only goal was to make money and be successful. I wanted more clients, bigger budgets, larger office space and more staff. It took three years, but my part-time design work grew into a two-person design studio and then into an advertising agency, which grew and grew! My business had succeeded beyond my wildest dreams. *Everyone* said I was successful. But I found myself angry at everything about and everyone involved in my business, and I didn't know why. Why wasn't I happy when I had achieved my goals?

I had never thought what success meant to me. After all, where would any sane person want her business to go but up? Up to more productivity, to more clients, and especially to more money – all the things I said I wanted. I thought I was having fun, but I felt hollow. I had poured everything into my business for ten years, until there was nothing left of me. There's nothing wrong with being committed to your work. In fact, you have to do that. But your business – the work, itself – has to give something back to you. If you keep giving without getting, pretty soon there's nothing left.

It took a year and a half of soul-searching to realize that what my business had become wasn't *my* idea of success. For me, neither money nor other people's acknowledgment that I was successful was enough. I didn't feel successful, because my achievements weren't based on what success meant to me.

When I listened to my anger, I realized that I resented my clients because the projects we did for them weren't the kind that I loved to do: designs with an artistic flair that involved illustrations. Instead, they needed materials, such as newspaper and magazine ads and sales brochures, that used photographs and simple designs. I also resented my employees because they did the design work. Even if it wasn't exactly the kind that I loved, at least it was designing. They got to sit at drawing boards all day while I had to sit at a big desk talking to clients and worrying about money. That was the problem. I was happiest when actually designing, not managing, especially if it involved illustrations and more sophisticated graphic design. Now, I could plan a new direction for my company.

About this time, my art director resigned, so I took over as creative/art director. What fun! Then I announced to all my employees, especially account executives soliciting clients, that the agency would only take on certain types of projects and accounts. We would slowly phase out those clients who had strictly advertising accounts, and solicit, instead, clients who preferred graphic design projects with a softer style that used illustrations rather than photographs. The employees were thrilled, but I suspect mainly because they saw my own excitement and enthusiasm return, making them more cheerful and positive as a result. A whole new energy surged through the agency. I had finally succeeded, because I had reshaped my business into one that would allow me to do those things that I truly enjoyed. It seems so simple now, but it still amazes me how few people ever realize that doing those things that will make you joyful is what success is all about.

Freedom to Succeed

Running a successful design business, even a part-time one, calls for design training and experience, planning, working capital, good business advice and a desire to succeed. While all these are important—and we'll come back to them later—wanting to succeed may be the most critical. No matter how talented you are, no matter how much money you have in the bank, you won't succeed unless you really want to.

I'm convinced that my business career—from freelancer to partner in a small design studio to executive director of my own advertising agency—advanced steadily because I finally decided to take myself and my business seriously. Along with that decision came the determination to become the best designer that I could be. That might not mean being the best designer in the area or winning awards for my designs, but it did mean trying to get better with each new project.

This was a change in attitude for me. Up to that point, I had been content with being "good enough." I used to think that I was just lucky when good things happened and opportunities came my way. But it wasn't luck; opportunities came my way because I earned them and was ready for them.

When I made the decision to work at being my best, it was like an antenna popped right out of my head. Suddenly I was tuned into concepts, and possibilities that I had never considered before. I came up with new ways to attract business and make new contacts. I made a conscious effort to expand my technical abilities. I even started to take a few chances as a designer, trying out ideas I had been afraid of before. And my antenna, vibrating with my new enthusiasm, picked up signals that I'm sure used to pass right by me. That's why I believe that opportunity only comes when you're ready to pick up the signals. Opportunity is always around, but until we have our antennae up, we just can't see it.

How Do You Spell Success?

Most people want to succeed. But that's only one part of the formula for success. You must also know what success means to you and believe that you can achieve it. Add all these together with dedicated hard work and your success is almost guaranteed. Assuming that you already want to succeed or you wouldn't be reading this book, it's time to define what success means to you.

We owe it to ourselves to understand what will make us feel successful *and* bring us happiness. Only then will all the sacrifice and effort be worth it. This chapter has two sets of exercises to help you define your own idea of success, confirm your confidence in your abilities, and establish the goals and actions that will keep you moving steadily toward your dreams.

I suggest that you don't just do these exercises once; go through the questions again at least once a year. As you reach your goals, you'll want to set new ones and perhaps even to redefine your idea of success. We all move through many levels of accomplishment and personal growth. As we do this, our attitudes about what's important to us and our businesses change. We need to adjust ourselves to those new attitudes and change our work lives to avoid the frustration, and even burnout, that can happen when we're pursuing goals that are no longer meaningful to us.

Exercise #1: Defining Success

Before you can understand what success is for you, you have to strip away all the influences of other people. This first exercise will help you identify and examine how you think the world perceives success. Then you can begin to accept or reject those concepts that have affected your behavior and beliefs. Once you've chosen those, make sure that what you've accepted feels right. If it doesn't, eliminate those messages and values. Through the process of elimination, you can get more in touch with what you feel in your heart. That feeling, even if it's hard to express, will lead you to your own definition of success.

Begin by answering the following questions for yourself on a separate sheet of paper. Take as much time as you need (you don't have to do it all at once).

Have a Written Plan and Review It Daily

~~~~~~~

It's not enough to think about your goals occasionally. Numerous studies show that people successful in reaching their goals often write out those goals as a list, with detailed plans for achieving them. They read through their lists daily and check off each completed step, revising their lists frequently. In addition to actively working toward their goals, many recite them several times a day as affirmations. This helps them focus on and develop a positive attitude about achieving their goals.

Instead of worrying about what might go wrong, they concentrate on how to make good things happen. For example, the affirmative person sets a goal of bringing in five new clients this year. She carefully plans her self-promotion efforts with that in mind. She doesn't get discouraged by negative responses; she moves on to the next prospect still confident about what she wants, and how she intends to get it. By the end of the year she has her five new clients. The negative person approaches the same goal very differently, because she's already convinced she can't do it. She agonizes over her self-promotion plans. She worries about blowing her presentations, and usually does because she makes mistakes out of sheer stage fright. At the year's end, she hasn't got her five new clients and tells everyone that she knew it wouldn't work out.

1. How does society define success?

2. What are the accepted symbols of that success?

3. How does your family define success?

4. How do your closest friends define success?

5. How does the business community of designers, clients and vendors with whom you work perceive success?

6. Now, make one list of anything you just wrote down with which you agree and another list of anything with which you disagree. Why do you agree or disagree with each?

7. Now, write a definition of success for you and your business. If you have difficulty with this question, don't try to answer it right now. You may need to explore your feelings about success, happiness and your business some more. Exercise #2 on pages 197-198 will help you. When you finish it, try to answer this question again. Even if you did answer it now, see if your definition still sounds good or if it needs revision.

Do What You Love and Love What You Do

Few people take the time to think about what would make them happy in their businesses. Why should they? They don't have other options. As long as their businesses keep making money, they're happy. Or are they? Those people would probably be very surprised to learn there are alternatives. But it's true: You do have a choice. You can make the things that are important to you part of your work life, too.

What brings you joy? If spending time with your family and friends is more important than having a million-dollar business that consumes all your time, then you aren't going to be happy even if you're making tons of money—and you shouldn't build that kind of business. In other words, get in touch with what you want, then set goals for yourself and your business that reflect it.

We can create the conditions that cultivate joy in our businesses, as well as in our personal lives. For example, some people love creating new businesses. As soon as one takes off, they need to move on to a new challenge. If that sounds like you, then you'll feel more successful if you have the kind of business that is growing not just in billings, but in new directions. Seek out clients who'll let you try different things. Or add on a different type of business, such as a video production company.

If you're attracted to the thought of earning a national reputation as a top designer, seek out the kinds of clients that can give you national exposure and enter every competition you can find. If you want a one-person studio at home, and to limit the number of clients or projects so you can enjoy your personal life, you'll achieve success by making less money and keeping your business small. (In other words, you'll succeed by refusing the world's definition of success.)

Some people find it easy to know what they feel and whether their business goals will bring them joy. But for those who have trouble focusing on what they feel and want, the exercise that follows has a series of questions to help you reflect on your feelings about money, clients, employees, your design work, your office space and various other aspects of your business. Once you're aware of how you feel about your business now, it'll be easier to figure out what you want for the future.

What Next? Goals and Plans

If you want to go somewhere, but don't know where, you'll spend all your time just wandering around. You may eventually end up somewhere, but there's a good chance you won't like it there. You need to pick your destination and then head for it. In business, your destination is achieving your goals. That's why you need to set specific goals for your business; goals that reflect your ideas of success.

If you do know where you want to go but not how to get there, chances are slim that you will. You need directions—or a good map. To get to your business destination—your goal—you need a plan of action. The more detailed and complete your action plans are, the easier it is to achieve your goal without getting lost or sidetracked. That means breaking them down into a series of specific steps with target dates for each.

Exercise #2: Goals and Action Plans

There are so many options to consider when we begin planning for the future! This exercise will help you get a better sense of what you want from your business and how to get it. The questions will help you identify what you like and dislike about your business and which possibilities for expansion or new directions for the future you do or don't want.

The exercise focuses on different areas of your business, posing three questions about each. The first helps you explore your preferences. The second asks you to list specific actions you can take to bring about your desired goal and to set a deadline for completing each. For the third question, you'll list the steps needed to accomplish each. List every step you can think of, no matter how small, and assign a deadline to each.

Try large sheets of paper that give you plenty of room. When you're done, you'll have a "Goals and Actions Plan" to help you stay on course and move steadily toward what you've identified as being important to you.

Question One:

How I Feel: What do I love most about my business as it is now? Why?
What I'll Do: What can I do to give me more time for what I love most?
How I'll Do It: Step #1:

Question Two:

How I Feel: What do I hate most about my business right now? Why?
What I'll Do: What can I do to eventually eliminate those things I hate?
How I'll Do It: Step #1:

Question Three:

How I Feel: If could choose, which of my present clients would I keep and why?

What I'll Do: What steps can I take to weed out those clients I don't want?
How I'll Do It: Step #1:

Question Four:

How I Feel: If I could have any other clients I wanted, who would I choose, and why?
What I'll Do: What can I do to get those clients or others like them?
How I'll Do It: Step #1:

Question Five:

How I Feel: Is there anything I'd like to change about the way I work with my clients?
What I'll Do: What can I do to improve those aspects of my client relationships?
How I'll Do It: Step #1:

Question Six:

How I Feel: Which of my design skills would I like to improve and why?
What I'll Do: What can I do to improve those skills?
How I'll Do It: Step #1:

Question Seven:

How I Feel: What new skills would I like to have or what new areas would I like to learn more about?
What I'll Do: What can I do to develop those skills or to learn new things?
How I'll Do It: Step #1:

Question Eight:

How I Feel: How do I feel about the kind of projects I'm presently getting from my clients, in terms of their content and creative challenges?
What I'll Do: If I'm not satisfied, what can I do to bring in different kinds of projects? If I am satisfied, what can I do to keep growing in these directions?
How I'll Do It: Step #1:

Question Nine:

How I Feel: Is there a particular specialization I'd like to become known for, but haven't had the opportunity or the time to pursue?

What I'll Do: What can I do to give myself the time and opportunities to expand in that direction?
How I'll Do It: Step #1:

Question Ten:

How I Feel: What would my ideal work environment be like? (Describe it in detail and include not only the physical layout, but also other people, if any, you'd like to work with and why.) How does this differ from my present situation?
What I'll Do: What can I do to create my ideal work environment? Is there anything I can change now?
How I'll Do It: Step #1:

Question Eleven:

How I Feel: If I had employees, what would they do? (If you already have employees, skip to Question Twelve. If you don't have and don't want employees, skip to Question Thirteen.)
What I'll Do: What can I do to bring my business to the point where it could support employees?
How I'll Do It: Step #1:

Question Twelve:

How I Feel: What do I like about having employees? (If you don't yet have employees, skip to Question Thirteen.)
What I'll Do: What can I do to change what I don't like about having employees?
How I'll Do It: Step #1:

Question Thirteen:

How I Feel: Do I want to expand my business (for example, client base, facilities or equipment)? If so, why and how?
What I'll Do: What actions can I take to expand it?
How I'll Do It: Step #1:

Question Fourteen:

How I Feel: If I won ten million dollars in the lottery, what would I like to change about my business?
What I'll Do: What changes can I make without the lottery jackpot?
How I'll Do It: Step #1:

Question Fifteen:

How I Feel: Which things that I enjoy, if any, are presently a part of my business?
What I'll Do: What can I do to incorporate into my business those things I do enjoy that aren't currently part of it?
How I'll Do It: Step #1:

Question Sixteen:

How I Feel: What are my financial goals?
What I'll Do: What do I need to do now to make those goals a reality?
How I'll Do It: Step #1:

If you couldn't answer question 7 in Exercise #1 (defining success for you and your business) before, go back and do it now. It should be a breeze. Since you've just identified some goals for your business, your definition of success should include them. If you did answer question 7, but your definition of success didn't include the things you cited as being important to pursue in this second exercise, go back and add to your answer or rewrite your definition.

Making It Happen

Exercise #2 gave you a good start on drawing up a business plan. This will be your road map toward success — however you've defined it for yourself. Although you do need a formal, detailed business plan when applying for a loan (see pages 7-11 for more on business plans), you should have a plan down on paper to remind you where you want to go and how you're going to get there. It doesn't matter what it looks like — as long as you can read and understand it!

Here's one approach. Start by putting down everything you know about your business and your market. (You're reorganizing your answers to the questions in Exercise #2 to make unified statements about your business.) Your key areas are revenues and profits, design strengths and weaknesses, and competition. Review your operations. How do you design and produce projects? How do you handle paperwork (and supervising staff if you have them)? (Your answers to questions 5 and 11-

13 can help here.) How do you market your work?

Evaluate your market. Review your answers to questions 3, 4, 6, 7 and 8; what are they telling you about your market and how potential clients might perceive you? Keep writing until you run out of things to say.

Now what? You've faced the facts, so the conclusions should follow easily. What are your business's strengths and weaknesses? What opportunities do you see? What problems? For example, you've built up a good client base but you don't find the projects interesting or challenging. Are your current clients unaware of your capabilities? Are you spending too much time designing and not enough selling? Your action plans for those questions should give you some insight into both the problems and the solutions. Or do you think your plans need some revision now that you have looked at them from a slightly different perspective?

Your action plans also describe strategies for capitalizing on opportunities and correcting problems. Review them carefully, then look for other options. Can you improve profitability by cutting overhead rather than bringing in new clients? Look for actions that might help you toward more than one goal. For example, you want both to add five new clients in the next year and become better known for your logo designs. One way to work toward both would be to enter your logos into competitions so more people see your work. You'd then follow up by actively pursuing design work that involved logos and show your logos as part of your presentations to potential clients.

Finally, organize your goals and action plans with a schedule. You don't have to work toward everything you want all at once. Instead, you need to set priorities by ranking your goals in order of importance or by determining which goal is dependent on another's being achieved first. For example, you may want a nicer office, but should put that goal on hold until you have a larger client base. From there, you can establish a tentative time line for taking on each goal that's not possible yet. Thinking of your goals and action plans in this way helps you stay focused on what is feasible and practical.

Now that you've got your plan, you've reached the hard part—sticking to it. Some goals will be easier than others to achieve, but you can't let yourself get discouraged if some take longer or are much harder to reach than you've anticipated. And be prepared to change your plans if you find your needs have changed or that a goal just isn't practical.

Increased income doesn't always mean in-

Red Alert

As you work on your business plan, do you feel fairly comfortable with the goals you've set and how you plan to achieve them? Or do you have a funny, uncomfortable feeling in the pit of your stomach? Feel like there's a headache coming on? Feeling a little edgy? If you feel that uncomfortable about your plans, you just might have a good reason.

Although any growth requires us to stretch our abilities, we also have a built-in warning device that alerts us when we're about to bite off far more than we can chew. It's like learning how much you can push yourself when you exercise. There's a fine line between a healthy stretch that feels uncomfortable and the pain that warns you're hurting yourself.

How can you tell when a business goal is too much of a stretch? If you're not sure what's bothering you, reread each "How I Feel" question and action plan from Exercise #2 aloud. This can help you be more in tune with the impact of the words you read. Focus on the one(s) that you feel uncomfortable about. First, determine whether the goal is really something you want. Then consider its feasibility. Can you achieve it with the resources you have now? If not, what would make it possible? Maybe your business needs to grow a little or you need more experience before tackling that particular goal. Or maybe your ego is running away with you. For example, you've set a goal of doubling your profits over the next year and plan to get all that growth from new business. You may be stretching too much. Since you'll get maybe one new client from every five presentations, you're planning to greatly increase time spent on that area without reducing your current workload (can't afford to lose work and money). Can you realistically plan to do that? If you're a very small shop, the answer is an emphatic "no" unless you can afford to take on temporary help to pick up the slack. *That's* the time to pay attention to your internal warning system.

No one gets through life without making a few ambitious mistakes, and when that happens, you just have to learn your lesson and go on—sadder but wiser. But you can reduce the frequency and severity of your mistakes by learning to listen to those internal warnings.

Long Long-Term Planning

Someday, you'll want to retire. That may seem like something you won't need to even think about for a long time. Wrong! Especially if your design business is your sole source of income. Think about it. When you stop working, the money stops coming in. So, what will you live on when you aren't working?

There are several ways to protect yourself against being retired and poor, but they all take some long-term planning. You can build up your savings and should. You can invest some money in a variety of options—especially tax-deferred ones (see below for more on investing carefully). You can also sell your design business, if your children won't be taking it over (in which case you'd arrange to get a good pension). Your company will be most valuable if you have worked to increase your assets and its market value. That means not only having a nice location and up-to-date equipment but building a solid client base and a stable staff (to carry on when you're gone). In fact, you'll probably get your best deal by selling to someone inside your business rather than outside.

 creased net profits. If your expenses increase with your income, the money will go out as fast as it comes in. Business growth has to be measured by its bottom line. Some goals seem terrific but actually reduce your profits. Others are less glamorous but yield long-term business growth. Still others, making your business more competitive or your work life happier, may be worth any sacrifice you'll have to make. Try to include in your action plans cost-cutting measures that will help offset any additional expenses. Just be clear about why you want certain goals for your business and understand the trade-offs involved in pursuing them.

Financial Plans for Your Business

The safest, but slowest way to raise money for business growth is to build up your savings until you can finance your expansion. The best way to save is setting goals. Budget a fixed percentage of your net profits, 10 percent is a good place to start, to pay for expansion projects. If, after six months, you find this amount is too much to carry, scale back and extend your time lines. Or, you may want to increase the amount you're saving, if you can do so comfortably, in order to reach your goals faster. Another way to increase your capital is investing your savings in such instruments as Certificates of Deposit (CDs), mutual funds or treasury bills that will pay a higher return on your money.

Investment Options and Risks

You should start investing slowly and cautiously, leaving a margin to cover unexpected variations in your cash flow. Gauge how much you can afford to invest against your ability to replace the money without causing yourself financial hardship in case an emergency occurs.

If you can afford the minimum deposit (usually $1,000), a one-year Certificate of Deposit (CD) can be good investment. Six-month CDs usually pay simple, not compound, interest on the total amount of your investment, giving a much smaller effective yield. Shop around for the bank or credit union with the highest interest rates.

When you've got more money to invest, try not to put all of it into any single investment at one time. It's better to stagger your maturity dates and limit the amounts to no more than $5,000 in any one-time deposit. That way, you'll have available a consistent source of investment income after your first year. Then you can use it to beef up a sagging cash flow, if you need it, or you can reinvest it. When you reinvest it, you can take advantage of the best interest rates, which may be better than the original ones. Or you can simply roll it over at the same rate within the grace period at the time of maturity. You can go for investments with longer maturity dates and higher yields when your cash flow stabilizes and your profits increase.

CDs and money market accounts are good, conservative investments on which you won't make a fortune but won't lose your shirt either. There are options that offer better returns on your investment but present greater risks—and larger losses if something goes wrong. These include money market mutual funds; government, municipal and corporate bonds; bond funds; stocks; stock funds; and treasury bills and notes. Each of these options has its advantages and disadvantages. For example, government bonds carry a low risk and are exempt from state and local taxes (you do pay federal) but they carry a lower interest rate than other kinds of bonds.

Mutual funds are your best bet for the bond and stock markets. The larger pool of investors reduces the amount any individual must commit in order to get a decent return. And since funds spread their members' money over a wide range of investments, using a fund also reduces your risk. For example, a well-diversified stock fund may hold over 100 stocks in different companies. If you aren't using a financial planner (see below for more on choosing one), magazines such as *Forbes* and *Business Week* do annual evaluations of the performance of all kinds of mutual funds. Once you've found several that interest you, send for their prospectuses and study the services offered and the fees charged. If you're concerned about the types of businesses your fund invests in, choose one that specializes in a particular industry or area, or look for one that handles only socially responsible industries.

Before you do any investing at all, know how much you can afford to invest — and how much you can afford to lose. A related issue is your comfort level with risk. Although you may be able to afford losing a thousand dollars from a financial standpoint, psychologically you may be comfortable only with a lower level of risk. In that case, you should go with a more stable form of investing, such as mutual bond funds. You can lose money if the interest rates rise, but you won't face the kind of fluctuations you have when playing the stock market.

Shop for investments as carefully as you would any other major purchase. Comparison shop and don't be afraid to ask questions. You can get good background information on investing in general from bankers, brokers and financial planners, or by consulting some of the many books available on the subject at your local library. You can learn about specific companies from the business magazines (*Forbes*, *Money* and *Business Week*) and *The Wall Street Journal*. Even if you plan to have someone else handle the actual investing for you, knowing a little about the various types of investments and how they work will help you evaluate your broker's or financial planner's performance.

You can never start too early to begin investing in a well thought out retirement plan. In fact, it's more important now than ever before, because people are living longer than even statistical estimations have predicted, and that trend will only increase during the coming years. Now you need to prepare to live on your retirement income for as long as thirty years, and perhaps even more. You must also be aware of the impact inflation will continue to have on your retirement funds. When you are ready to begin living on the money you've set aside over the years, it's purchasing power will be worth far less than it was at the time you invested it. So you will need more money in the future to live at your present standard. Therefore, you must begin planning for your retirement as soon as possible. Don't wait until you are making more money. Start now.

To demonstrate how little it can take to provide for your retirement needs, consider this: If you were to deposit only $2,000 a year (which is the total amount allowed to an individual in a given year at the time of this writing) into an Individual Retirement Account (IRA) for thirty years, and you were able to earn an average rate of 8 percent, compounded daily, at the end of thirty years that IRA would be worth a whopping $266,846.35. To do this, however, you would have to open your first IRA account by age thrity-seven, and not touch it until you reached sixty-seven. But you can begin ealier. If you begin as early as twenty-two, you can amass $961,716.11 by the time you hit sixty-seven. So you can see that an IRA alone can put you in a good position when you're ready to retire. Now, if you are able to combine an IRA with other investment vehicles as you get older and have more money to invest, you could be sitting on Wealthy Street in your golden years.

What are those other investment vehicles? Aside from an IRA, you can open a Keogh Plan that is specifically designed for the self-employed person. The minimum deposit with a Keogh is a percent of your annual earned income, which makes this plan very attractive because you are not limited to the $2,000 maximum of the IRA. With either plan, as with all retirement investments, you pay no income tax on the interest earned, and you get to deduct the amount deposited each year from your gross income. That, too, is a real added incentive to begin your participation in a retirement plan as early in your career as possible.

The only catch is that the money invested in an IRA or a Keogh account must remain there until you reach age fifty-nine-and-a-half. If you try to withdraw it earlier, you will have to pay a penalty plus claim the interest as income on your taxes. The only exception would be if you were disabled and unable to work; then you could withdraw your money

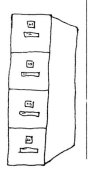

at no penalty. And best of all, either of these retirement plans can be set up at any local bank. So you don't need a broker or financial planner to get started.

The only restriction to opening an IRA is that you cannot participate at the same time in another pension plan, whether it's a Keogh or a company pension plan, such as a Simplified Employee Pension plan (SEP) or have coverage with another employer's pension plan.

The same restrictions do not apply to a Keogh Plan. For example, if you work for another company full- or part-time and you run your design business part time, you can open a Keogh based on that part-time, self-employed income. Keoghs offer another advantage. You pay less tax on your Keogh money at the time of retiring if you withdraw all of it at the same time, because you get to do what's called ten-year forward averaging. This means the money is taxed as if it were being withdrawn over a ten-year period.

You can also invest in a SEP plan if your business is incorporated. This allows you to deduct a percent of your income and put it into tax-deferred government bonds, stocks and mutual funds. However, you must go through a broker to set up this type of pension plan.

If you choose to work with a broker to develop a pension plan, you can allow him or her to place you in a mutual funds program where the decisions regarding the exact stocks and bonds you invest in are made for you, or you can get into a self-directed IRA or SEP plan. This allows you to choose what companies you wish to invest in or which bonds you want to purchase.

Brokers, Bankers and Financial Planners

Some people swear by their brokers and would never think of making an investment without them. Others, and I'm one, prefer to handle their own investments. I've always felt that brokers were more concerned with finding the investment that would give them the best commission rather than what was right for me. That may not be fair, and certainly

they should be paid for the expertise they offer, but I do feel I'm better off looking after my own money. I'm not investing large sums (which makes it hard to justify the commission and annual fee) and do have the time to do my homework for the investments I want.

Whether you or someone else manages your investments, you should keep an accurate record of all of them: when they come due and where they are (banks, credit unions, brokerage firms). Your bank, broker or planner will notify you about any changes in and roll-over dates for your investments. But you need to know when you can count on investment income (in case you need it). You'll also use that information to determine your net worth for financial statements or when applying for a business loan.

Although stockbrokers focus almost exclusively on your investments, financial planners work with your banker, accountant, insurance agent and broker to produce a long-term plan for your finances. Some accountants with financial planning backgrounds can make recommendations to you, but most are not trained for it. This plan covers all your needs, including how much you should save and how much insurance coverage you need. Financial planners can recommend a combination of investments to get the most interest without paying hefty, unnecessary taxes.

Begin your search for a financial planner by asking friends and business associates for recommendations. Make sure those planners are Registered Investment Advisors (registered with the Securities and Exchange Commission) and then ask to see any literature they may have, including a copy of the form they filed with the SEC that details the firm's investment philosophy and the background and experience of its principal planners. If a firm or person looks good to you, set up an interview.

Ask about fees, because there are three types of financial planners — commission-based, fee-based, and those who get a combination of fee and commission. I would be wary of commission-based planners for the same reason I'm wary of stockbrokers: They might make recommendations based on

their potential commissions rather than your needs. Most typical is the combination of yearly fee and commissions; if you don't have a lot of money to invest but need good advice, this is an especially good arrangement. And the fee is usually tax deductible.

You should also ask about the planner's credentials; certification in the Registry of Financial Planning Practitioners (most prestigious) or as a Certified Financial Planner and Chartered Financial Consultant tells you they adhere to certain standards. Look for a degree in law, finance or accounting as well. Although membership in the International Association for Financial Planning or the Institute for Certified Financial Planners shows that she keeps up with trends and belongs to a wide network of colleagues, inquire carefully about the methods she uses to investigate potential investments for you. You don't want someone who just sits in the office and reads prospectuses.

To learn about the types of clients the planner has and investments she recommends, ask to see a typical client profile and financial plan. You want to see one for someone similar to you in income, net worth, etc. This will give you an idea of the strategies this planner uses and how familiar she is with the needs of someone in your financial position.

The final consideration is the amount of trust and rapport you feel with this person, because you'll have to tell him or her everything so she can make the best plan for you. If you don't feel comfortable with or about a planner, then she isn't right for you. Just keep looking till you find one who is.

Index

A

B

C

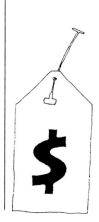